Catalan
Verb Conjugator

The most common verbs
fully conjugated

∝ FLUO: LANGUAGES

Catalan Verb Conjugator:
The most common verbs fully conjugated

by Joan Milà

First Edition: April 2018

Contents

Contents

Contents

Contents

Contents

Abbreviations

ind	Indicative
sub	Subjunctive
imp	Imperative
inf	Infinitive
ger	Gerund
pp	Past Participle
pre	Present
imp	Imperfect
prt	Preterite
fut	Future
con	Conditional

A

abandonar /abandon/ • **ind** _pre_ abandono, abandones, abando-
na, abandonem, abandoneu, abandonen _imp_ abandonava, abandonaves,
abandonava, abandonàvem, abandonàveu, abandonaven _prt_ abandoní,
abandonares, abandonà, abandonàrem, abandonàreu, abandonaren _fut_
abandonaré, abandonaràs, abandonarà, abandonarem, abandonareu, aban-
donaran _con_ abandonaria, abandonaries, abandonaria, abandonaríem,
abandonaríeu, abandonarien • **sub** _pre_ abandoni, abandonis, abandoni, abandonem, abandoneu, abandonin _imp_ abandonés, abandonessis,
abandonés, abandonéssim, abandonéssiu, abandonessin • **imp** -, aban-
dona, abandoni, abandonem, abandoneu, abandonin • **inf** abandonar •
ger abandonant • **pp** _sing_ abandonat / abandonada _plur_ abandonats /
abandonades

abastar /cover/ • **ind** _pre_ abasto, abastes, abasta, abastem, abasteu,
abasten _imp_ abastava, abastaves, abastava, abastàvem, abastàveu, abas-
taven _prt_ abastí, abastares, abastà, abastàrem, abastàreu, abastaren _fut_
abastaré, abastaràs, abastarà, abastarem, abastareu, abastaran _con_ abastaria, abastaries, abastaria, abastaríem, abastaríeu, abastarien • **sub** _pre_
abasti, abastis, abasti, abastem, abasteu, abastin _imp_ abastés, abastessis,
abastés, abastéssim, abastéssiu, abastessin • **imp** -, abasta, abasti, abastem, abasteu, abastin • **inf** abastar • **ger** abastant • **pp** _sing_ abastat /
abastada _plur_ abastats / abastades

abatre /drop down/ • **ind** _pre_ abato, abats, abat, abatem, abateu,
abaten _imp_ abatia, abaties, abatia, abatíem, abatíeu, abatien _prt_ abatí,
abateres, abaté, abatérem, abatéreu, abateren _fut_ abatré, abatràs, aba-
trà, abatrem, abatreu, abatran _con_ abatria, abatries, abatria, abatríem,
abatríeu, abatrien • **sub** _pre_ abati, abatis, abati, abatem, abateu, abatin
imp abatés, abatessis, abatés, abatéssim, abatéssiu, abatessin • **imp** -,
abat, abati, abatem, abateu, abatin • **inf** abatre • **ger** abatent • **pp** _sing_
abatut / abatuda _plur_ abatuts / abatudes

acabar /end up/ • **ind** _pre_ acabo, acabes, acaba, acabem, acabeu,
acaben _imp_ acabava, acabaves, acabava, acabàvem, acabàveu, acabaven
prt acabí, acabares, acabà, acabàrem, acabàreu, acabaren _fut_ acabaré,
acabaràs, acabarà, acabarem, acabareu, acabaran _con_ acabaria, acabari-
es, acabaria, acabaríem, acabaríeu, acabarien • **sub** _pre_ acabi, acabis,

acabi, acabem, acabeu, acabin _imp_ acabés, acabessis, acabés, acabéssim, acabéssiu, acabessin • **imp** -, acaba, acabi, acabem, acabeu, acabin • **inf** acabar • **ger** acabant • **pp** _sing_ acabat / acabada _plur_ acabats / acabades

accedir /access/ • **ind** _pre_ accedeixo, accedeixes, accedeix, accedim, accediu, accedeixen _imp_ accedia, accedies, accedia, accedíem, accedíeu, accedien _prt_ accedí, accedires, accedí, accedírem, accedíreu, accediren _fut_ accediré, accediràs, accedirà, accedirem, accedireu, accediran _con_ accediria, accediries, accediria, accediríem, accediríeu, accedirien • **sub** _pre_ accedeixi, accedeixis, accedeixi, accedim, accediu, accedeixin _imp_ accedís, accedissis, accedís, accedíssim, accedíssiu, accedissin • **imp** -, accedeix, accedeixi, accedim, accediu, accedeixin • **inf** accedir • **ger** accedint • **pp** _sing_ accedit / accedida _plur_ accedits / accedides

acceptar /accept/ • **ind** _pre_ accepto, acceptes, accepta, acceptem, accepteu, accepten _imp_ acceptava, acceptaves, acceptava, acceptàvem, acceptàveu, acceptaven _prt_ acceptí, acceptares, acceptà, acceptàrem, acceptàreu, acceptaren _fut_ acceptaré, acceptaràs, acceptarà, acceptarem, acceptareu, acceptaran _con_ acceptaria, acceptaries, acceptaria, acceptaríem, acceptaríeu, acceptarien • **sub** _pre_ accepti, acceptis, accepti, acceptem, accepteu, acceptin _imp_ acceptés, acceptessis, acceptés, acceptéssim, acceptéssiu, acceptessin • **imp** -, accepta, accepti, acceptem, accepteu, acceptin • **inf** acceptar • **ger** acceptant • **pp** _sing_ acceptat / acceptada _plur_ acceptats / acceptades

aclarir /clear up/ • **ind** _pre_ aclareixo, aclareixes, aclareix, aclarim, aclariu, aclareixen _imp_ aclaria, aclaries, aclaria, aclaríem, aclaríeu, aclarien _prt_ aclarí, aclarires, aclarí, aclarírem, aclaríreu, aclariren _fut_ aclariré, aclariràs, aclarirà, aclarirem, aclarireu, aclariran _con_ aclariria, aclariries, aclariria, aclaririem, aclariríeu, aclaririen • **sub** _pre_ aclareixi, aclareixis, aclareixi, aclarim, aclariu, aclareixin _imp_ aclarís, aclarissis, aclarís, aclaríssim, aclaríssiu, aclarissin • **imp** -, aclareix, aclareixi, aclarim, aclariu, aclareixin • **inf** aclarir • **ger** aclarint • **pp** _sing_ aclarit / aclarida _plur_ aclarits / aclarides

acomiadar /say goodbye, dismiss/ • **ind** _pre_ acomiado, acomiades, acomiada, acomiadem, acomiadeu, acomiaden _imp_ acomiadava, acomiadaves, acomiadava, acomiadàvem, acomiadàveu, acomiadaven _prt_ acomiadí, acomiadares, acomiadà, acomiadàrem, acomiadàreu, acomiadaren _fut_ acomiadaré, acomiadaràs, acomiadarà, acomiadarem, acomiadareu, acomiadaran _con_ acomiadaria, acomiadaries, acomiadaria, acomiadaríem, acomiadaríeu, acomiadarien • **sub** _pre_ acomiadi, acomiadis, aco-

miadi, acomiadem, acomiadeu, acomiadin *imp* acomiadés, acomiadessis, acomiadés, acomiadéssim, acomiadéssiu, acomiadessin • **imp** -, acomiada, acomiadi, acomiadem, acomiadeu, acomiadin • **inf** acomiadar • **ger** acomiadant • **pp** *sing* acomiadat / acomiadada *plur* acomiadats / acomiadades

acompanyar /accompany/ • **ind** *pre* acompanyo, acompanyes, acompanya, acompanyem, acompanyeu, acompanyen *imp* acompanyava, acompanyaves, acompanyava, acompanyàvem, acompanyàveu, acompanyaven *prt* acompanyí, acompanyares, acompanyà, acompanyàrem, acompanyàreu, acompanyaren *fut* acompanyaré, acompanyaràs, acompanyarà, acompanyarem, acompanyareu, acompanyaran *con* acompanyaria, acompanyaries, acompanyaria, acompanyaríem, acompanyaríeu, acompanyarien • **sub** *pre* acompanyi, acompanyis, acompanyi, acompanyem, acompanyeu, acompanyin *imp* acompanyés, acompanyessis, acompanyés, acompanyéssim, acompanyéssiu, acompanyessin • **imp** -, acompanya, acompanyi, acompanyem, acompanyeu, acompanyin • **inf** acompanyar • **ger** acompanyant • **pp** *sing* acompanyat / acompanyada *plur* acompanyats / acompanyades

aconseguir /achieve/ • **ind** *pre* aconsegueixo, aconsegueixes, aconsegueix, aconseguim, aconseguiu, aconsegueixen *imp* aconseguia, aconseguies, aconseguia, aconseguíem, aconseguíeu, aconseguien *prt* aconseguí, aconseguires, aconseguí, aconseguírem, aconseguíreu, aconseguiren *fut* aconseguiré, aconseguiràs, aconseguirà, aconseguirem, aconseguireu, aconseguiran *con* aconseguiria, aconseguiries, aconseguiria, aconseguiríem, aconseguiríeu, aconseguirien • **sub** *pre* aconsegueixi, aconsegueixis, aconsegueixi, aconseguim, aconseguiu, aconsegueixin *imp* aconseguís, aconseguissis, aconseguís, aconseguíssim, aconseguíssiu, aconseguissin • **imp** -, aconsegueix, aconsegueixi, aconseguim, aconseguiu, aconsegueixin • **inf** aconseguir • **ger** aconseguint • **pp** *sing* aconseguit / aconseguida *plur* aconseguits / aconseguides

acordar /agree/ • **ind** *pre* acordo, acordes, acorda, acordem, acordeu, acorden *imp* acordava, acordaves, acordava, acordàvem, acordàveu, acordaven *prt* acordí, acordares, acordà, acordàrem, acordàreu, acordaren *fut* acordaré, acordaràs, acordarà, acordarem, acordareu, acordaran *con* acordaria, acordaries, acordaria, acordaríem, acordaríeu, acordarien • **sub** *pre* acordi, acordis, acordi, acordem, acordeu, acordin *imp* acordés, acordessis, acordés, acordéssim, acordéssiu, acordessin • **imp** -, acorda, acordi, acordem, acordeu, acordin • **inf** acordar • **ger** acordant • **pp** *sing* acordat / acordada *plur* acordats / acordades

acostar /bring closer/ • **ind** _pre_ acosto, acostes, acosta, acostem, acosteu, acosten _imp_ acostava, acostaves, acostava, acostàvem, acostàveu, acostaven _prt_ acostí, acostares, acostà, acostàrem, acostàreu, acostaren _fut_ acostaré, acostaràs, acostarà, acostarem, acostareu, acostaran _con_ acostaria, acostaries, acostaria, acostaríem, acostaríeu, acostarien • **sub** _pre_ acosti, acostis, acosti, acostem, acosteu, acostin _imp_ acostés, acostessis, acostés, acostéssim, acostéssiu, acostessin • **imp** -, acosta, acosti, acostem, acosteu, acostin • **inf** acostar • **ger** acostant • **pp** _sing_ acostat / acostada _plur_ acostats / acostades

activar /activate/ • **ind** _pre_ activo, actives, activa, activem, activeu, activen _imp_ activava, activaves, activava, activàvem, activàveu, activaven _prt_ activí, activares, activà, activàrem, activàreu, activaren _fut_ activaré, activaràs, activarà, activarem, activareu, activaran _con_ activaria, activaries, activaria, activaríem, activaríeu, activarien • **sub** _pre_ activi, activis, activi, activem, activeu, activin _imp_ activés, activessis, activés, activéssim, activéssiu, activessin • **imp** -, activa, activi, activem, activeu, activin • **inf** activar • **ger** activant • **pp** _sing_ activat / activada _plur_ activats / activades

actuar /act/ • **ind** _pre_ actuo, actues, actua, actuem, actueu, actuen _imp_ actuava, actuaves, actuava, actuàvem, actuàveu, actuaven _prt_ actuí, actuares, actuà, actuàrem, actuàreu, actuaren _fut_ actuaré, actuaràs, actuarà, actuarem, actuareu, actuaran _con_ actuaria, actuaries, actuaria, actuaríem, actuaríeu, actuarien • **sub** _pre_ actuï, actuïs, actuï, actuem, actueu, actuïn _imp_ actués, actuessis, actués, actuéssim, actuéssiu, actuessin • **imp** -, actua, actuï, actuem, actueu, actuïn • **inf** actuar • **ger** actuant • **pp** _sing_ actuat / actuada _plur_ actuats / actuades

acudir /attend, go/ • **ind** _pre_ acudeixo, acudeixes, acudeix, acudim, acudiu, acudeixen _imp_ acudia, acudies, acudia, acudíem, acudíeu, acudien _prt_ acudí, acudires, acudí, acudírem, acudíreu, acudiren _fut_ acudiré, acudiràs, acudirà, acudirem, acudireu, acudiran _con_ acudiria, acudiries, acudiria, acudiríem, acudiríeu, acudirien • **sub** _pre_ acudeixi, acudeixis, acudeixi, acudim, acudiu, acudeixin _imp_ acudís, acudissis, acudís, acudíssim, acudíssiu, acudissin • **imp** -, acudeix, acudeixi, acudim, acudiu, acudeixin • **inf** acudir • **ger** acudint • **pp** _sing_ acudit / acudida _plur_ acudits / acudides

admetre /admit/ • **ind** _pre_ admeto, admets, admet, admetem, admeteu, admeten _imp_ admetia, admeties, admetia, admetíem, admetíeu, admetien _prt_ admetí, admeteres, admeté, admetérem, admetéreu, admeteren _fut_ admetré, admetràs, admetrà, admetrem, admetreu, admetran _con_ admetria, admetries, admetria, admetríem, admetríeu, admetrien • **sub** _pre_ admeti, admetis, admeti, admetem, admeteu, admetin _imp_ admetés, admetessis, admetés, admetéssim, admetéssiu, admetessin • **imp** -, admet, admeti, admetem, admeteu, admetin • **inf** admetre • **ger** admetent • **pp** _sing_ admès / admesa _plur_ admesos / admeses

adoptar /adopt/ • **ind** _pre_ adopto, adoptes, adopta, adoptem, adopteu, adopten _imp_ adoptava, adoptaves, adoptava, adoptàvem, adoptàveu, adoptaven _prt_ adoptí, adoptares, adoptà, adoptàrem, adoptàreu, adoptaren _fut_ adoptaré, adoptaràs, adoptarà, adoptarem, adoptareu, adoptaran _con_ adoptaria, adoptaries, adoptaria, adoptaríem, adoptaríeu, adoptarien • **sub** _pre_ adopti, adoptis, adopti, adoptem, adopteu, adoptin _imp_ adoptés, adoptessis, adoptés, adoptéssim, adoptéssiu, adoptessin • **imp** -, adopta, adopti, adoptem, adopteu, adoptin • **inf** adoptar • **ger** adoptant • **pp** _sing_ adoptat / adoptada _plur_ adoptats / adoptades

adquirir /acquire/ • **ind** _pre_ adquireixo, adquireixes, adquireix, adquirim, adquiriu, adquireixen _imp_ adquiria, adquiries, adquiria, adquiríem, adquiríeu, adquirien _prt_ adquirí, adquirires, adquirí, adquirírem, adquiríreu, adquiriren _fut_ adquiriré, adquiriràs, adquirirà, adquirirem, adquirireu, adquiriran _con_ adquiriria, adquiriries, adquiriria, adquiriríem, adquiriríeu, adquiririen • **sub** _pre_ adquireixi, adquireixis, adquireixi, adquirim, adquiriu, adquireixin _imp_ adquirís, adquirissis, adquirís, adquiríssim, adquiríssiu, adquirissin • **imp** -, adquireix, adquireixi, adquirim, adquiriu, adquireixin • **inf** adquirir • **ger** adquirint • **pp** _sing_ adquirit / adquirida _plur_ adquirits / adquirides

advertir /warn/ • **ind** _pre_ adverteixo, adverteixes, adverteix, advertim, advertiu, adverteixen _imp_ advertia, adverties, advertia, advertíem, advertíeu, advertien _prt_ advertí, advertires, advertí, advertírem, advertíreu, advertiren _fut_ advertiré, advertiràs, advertirà, advertirem, advertireu, advertiran _con_ advertiria, advertiries, advertiria, advertiríem, advertiríeu, advertirien • **sub** _pre_ adverteixi, adverteixis, adverteixi, advertim, advertiu, adverteixin _imp_ advertís, advertissis, advertís, advertíssim, advertíssiu, advertissin • **imp** -, adverteix, adverteixi, advertim, advertiu, adverteixin • **inf** advertir • **ger** advertint • **pp** _sing_ advertit / advertida _plur_ advertits / advertides

afectar /affect/ • **ind** _pre_ afecto, afectes, afecta, afectem, afecteu, afecten _imp_ afectava, afectaves, afectava, afectàvem, afectàveu, afectaven _prt_ afectí, afectares, afectà, afectàrem, afectàreu, afectaren _fut_ afectaré, afectaràs, afectarà, afectarem, afectareu, afectaran _con_ afectaria, afectaries, afectaria, afectaríem, afectaríeu, afectarien • **sub** _pre_ afecti, afectis, afecti, afectem, afecteu, afectin _imp_ afectés, afectessis, afectés, afectéssim, afectéssiu, afectessin • **imp** -, afecta, afecti, afectem, afecteu, afectin • **inf** afectar • **ger** afectant • **pp** _sing_ afectat / afectada _plur_ afectats / afectades

afegir /add/ • **ind** _pre_ afegeixo, afegeixes, afegeix, afegim, afegiu, afegeixen _imp_ afegia, afegies, afegia, afegíem, afegíeu, afegien _prt_ afegí, afegires, afegí, afegírem, afegíreu, afegiren _fut_ afegiré, afegiràs, afegirà, afegirem, afegireu, afegiran _con_ afegiria, afegiries, afegiria, afegiríem, afegiríeu, afegirien • **sub** _pre_ afegeixi, afegeixis, afegeixi, afegim, afegiu, afegeixin _imp_ afegís, afegissis, afegís, afegíssim, afegíssiu, afegissin • **imp** -, afegeix, afegeixi, afegim, afegiu, afegeixin • **inf** afegir • **ger** afegint • **pp** _sing_ afegit / afegida _plur_ afegits / afegides

agafar /grab/ • **ind** _pre_ agafo, agafes, agafa, agafem, agafeu, agafen _imp_ agafava, agafaves, agafava, agafàvem, agafàveu, agafaven _prt_ agafí, agafares, agafà, agafàrem, agafàreu, agafaren _fut_ agafaré, agafaràs, agafarà, agafarem, agafareu, agafaran _con_ agafaria, agafaries, agafaria, agafaríem, agafaríeu, agafarien • **sub** _pre_ agafi, agafis, agafi, agafem, agafeu, agafin _imp_ agafés, agafessis, agafés, agaféssim, agaféssiu, agafessin • **imp** -, agafa, agafi, agafem, agafeu, agafin • **inf** agafar • **ger** agafant • **pp** _sing_ agafat / agafada _plur_ agafats / agafades

agradar /like/ • **ind** _pre_ agrado, agrades, agrada, agradem, agradeu, agraden _imp_ agradava, agradaves, agradava, agradàvem, agradàveu, agradaven _prt_ agradí, agradares, agradà, agradàrem, agradàreu, agradaren _fut_ agradaré, agradaràs, agradarà, agradarem, agradareu, agradaran _con_ agradaria, agradaries, agradaria, agradaríem, agradaríeu, agradarien • **sub** _pre_ agradi, agradis, agradi, agradem, agradeu, agradin _imp_ agradés, agradessis, agradés, agradéssim, agradéssiu, agradessin • **imp** -, agrada, agradi, agradem, agradeu, agradin • **inf** agradar • **ger** agradant • **pp** _sing_ agradat / agradada _plur_ agradats / agradades

agrair /thank/ • **ind** _pre_ agraeixo, agraeixes, agraeix, agraïm, agraïu, agraeixen _imp_ agraïa, agraïes, agraïa, agraíem, agraíeu, agraïen _prt_ agraí, agraïres, agraí, agraírem, agraíreu, agraïren _fut_ agrairé, agrairàs, agrairà, agrairem, agraireu, agrairan _con_ agrairia, agrairies, agrairia, agrairíem, agrairíeu, agrairien • **sub** _pre_ agraeixi, agraeixis, agraeixi, agraïm, agraïu, agraeixin _imp_ agraís, agraïssis, agraís, agraíssim, agraíssiu, agraïssin • **imp** -, agraeix, agraeixi, agraïm, agraïu, agraeixin • **inf** agrair • **ger** agraint • **pp** _sing_ agraït / agraïda _plur_ agraïts / agraïdes

aguantar /hold/ • **ind** _pre_ aguanto, aguantes, aguanta, aguantem, aguanteu, aguanten *imp* aguantava, aguantaves, aguantava, aguantàvem, aguantàveu, aguantaven *prt* aguantí, aguantares, aguantà, aguantàrem, aguantàreu, aguantaren *fut* aguantaré, aguantaràs, aguantarà, aguantarem, aguantareu, aguantaran *con* aguantaria, aguantaries, aguantaria, aguantaríem, aguantaríeu, aguantarien • **sub** *pre* aguanti, aguantis, aguanti, aguantem, aguanteu, aguantin *imp* aguantés, aguantessis, aguantés, aguantéssim, aguantéssiu, aguantessin • **imp** -, aguanta, aguanti, aguantem, aguanteu, aguantin • **inf** aguantar • **ger** aguantant • **pp** *sing* aguantat / aguantada *plur* aguantats / aguantades

aixecar /lift up/ • **ind** *pre* aixeco, aixeques, aixeca, aixequem, aixequeu, aixequen *imp* aixecava, aixecaves, aixecava, aixecàvem, aixecàveu, aixecaven *prt* aixequí, aixecares, aixecà, aixecàrem, aixecàreu, aixecaren *fut* aixecaré, aixecaràs, aixecarà, aixecarem, aixecareu, aixecaran *con* aixecaria, aixecaries, aixecaria, aixecaríem, aixecaríeu, aixecarien • **sub** *pre* aixequi, aixequis, aixequi, aixequem, aixequeu, aixequin *imp* aixequés, aixequessis, aixequés, aixequéssim, aixequéssiu, aixequessin • **imp** -, aixeca, aixequi, aixequem, aixequeu, aixequin • **inf** aixecar • **ger** aixecant • **pp** *sing* aixecat / aixecada *plur* aixecats / aixecades

ajudar /help/ • **ind** *pre* ajudo, ajudes, ajuda, ajudem, ajudeu, ajuden *imp* ajudava, ajudaves, ajudava, ajudàvem, ajudàveu, ajudaven *prt* ajudí, ajudares, ajudà, ajudàrem, ajudàreu, ajudaren *fut* ajudaré, ajudaràs, ajudarà, ajudarem, ajudareu, ajudaran *con* ajudaria, ajudaries, ajudaria, ajudaríem, ajudaríeu, ajudarien • **sub** *pre* ajudi, ajudis, ajudi, ajudem, ajudeu, ajudin *imp* ajudés, ajudessis, ajudés, ajudéssim, ajudéssiu, ajudessin • **imp** -, ajuda, ajudi, ajudem, ajudeu, ajudin • **inf** ajudar • **ger** ajudant • **pp** *sing* ajudat / ajudada *plur* ajudats / ajudades

alimentar /feed/ • **ind** *pre* alimento, alimentes, alimenta, alimentem, alimenteu, alimenten *imp* alimentava, alimentaves, alimentava, alimentàvem, alimentàveu, alimentaven *prt* alimentí, alimentares, alimentà, alimentàrem, alimentàreu, alimentaren *fut* alimentaré, alimentaràs, alimentarà, alimentarem, alimentareu, alimentaran *con* alimentaria, alimentaries, alimentaria, alimentaríem, alimentaríeu, alimentarien • **sub** *pre* alimenti, alimentis, alimenti, alimentem, alimenteu, alimentin *imp* alimentés, alimentessis, alimentés, alimentéssim, alimentéssiu, alimentessin • **imp** -, alimenta, alimenti, alimentem, alimenteu, alimentin • **inf** alimentar • **ger** alimentant • **pp** *sing* alimentat / alimentada *plur* alimentats / alimentades

alliberar /liberate/ • **ind** *pre* allibero, alliberes, allibera, alliberem, allibereu, alliberen *imp* alliberava, alliberaves, alliberava, alliberàvem, alliberàveu, alliberaven _prt_ alliberí, alliberares, alliberà, alliberàrem, alliberàreu, alliberaren _fut_ alliberaré, alliberaràs, alliberarà, alliberarem, alliberareu, alliberaran _con_ alliberaria, alliberaries, alliberaria, alliberaríem, alliberaríeu, alliberarien • **sub** _pre_ alliberi, alliberis, alliberi, alliberem, alliebreu, alliberin _imp_ alliberés, alliberessis, alliberés, alliberéssim, alliberéssiu, alliberessin • **imp** -, allibera, alliberi, alliberem, alliebreu, alliberin • **inf** alliberar • **ger** alliberant • **pp** _sing_ alliberat / alliberada _plur_ alliberats / alliberades

allunyar /move away/ • **ind** _pre_ allunyo, allunyes, allunya, allunyem, allunyeu, allunyen _imp_ allunyava, allunyaves, allunyava, allunyàvem, allunyàveu, allunyaven _prt_ allunyí, allunyares, allunyà, allunyàrem, allunyàreu, allunyaren _fut_ allunyaré, allunyaràs, allunyarà, allunyarem, allunyareu, allunyaran _con_ allunyaria, allunyaries, allunyaria, allunyaríem, allunyaríeu, allunyarien • **sub** _pre_ allunyi, allunyis, allunyi, allunyem, allunyeu, allunyin _imp_ allunyés, allunyessis, allunyés, allunyéssim, allunyéssiu, allunyessin • **imp** -, allunya, allunyi, allunyem, allunyeu, allunyin • **inf** allunyar • **ger** allunyant • **pp** _sing_ allunyat / allunyada _plur_ allunyats / allunyades

amagar /hide/ • **ind** _pre_ amago, amagues, amaga, amaguem, amagueu, amaguen _imp_ amagava, amagaves, amagava, amagàvem, amagàveu, amagaven _prt_ amaguí, amagares, amagà, amagàrem, amagàreu, amagaren _fut_ amagaré, amagaràs, amagarà, amagarem, amagareu, amagaran _con_ amagaria, amagaries, amagaria, amagaríem, amagaríeu, amagarien • **sub** _pre_ amagui, amaguis, amagui, amaguem, amagueu, amaguin _imp_ amagués, amaguessis, amagués, amaguéssim, amaguéssiu, amaguessin • **imp** -, amaga, amagui, amaguem, amagueu, amaguin • **inf** amagar • **ger** amagant • **pp** _sing_ amagat / amagada _plur_ amagats / amagades

analitzar /analyze/ • **ind** _pre_ analitzo, analitzes, analitza, analitzem, analitzeu, analitzen _imp_ analitzava, analitzaves, analitzava, analitzàvem, analitzàveu, analitzaven _prt_ analitzí, analitzares, analitzà, analitzàrem, analitzàreu, analitzaren _fut_ analitzaré, analitzaràs, analitzarà, analitzarem, analitzareu, analitzaran _con_ analitzaria, analitzaries, analitzaria, analitzaríem, analitzaríeu, analitzarien • **sub** _pre_ analitzi, analitzis, analitzi, analitzem, analitzeu, analitzin _imp_ analitzés, analitzessis, analitzés, analitzéssim, analitzéssiu, analitzessin • **imp** -, analitza, analitzi, analitzem, analitzeu, analitzin • **inf** analitzar • **ger** analitzant • **pp** _sing_ analitzat / analitzada _plur_ analitzats / analitzades

anar /go/ • **ind** _pre_ vaig, vas, va, anem, aneu, van _imp_ anava, anaves, anava, anàvem, anàveu, anaven _prt_ aní, anares, anà, anàrem, anàreu, anaren _fut_ aniré, aniràs, anirà, anirem, anireu, aniran _con_ aniria, aniries, aniria, aniríem, aniríeu, anirien • **sub** _pre_ vagi, vagis, vagi, anem, aneu, vagin _imp_ anés, anessis, anés, anéssim, anéssiu, anessin • **imp** -, vés, vagi, anem, aneu, vagin • **inf** anar • **ger** anant • **pp** _sing_ anat / anada _plur_ anats / anades

animar /cheer up/ • **ind** _pre_ animo, animes, anima, animem, animeu, animen _imp_ animava, animaves, animava, animàvem, animàveu, animaven _prt_ animí, animares, animà, animàrem, animàreu, animaren _fut_ animaré, animaràs, animarà, animarem, animareu, animaran _con_ animaria, animaries, animaria, animaríem, animaríeu, animarien • **sub** _pre_ animi, animis, animi, animem, animeu, animin _imp_ animés, animessis, animés, animéssim, animéssiu, animessin • **imp** -, anima, animi, animem, animeu, animin • **inf** animar • **ger** animant • **pp** _sing_ animat / animada _plur_ animats / animades

anomenar /call/ • **ind** _pre_ anomeno, anomenes, anomena, anomenem, anomeneu, anomenen _imp_ anomenava, anomenaves, anomenava, anomenàvem, anomenàveu, anomenaven _prt_ anomení, anomenares, anomenà, anomenàrem, anomenàreu, anomenaren _fut_ anomenaré, anomenaràs, anomenarà, anomenarem, anomenareu, anomenaran _con_ anomenaria, anomenaries, anomenaria, anomenaríem, anomenaríeu, anomenarien • **sub** _pre_ anomeni, anomenis, anomeni, anomenem, anomeneu, anomenin _imp_ anomenés, anomenessis, anomenés, anomenéssim, anomenéssiu, anomenessin • **imp** -, anomena, anomeni, anomenem, anomeneu, anomenin • **inf** anomenar • **ger** anomenant • **pp** _sing_ anomenat / anomenada _plur_ anomenats / anomenades

anunciar /advertise/ • **ind** _pre_ anuncio, anuncies, anuncia, anunciem, anuncieu, anuncien _imp_ anunciava, anunciaves, anunciava, anunciàvem, anunciàveu, anunciaven _prt_ anuncií, anunciares, anuncià, anunciàrem, anunciàreu, anunciaren _fut_ anunciaré, anunciaràs, anunciarà, anunciarem, anunciareu, anunciaran _con_ anunciaria, anunciaries, anunciaria, anunciaríem, anunciaríeu, anunciarien • **sub** _pre_ anuncïi, anuncïis, anuncïi, anunciem, anuncieu, anuncïin _imp_ anunciés, anunciessis, anunciés, anunciéssim, anunciéssiu, anunciessin • **imp** -, anuncia, anuncïi, anunciem, anuncieu, anuncïin • **inf** anunciar • **ger** anunciant • **pp** _sing_ anunciat / anunciada _plur_ anunciats / anunciades

apagar /turn off/ • **ind** _pre_ apago, apagues, apaga, apaguem, apagueu, apaguen _imp_ apagava, apagaves, apagava, apagàvem, apagàveu, apagaven _prt_ apaguí, apagares, apagà, apagàrem, apagàreu, apagaren _fut_ apagaré, apagaràs, apagarà, apagarem, apagareu, apagaran _con_ apagaria, apagaries, apagaria, apagaríem, apagaríeu, apagarien • **sub** _pre_ apagui, apaguis, apagui, apaguem, apagueu, apaguin *imp* apagués, apaguessis, apagués, apaguéssim, apaguéssiu, apaguessin • **imp** -, apaga, apagui, apaguem, apagueu, apaguin • **inf** apagar • **ger** apagant • **pp** *sing* apagat / apagada *plur* apagats / apagades

apartar /get away/ • **ind** *pre* aparto, apartes, aparta, apartem, aparteu, aparten *imp* apartava, apartaves, apartava, apartàvem, apartàveu, apartaven *prt* apartí, apartares, apartà, apartàrem, apartàreu, apartaren *fut* apartaré, apartaràs, apartarà, apartarem, apartareu, apartaran *con* apartaria, apartaries, apartaria, apartaríem, apartaríeu, apartarien • **sub** *pre* aparti, apartis, aparti, apartem, aparteu, apartin *imp* apartés, apartessis, apartés, apartéssim, apartéssiu, apartessin • **imp** -, aparta, aparti, apartem, aparteu, apartin • **inf** apartar • **ger** apartant • **pp** *sing* apartat / apartada *plur* apartats / apartades

aplicar /apply/ • **ind** *pre* aplico, apliques, aplica, apliquem, apliqueu, apliquen *imp* aplicava, aplicaves, aplicava, aplicàvem, aplicàveu, aplicaven *prt* apliquí, aplicares, aplicà, aplicàrem, aplicàreu, aplicaren *fut* aplicaré, aplicaràs, aplicarà, aplicarem, aplicareu, aplicaran *con* aplicaria, aplicaries, aplicaria, aplicaríem, aplicaríeu, aplicarien • **sub** *pre* apliqui, apliquis, apliqui, apliquem, apliqueu, apliquin *imp* apliqués, apliquessis, apliqués, apliquéssim, apliquéssiu, apliquessin • **imp** -, aplica, apliqui, apliquem, apliqueu, apliquin • **inf** aplicar • **ger** aplicant • **pp** *sing* aplicat / aplicada *plur* aplicats / aplicades

apostar /bet/ • **ind** *pre* aposto, apostes, aposta, apostem, aposteu, aposten *imp* apostava, apostaves, apostava, apostàvem, apostàveu, apostaven *prt* apostí, apostares, apostà, apostàrem, apostàreu, apostaren *fut* apostaré, apostaràs, apostarà, apostarem, apostareu, apostaran *con* apostaria, apostaries, apostaria, apostaríem, apostaríeu, apostarien • **sub** *pre* aposti, apostis, aposti, apostem, aposteu, apostin *imp* apostés, apostessis, apostés, apostéssim, apostéssiu, apostessin • **imp** -, aposta, aposti, apostem, aposteu, apostin • **inf** apostar • **ger** apostant • **pp** *sing* apostat / apostada *plur* apostats / apostades

aprendre /learn/ • **ind** *pre* aprenc, aprens, aprèn, aprenem, apreneu, aprenen *imp* aprenia, aprenies, aprenia, apreníem, apreníeu, aprenien *prt* aprenguí, aprengueres, aprengué, aprenguérem, aprenguéreu, aprengueren *fut* aprendré, aprendràs, aprendrà, aprendrem, aprendreu, aprendran *con* aprendria, aprendries, aprendria, aprendríem, aprendríeu, aprendrien • **sub** *pre* aprengui, aprenguis, aprengui, aprenguem, aprengueu, aprenguin *imp* aprengués, aprenguessis, aprengués, aprenguéssim, aprenguéssiu, aprenguessin • **imp** -, aprèn, aprengui, aprenguem, apre-

neu, aprenguin • **inf** aprendre • **ger** aprenent • **pp** _sing_ après / apresa
plur apresos / apreses

aprofitar /take advantage/ • **ind** _pre_ aprofito, aprofites, aprofita,
aprofitem, aprofiteu, aprofiten _imp_ aprofitava, aprofitaves, aprofitava,
aprofitàvem, aprofitàveu, aprofitaven _prt_ aprofití, aprofitares, aprofità,
aprofitàrem, aprofitàreu, aprofitaren _fut_ aprofitaré, aprofitaràs, aprofi-
tarà, aprofitarem, aprofitareu, aprofitaran _con_ aprofitaria, aprofitaries,
aprofitaria, aprofitaríem, aprofitaríeu, aprofitarien • **sub** _pre_ aprofiti,
aprofitis, aprofiti, aprofitem, aprofiteu, aprofitin _imp_ aprofités, aprofites-
sis, aprofités, aprofitéssim, aprofitéssiu, aprofitessin • **imp** -, aprofita,
aprofiti, aprofitem, aprofiteu, aprofitin • **inf** aprofitar • **ger** aprofitant
• **pp** _sing_ aprofitat / aprofitada _plur_ aprofitats / aprofitades

apropar /approach/ • **ind** _pre_ apropo, apropes, apropa, apropem,
apropeu, apropen _imp_ apropava, apropaves, apropava, apropàvem, apro-
pàveu, apropaven _prt_ apropí, apropares, apropà, apropàrem, apropàreu,
aproparen _fut_ aproparé, aproparàs, apropparà, aproparem, apropareu,
aproparan _con_ aproparia, aproparies, aproparia, aproparíem, aproparíeu,
aproparien • **sub** _pre_ apropi, apropis, apropi, apropem, apropeu, apropin _imp_ apropés, apropessis, apropés, apropéssim, apropéssiu, apropes-
sin • **imp** -, apropa, apropi, apropem, apropeu, apropin • **inf** apropar •
ger apropant • **pp** _sing_ apropat / apropada _plur_ apropats / apropades

aprovar /approve/ • **ind** _pre_ aprovo, aproves, aprova, aprovem,
aproveu, aproven _imp_ aprovava, aprovaves, aprovava, aprovàvem, apro-
vàveu, aprovaven _prt_ aproví, aprovares, aprovà, aprovàrem, aprovàreu,
aprovaren _fut_ aprovaré, aprovaràs, aprovarà, aprovarem, aprovareu,
aprovaran _con_ aprovaria, aprovaries, aprovaria, aprovaríem, aprovaríeu,
aprovarien • **sub** _pre_ aprovi, aprovis, aprovi, aprovem, aproveu, aprovin
imp aprovés, aprovessis, aprovés, aprovéssim, aprovéssiu, aprovessin •
imp -, aprova, aprovi, aprovem, aproveu, aprovin • **inf** aprovar • **ger**
aprovant • **pp** _sing_ aprovat / aprovada _plur_ aprovats / aprovades

apuntar /point out/ • **ind** _pre_ apunto, apuntes, apunta, apuntem,
apunteu, apunten _imp_ apuntava, apuntaves, apuntava, apuntàvem, apun-
tàveu, apuntaven _prt_ apuntí, apuntares, apuntà, apuntàrem, apuntàreu,
apuntaren _fut_ apuntaré, apuntaràs, apuntarà, apuntarem, apuntareu, apun-
taran _con_ apuntaria, apuntaries, apuntaria, apuntaríem, apuntaríeu, apun-
tarien • **sub** _pre_ apunti, apuntis, apunti, apuntem, apunteu, apuntin _imp_
apuntés, apuntessis, apuntés, apuntéssim, apuntéssiu, apuntessin • **imp**
-, apunta, apunti, apuntem, apunteu, apuntin • **inf** apuntar • **ger** apun-
tant • **pp** _sing_ apuntat / apuntada _plur_ apuntats / apuntades

apunyalar /stab/ • **ind** _pre_ apunyalo, apunyales, apunyala, apunyalem, apunyaleu, apunyalen _imp_ apunyalava, apunyalaves, apunyalava, apunyalàvem, apunyalàveu, apunyalaven _prt_ apunyalí, apunyalares, apunyalà, apunyalàrem, apunyalàreu, apunyalaren _fut_ apunyalaré, apunyalaràs, apunyalarà, apunyalarem, apunyalareu, apunyalaran _con_ apunyalaria, apunyalaries, apunyalaria, apunyalaríem, apunyalaríeu, apunyalarien • **sub** _pre_ apunyali, apunyalis, apunyali, apunyalem, apunyaleu, apunyalin _imp_ apunyalés, apunyalessis, apunyalés, apunyaléssim, apunyaléssiu, apunyalessin • **imp** -, apunyala, apunyali, apunyalem, apunyaleu, apunyalin • **inf** apunyalar • **ger** apunyalant • **pp** _sing_ apunyalat / apunyalada _plur_ apunyalats / apunyalades

arreglar /fix/ • **ind** _pre_ arreglo, arregles, arregla, arreglem, arregleu, arreglen _imp_ arreglava, arreglaves, arreglava, arreglàvem, arreglàveu, arreglaven _prt_ arreglí, arreglares, arreglà, arreglàrem, arreglàreu, arreglaren _fut_ arreglaré, arreglaràs, arreglarà, arreglarem, arreglareu, arreglaran _con_ arreglaria, arreglaries, arreglaria, arreglaríem, arreglaríeu, arreglarien • **sub** _pre_ arregli, arreglis, arregli, arreglem, arregleu, arreglin _imp_ arreglés, arreglessis, arreglés, arregléssim, arregléssiu, arreglessin • **imp** -, arregla, arregli, arreglem, arregleu, arreglin • **inf** arreglar • **ger** arreglant • **pp** _sing_ arreglat / arreglada _plur_ arreglats / arreglades

arrencar /rip, take off, start up/ • **ind** _pre_ arrenco, arrenques, arrenca, arrenquem, arrenqueu, arrenquen _imp_ arrencava, arrencaves, arrencava, arrencàvem, arrencàveu, arrencaven _prt_ arrenquí, arrencares, arrencà, arrencàrem, arrencàreu, arrencaren _fut_ arrencaré, arrencaràs, arrencarà, arrencarem, arrencareu, arrencaran _con_ arrencaria, arrencaries, arrencaria, arrencaríem, arrencaríeu, arrencarien • **sub** _pre_ arrenqui, arrenquis, arrenqui, arrenquem, arrenqueu, arrenquin _imp_ arrenqués, arrenquessis, arrenqués, arrenquéssim, arrenquéssiu, arrenquessin • **imp** -, arrenca, arrenqui, arrenquem, arrenqueu, arrenquin • **inf** arrencar • **ger** arrencant • **pp** _sing_ arrencat / arrencada _plur_ arrencats / arrencades

arrestar /arrest/ • **ind** _pre_ arresto, arrestes, arresta, arrestem, arresteu, arresten _imp_ arrestava, arrestaves, arrestava, arrestàvem, arrestàveu, arrestaven _prt_ arrestí, arrestares, arrestà, arrestàrem, arrestàreu, arrestaren _fut_ arrestaré, arrestaràs, arrestarà, arrestarem, arrestareu, arrestaran _con_ arrestaria, arrestaries, arrestaria, arrestaríem, arrestaríeu, arrestarien • **sub** _pre_ arresti, arrestis, arresti, arrestem, arresteu, arrestin _imp_ arrestés, arrestessis, arrestés, arrestéssim, arrestéssiu, arrestessin • **imp** -, arresta, arresti, arrestem, arresteu, arrestin • **inf** arrestar • **ger** arrestant • **pp** _sing_ arrestat / arrestada _plur_ arrestats /

arrestades

arribar /arrive/ • **ind** _pre_ arribo, arribes, arriba, arribem, arribeu, arriben _imp_ arribava, arribaves, arribava, arribàvem, arribàveu, arribaven _prt_ arribí, arribares, arribà, arribàrem, arribàreu, arribaren _fut_ arribaré, arribaràs, arribarà, arribarem, arribareu, arribaran _con_ arribaria, arribaries, arribaria, arribaríem, arribaríeu, arribarien • **sub** _pre_ arribi, arribis, arribi, arribem, arribeu, arribin _imp_ arribés, arribessis, arribés, arribéssim, arribéssiu, arribessin • **imp** -, arriba, arribi, arribem, arribeu, arribin • **inf** arribar • **ger** arribant • **pp** _sing_ arribat / arribada _plur_ arribats / arribades

arriscar /risk/ • **ind** _pre_ arrisco, arrisques, arrisca, arrisquem, arrisqueu, arrisquen _imp_ arriscava, arriscaves, arriscava, arriscàvem, arriscàveu, arriscaven _prt_ arrisquí, arriscares, arriscà, arriscàrem, arriscàreu, arriscaren _fut_ arriscaré, arriscaràs, arriscarà, arriscarem, arriscareu, arriscaran _con_ arriscaria, arriscaries, arriscaria, arriscaríem, arriscaríeu, arriscarien • **sub** _pre_ arrisqui, arrisquis, arrisqui, arrisquem, arrisqueu, arrisquin _imp_ arrisqués, arrisquessis, arrisqués, arrisquéssim, arrisquéssiu, arrisquessin • **imp** -, arrisca, arrisqui, arrisquem, arrisqueu, arrisquin • **inf** arriscar • **ger** arriscant • **pp** _sing_ arriscat / arriscada _plur_ arriscats / arriscades

arrossegar /drag/ • **ind** _pre_ arrossego, arrossegues, arrossega, arrosseguem, arrossegueu, arrosseguen _imp_ arrossegava, arrossegaves, arrossegava, arrossegàvem, arrossegàveu, arrossegaven _prt_ arrosseguí, arrossegares, arrossegà, arrossegàrem, arrossegàreu, arrossegaren _fut_ arrossegaré, arrossegaràs, arrossegarà, arrossegarem, arrossegareu, arrossegaran _con_ arrossegaria, arrossegaries, arrossegaria, arrossegaríem, arrossegaríeu, arrossegarien • **sub** _pre_ arrossegui, arrosseguis, arrossegui, arrosseguem, arrossegueu, arrosseguin _imp_ arrossegués, arrosseguessis, arrossegués, arrosseguéssim, arrosseguéssiu, arrosseguessin • **imp** -, arrossega, arrossegui, arrosseguem, arrossegueu, arrosseguin • **inf** arrossegar • **ger** arrossegant • **pp** _sing_ arrossegat / arrossegada _plur_ arrossegats / arrossegades

assabentar /find out/ • **ind** _pre_ assabento, assabentes, assabenta, assabentem, assabenteu, assabenten _imp_ assabentava, assabentaves, assabentava, assabentàvem, assabentàveu, assabentaven _prt_ assabentí, assabentares, assabentà, assabentàrem, assabentàreu, assabentaren _fut_ assabentaré, assabentaràs, assabentarà, assabentarem, assabentareu, assabentaran _con_ assabentaria, assabentaries, assabentaria, assabentaríem, assabentaríeu, assabentarien • **sub** _pre_ assabenti, assabentis, assabenti, assabentem, assabenteu, assabentin *imp* assabentés, assabentessis, assabentés, assabentéssim, assabentéssiu, assabentessin • **imp** -, assabenta, assabenti, assabentem, assabenteu, assabentin • **inf** assabentar • **ger** assabentant • **pp** *sing* assabentat / assabentada *plur* assabentats / assabentades

assaltar /assault/ • **ind** *pre* assalto, assaltes, assalta, assaltem, assalteu, assalten *imp* assaltava, assaltaves, assaltava, assaltàvem, assaltàveu, assaltaven *prt* assaltí, assaltares, assaltà, assaltàrem, assaltàreu, assaltaren *fut* assaltaré, assaltaràs, assaltarà, assaltarem, assaltareu, assaltaran *con* assaltaria, assaltaries, assaltaria, assaltaríem, assaltaríeu, assaltarien • **sub** *pre* assalti, assaltis, assalti, assaltem, assalteu, assaltin *imp* assaltés, assaltessis, assaltés, assaltéssim, assaltéssiu, assaltessin • **imp** -, assalta, assalti, assaltem, assalteu, assaltin • **inf** assaltar • **ger** assaltant • **pp** *sing* assaltat / assaltada *plur* assaltats / assaltades

assassinar /assassinate/ • **ind** *pre* assassino, assassines, assassina, assassinem, assassineu, assassinen *imp* assassinava, assassinaves, assassinava, assassinàvem, assassinàveu, assassinaven *prt* assassiní, assassinares, assassinà, assassinàrem, assassinàreu, assassinaren *fut* assassinaré, assassinaràs, assassinarà, assassinarem, assassinareu, assassinaran *con* assassinaria, assassinaries, assassinaria, assassinaríem, assassinaríeu, assassinarien • **sub** *pre* assassini, assassinis, assassini, assassinem, assassineu, assassinin *imp* assassinés, assassinessis, assassinés, assassinéssim, assassinéssiu, assassinessin • **imp** -, assassina, assassini, assassinem, assassineu, assassinin • **inf** assassinar • **ger** assassinant • **pp** *sing* assassinat / assassinada *plur* assassinats / assassinades

assegurar /ensure/ • **ind** *pre* asseguro, assegures, assegura, assegurem, assegureu, asseguren *imp* assegurava, asseguraves, assegurava, asseguràvem, asseguràveu, asseguraven *prt* assegurí, assegurares, assegurà, asseguràrem, asseguràreu, asseguraren *fut* asseguraré, asseguraràs, assegurarà, assegurarem, assegurareu, asseguraran *con* asseguraria, asseguraries, asseguraria, asseguraríem, asseguraríeu, assegurarien • **sub** *pre* asseguri, asseguris, asseguri, assegurem, assegureu, assegurin *imp* assegurés, asseguressis, assegurés, asseguréssim, asseguréssiu, asseguressin • **imp** -, assegura, asseguri, assegurem, assegureu, assegurin • **inf** assegurar • **ger** assegurant • **pp** *sing* assegurat / assegurada *plur* assegurats / assegurades

asseure /sit down/ • **ind** *pre* assec, asseus, asseu, asseiem, asseieu, asseuen *imp* asseia, asseies, asseia, assèiem, assèieu, asseien *prt* asseguí, assegueres, assegué, asseguérem, asseguéreu, assegueren *fut* asseuré, asseuràs, asseurà, asseurem, asseureu, asseuran _con_ asseuria, asseuries, asseuria, asseuríem, asseuríeu, asseurien • **sub** _pre_ assegui, asseguis, assegui, asseguem, assegueu, asseguin _imp_ assegués, asseguessis, assegués, asseguéssim, asseguéssiu, asseguessin • **imp** -, asseu, assegui, asseguem, asseieu, asseguin • **inf** asseure • **ger** asseient • **pp** _sing_ assegut / asseguda _plur_ asseguts / assegudes

assistir /attend/ • **ind** _pre_ assisteixo, assisteixes, assisteix, assistim, assistiu, assisteixen _imp_ assistia, assisties, assistia, assistíem, assistíeu, assistien _prt_ assistí, assistires, assistí, assistírem, assistíreu, assistiren _fut_ assistiré, assistiràs, assistirà, assistirem, assistireu, assistiran _con_ assistiria, assistiries, assistiria, assistiríem, assistiríeu, assistirien • **sub** _pre_ assisteixi, assisteixis, assisteixi, assistim, assistiu, assisteixin _imp_ assistís, assistissis, assistís, assistíssim, assistíssiu, assistissin • **imp** -, assisteix, assisteixi, assistim, assistiu, assisteixin • **inf** assistir • **ger** assistint • **pp** _sing_ assistit / assistida _plur_ assistits / assistides

assolir /achieve/ • **ind** _pre_ assoleixo, assoleixes, assoleix, assolim, assoliu, assoleixen _imp_ assolia, assolies, assolia, assolíem, assolíeu, assolien _prt_ assolí, assolires, assolí, assolírem, assolíreu, assoliren _fut_ assoliré, assoliràs, assolirà, assolirem, assolireu, assoliran _con_ assoliria, assoliries, assoliria, assoliríem, assoliríeu, assolirien • **sub** _pre_ assoleixi, assoleixis, assoleixi, assolim, assoliu, assoleixin _imp_ assolís, assolissis, assolís, assolíssim, assolíssiu, assolissin • **imp** -, assoleix, assoleixi, assolim, assoliu, assoleixin • **inf** assolir • **ger** assolint • **pp** _sing_ assolit / assolida _plur_ assolits / assolides

assumir /assume/ • **ind** _pre_ assumeixo, assumeixes, assumeix, assumim, assumiu, assumeixen _imp_ assumia, assumies, assumia, assumíem, assumíeu, assumien _prt_ assumí, assumires, assumí, assumírem, assumíreu, assumiren _fut_ assumiré, assumiràs, assumirà, assumirem, assumireu, assumiran _con_ assumiria, assumiries, assumiria, assumiríem, assumiríeu, assumirien • **sub** _pre_ assumeixi, assumeixis, assumeixi, assumim, assumiu, assumeixin _imp_ assumís, assumissis, assumís, assumíssim, assumíssiu, assumissin • **imp** -, assumeix, assumeixi, assumim, assumiu, assumeixin • **inf** assumir • **ger** assumint • **pp** _sing_ assumit / assumida _plur_ assumits / assumides

atacar /attack/ • **ind** _pre_ ataco, ataques, ataca, ataquem, ataqueu, ataquen _imp_ atacava, atacaves, atacava, atacàvem, atacàveu, atacaven _prt_ ataquí, atacares, atacà, atacàrem, atacàreu, atacaren _fut_ atacaré, atacaràs, atacarà, atacarem, atacareu, atacaran _con_ atacaria, atacaries, atacaria, atacaríem, atacaríeu, atacarien • **sub** _pre_ ataqui, ataquis, ataqui, ataquem, ataqueu, ataquin _imp_ ataqués, ataquessis, ataqués, ataquéssim, ataquéssiu, ataquessin • **imp** -, ataca, ataqui, ataquem, ataqueu, ataquin • **inf** atacar • **ger** atacant • **pp** _sing_ atacat / atacada _plur_ atacats / atacades

atendre /attend/ • **ind** _pre_ atenc, atens, atén, atenem, ateneu, atenen _imp_ atenia, atenies, atenia, ateníem, ateníeu, atenien _prt_ atenguí, atengueres, atengué, atenguérem, atenguéreu, atengueren _fut_ atendré, atendràs, atendrà, atendrem, atendreu, atendran _con_ atendria, atendries, atendria, atendríem, atendríeu, atendrien • **sub** _pre_ atengui, atenguis, atengui, atenguem, atengueu, atenguin _imp_ atengués, atenguessis, atengués, atenguéssim, atenguéssiu, atenguessin • **imp** -, atén, atengui, atenguem, ateneu, atenguin • **inf** atendre • **ger** atenent • **pp** _sing_ atès / atesa _plur_ atesos / ateses

aterrar /land/ • **ind** _pre_ aterro, aterres, aterra, aterrem, aterreu, aterren _imp_ aterrava, aterraves, aterrava, aterràvem, aterràveu, aterraven _prt_ aterrí, aterrares, aterrà, aterràrem, aterràreu, aterraren _fut_ aterraré, aterraràs, aterrarà, aterrarem, aterrareu, aterraran _con_ aterraria, aterraries, aterraria, aterraríem, aterraríeu, aterrarien • **sub** _pre_ aterri, aterris, aterri, aterrem, aterreu, aterrin _imp_ aterrés, aterressis, aterrés, aterréssim, aterréssiu, aterressin • **imp** -, aterra, aterri, aterrem, aterreu, aterrin • **inf** aterrar • **ger** aterrant • **pp** _sing_ aterrat / aterrada _plur_ aterrats / aterrades

atrapar /catch/ • **ind** _pre_ atrapo, atrapes, atrapa, atrapem, atrapeu, atrapen _imp_ atrapava, atrapaves, atrapava, atrapàvem, atrapàveu, atrapaven _prt_ atrapí, atrapares, atrapà, atrapàrem, atrapàreu, atraparen _fut_ atraparé, atraparàs, atraparà, atraparem, atrapareu, atraparan _con_ atraparia, atraparies, atraparia, atraparíem, atraparíeu, atraparien • **sub** _pre_ atrapi, atrapis, atrapi, atrapem, atrapeu, atrapin _imp_ atrapés, atrapessis, atrapés, atrapéssim, atrapéssiu, atrapessin • **imp** -, atrapa, atrapi, atrapem, atrapeu, atrapin • **inf** atrapar • **ger** atrapant • **pp** _sing_ atrapat / atrapada _plur_ atrapats / atrapades

atraure /attract/ • **ind** _pre_ atrac, atraus, atrau, atraiem, atraieu, atrauen _imp_ atreia, atreies, atreia, atrèiem, atrèieu, atreien _prt_ atraguí, atragueres, atragué, atraguérem, atraguéreu, atragueren _fut_ atrauré, atrauràs, atraurà, atraurem, atraureu, atrauran _con_ atrauria, atrauries, atrauria, atrauríem, atrauríeu, atraurien • **sub** _pre_ atragui, atraguis, atragui, atraguem, atragueu, atraguin _imp_ atragués, atraguessis, atragués, atraguéssim, atraguéssiu, atraguessin • **imp** -, atrau, atragui, atraguem, atraieu, atraguin • **inf** atraure • **ger** atraient • **pp** _sing_ atret / atreta

plur atrets / atretes

aturar /stop/ • **ind** *pre* aturo, atures, atura, aturem, atureu, aturen *imp* aturava, aturaves, aturava, aturàvem, aturàveu, aturaven *prt* aturí, aturares, aturà, aturàrem, aturàreu, aturaren *fut* aturaré, aturaràs, aturarà, aturarem, aturareu, aturaran *con* aturaria, aturaries, aturaria, aturaríem, aturaríeu, aturarien • **sub** *pre* aturi, aturis, aturi, aturem, atureu, aturin *imp* aturés, aturessis, aturés, aturéssim, aturéssiu, aturessin • **imp** -, atura, aturi, aturem, atureu, aturin • **inf** aturar • **ger** aturant • **pp** *sing* aturat / aturada *plur* aturats / aturades

avisar /warn/ • **ind** *pre* aviso, avises, avisa, avisem, aviseu, avisen *imp* avisava, avisaves, avisava, avisàvem, avisàveu, avisaven *prt* avisí, avisares, avisà, avisàrem, avisàreu, avisaren *fut* avisaré, avisaràs, avisarà, avisarem, avisareu, avisaran *con* avisaria, avisaries, avisaria, avisaríem, avisaríeu, avisarien • **sub** *pre* avisi, avisis, avisi, avisem, aviseu, avisin *imp* avisés, avisessis, avisés, aviséssim, aviséssiu, avisessin • **imp** -, avisa, avisi, avisem, aviseu, avisin • **inf** avisar • **ger** avisant • **pp** *sing* avisat / avisada *plur* avisats / avisades

B

baixar /go down, download/ • **ind** *pre* baixo, baixes, baixa, baixem, baixeu, baixen *imp* baixava, baixaves, baixava, baixàvem, baixàveu, baixaven *prt* baixí, baixares, baixà, baixàrem, baixàreu, baixaren *fut* baixaré, baixaràs, baixarà, baixarem, baixareu, baixaran *con* baixaria, baixaries, baixaria, baixaríem, baixaríeu, baixarien • **sub** *pre* baixi, baixis, baixi, baixem, baixeu, baixin *imp* baixés, baixessis, baixés, baixéssim, baixéssiu, baixessin • **imp** -, baixa, baixi, baixem, baixeu, baixin • **inf** baixar • **ger** baixant • **pp** *sing* baixat / baixada *plur* baixats / baixades

ballar /dance/ • **ind** *pre* ballo, balles, balla, ballem, balleu, ballen *imp* ballava, ballaves, ballava, ballàvem, ballàveu, ballaven *prt* ballí, ballares, ballà, ballàrem, ballàreu, ballaren *fut* ballaré, ballaràs, ballarà, ballarem, ballareu, ballaran *con* ballaria, ballaries, ballaria, ballaríem, ballaríeu, ballarien • **sub** *pre* balli, ballis, balli, ballem, balleu, ballin *imp* ballés, ballessis, ballés, balléssim, balléssiu, ballessin • **imp** -, balla, balli, ballem, balleu, ballin • **inf** ballar • **ger** ballant • **pp** *sing* ballat / ballada *plur* ballats / ballades

B

barallar /fight/ • **ind** _pre_ barallo, baralles, baralla, barallem, baralleu, barallen _imp_ barallava, barallaves, barallava, barallàvem, barallàveu, barallaven _prt_ barallí, barallares, barallà, barallàrem, barallàreu, barallaren _fut_ barallaré, barallaràs, barallarà, barallarem, barallareu, barallaran _con_ barallaria, barallaries, barallaria, barallaríem, barallaríeu, barallarien • **sub** _pre_ baralli, barallis, baralli, barallem, baralleu, barallin _imp_ barallés, barallessis, barallés, baralléssim, baralléssiu, barallessin • **imp** -, baralla, baralli, barallem, baralleu, barallin • **inf** barallar • **ger** barallant • **pp** _sing_ barallat / barallada _plur_ barallats / barallades

besar /kiss/ • **ind** _pre_ beso, beses, besa, besem, beseu, besen _imp_ besava, besaves, besava, besàvem, besàveu, besaven _prt_ besí, besares, besà, besàrem, besàreu, besaren _fut_ besaré, besaràs, besarà, besarem, besareu, besaran _con_ besaria, besaries, besaria, besaríem, besaríeu, besarien • **sub** _pre_ besi, besis, besi, besem, beseu, besin _imp_ besés, besessis, besés, beséssim, beséssiu, besessin • **imp** -, besa, besi, besem, beseu, besin • **inf** besar • **ger** besant • **pp** _sing_ besat / besada _plur_ besats / besades

beure /drink/ • **ind** _pre_ bec, beus, beu, bevem, beveu, beuen _imp_ bevia, bevies, bevia, bevíem, bevíeu, bevien _prt_ beguí, begueres, begué, beguérem, beguéreu, begueren _fut_ beuré, beuràs, beurà, beurem, beureu, beuran _con_ beuria, beuries, beuria, beuríem, beuríeu, beurien • **sub** _pre_ begui, beguis, begui, beguem, begueu, beguin _imp_ begués, beguessis, begués, beguéssim, beguéssiu, beguessin • **imp** -, beu, begui, beguem, beveu, beguin • **inf** beure • **ger** bevent • **pp** _sing_ begut / beguda _plur_ beguts / begudes

bombardejar /bombard/ • **ind** _pre_ bombardejo, bombardeges, bombardeja, bombardegem, bombardegeu, bombardegen _imp_ bombardejava, bombardejaves, bombardejava, bombardejàvem, bombardejàveu, bombardejaven _prt_ bombardegí, bombardejares, bombardejà, bombardejàrem, bombardejàreu, bombardejaren _fut_ bombardejaré, bombardejaràs, bombardejarà, bombardejarem, bombardejareu, bombardejaran _con_ bombardejaria, bombardejaries, bombardejaria, bombardejaríem, bombardejaríeu, bombardejarien • **sub** _pre_ bombardegi, bombardegis, bombardegi, bombardegem, bombardegeu, bombardegin _imp_ bombardegés, bombardegessis, bombardegés, bombardegéssim, bombardegéssiu, bombardegessin • **imp** -, bombardeja, bombardegi, bombardegem, bombardegeu, bombardegin • **inf** bombardejar • **ger** bombardejant • **pp** _sing_ bombardejat / bombardejada _plur_ bombardejats / bombardejades

buidar /empty/ • **ind** _pre_ buido, buides, buida, buidem, buideu, buiden _imp_ buidava, buidaves, buidava, buidàvem, buidàveu, buidaven _prt_ buidí, buidares, buidà, buidàrem, buidàreu, buidaren _fut_ buidaré, buidaràs, buidarà, buidarem, buidareu, buidaran _con_ buidaria, buidaries, buidaria, buidaríem, buidaríeu, buidarien • **sub** _pre_ buidi, buidis, buidi, buidem, buideu, buidin _imp_ buidés, buidessis, buidés, buidéssim, buidéssiu, buidessin • **imp** -, buida, buidi, buidem, buideu, buidin • **inf** buidar • **ger** buidant • **pp** _sing_ buidat / buidada _plur_ buidats / buidades

buscar /search/ • **ind** _pre_ busco, busques, busca, busquem, busqueu, busquen _imp_ buscava, buscaves, buscava, buscàvem, buscàveu, buscaven _prt_ busquí, buscares, buscà, buscàrem, buscàreu, buscaren _fut_ buscaré, buscaràs, buscarà, buscarem, buscareu, buscaran _con_ buscaria, buscaries, buscaria, buscaríem, buscaríeu, buscarien • **sub** _pre_ busqui, busquis, busqui, busquem, busqueu, busquin _imp_ busqués, busquessis, busqués, busquéssim, busquéssiu, busquessin • **imp** -, busca, busqui, busquem, busqueu, busquin • **inf** buscar • **ger** buscant • **pp** _sing_ buscat / buscada _plur_ buscats / buscades

C

cagar /shit/ • **ind** _pre_ cago, cagues, caga, caguem, cagueu, caguen _imp_ cagava, cagaves, cagava, cagàvem, cagàveu, cagaven _prt_ caguí, cagares, cagà, cagàrem, cagàreu, cagaren _fut_ cagaré, cagaràs, cagarà, cagarem, cagareu, cagaran _con_ cagaria, cagaries, cagaria, cagaríem, cagaríeu, cagarien • **sub** _pre_ cagui, caguis, cagui, caguem, cagueu, caguin _imp_ cagués, caguessis, cagués, caguéssim, caguéssiu, caguessin • **imp** -, caga, cagui, caguem, cagueu, caguin • **inf** cagar • **ger** cagant • **pp** _sing_ cagat / cagada _plur_ cagats / cagades

callar /shut up/ • **ind** _pre_ callo, calles, calla, callem, calleu, callen _imp_ callava, callaves, callava, callàvem, callàveu, callaven _prt_ callí, callares, callà, callàrem, callàreu, callaren _fut_ callaré, callaràs, callarà, callarem, callareu, callaran _con_ callaria, callaries, callaria, callaríem, callaríeu, callarien • **sub** _pre_ calli, callis, calli, callem, calleu, callin _imp_ callés, callessis, callés, calléssim, calléssiu, callessin • **imp** -, calla, calli, callem, calleu, callin • **inf** callar • **ger** callant • **pp** _sing_ callat / callada _plur_ callats / callades

calmar /calm down/ • **ind** _pre_ calmo, calmes, calma, calmem, calmeu, calmen _imp_ calmava, calmaves, calmava, calmàvem, calmàveu, calmaven _prt_ calmí, calmares, calmà, calmàrem, calmàreu, calmaren _fut_ calmaré, calmaràs, calmarà, calmarem, calmareu, calmaran _con_ calmaria, calmaries, calmaria, calmaríem, calmaríeu, calmarien • **sub** _pre_ calmi, calmis, calmi, calmem, calmeu, calmin _imp_ calmés, calmessis, calmés, calméssim, calméssiu, calmessin • **imp** -, calma, calmi, calmem, calmeu, calmin • **inf** calmar • **ger** calmant • **pp** _sing_ calmat / calmada _plur_ calmats / calmades

caminar /walk/ • **ind** _pre_ camino, camines, camina, caminem, camineu, caminen _imp_ caminava, caminaves, caminava, caminàvem, caminàveu, caminaven _prt_ caminí, caminares, caminà, caminàrem, caminàreu, caminaren _fut_ caminaré, caminaràs, caminarà, caminarem, caminareu, caminaran _con_ caminaria, caminaries, caminaria, caminaríem, caminaríeu, caminarien • **sub** _pre_ camini, caminis, camini, caminem, camineu, caminin _imp_ caminés, caminessis, caminés, caminéssim, caminéssiu, caminessin • **imp** -, camina, camini, caminem, camineu, caminin • **inf** caminar • **ger** caminant • **pp** _sing_ caminat / caminada _plur_ caminats / caminades

cantar /sing/ • **ind** _pre_ canto, cantes, canta, cantem, canteu, canten _imp_ cantava, cantaves, cantava, cantàvem, cantàveu, cantaven _prt_ cantí, cantares, cantà, cantàrem, cantàreu, cantaren _fut_ cantaré, cantaràs, cantarà, cantarem, cantareu, cantaran _con_ cantaria, cantaries, cantaria, cantaríem, cantaríeu, cantarien • **sub** _pre_ canti, cantis, canti, cantem, canteu, cantin _imp_ cantés, cantessis, cantés, cantéssim, cantéssiu, cantessin • **imp** -, canta, canti, cantem, canteu, cantin • **inf** cantar • **ger** cantant • **pp** _sing_ cantat / cantada _plur_ cantats / cantades

canviar /change/ • **ind** _pre_ canvio, canvies, canvia, canviem, canvieu, canvien _imp_ canviava, canviaves, canviava, canviàvem, canviàveu, canviaven _prt_ canvií, canviares, canvià, canviàrem, canviàreu, canviaren _fut_ canviaré, canviaràs, canviarà, canviarem, canviareu, canviaran _con_ canviaria, canviaries, canviaria, canviaríem, canviaríeu, canviarien • **sub** _pre_ canvïi, canvïis, canvïi, canviem, canvieu, canvïin _imp_ canviés, canviessis, canviés, canviéssim, canviéssiu, canviessin • **imp** -, canvia, canvïi, canviem, canvieu, canvïin • **inf** canviar • **ger** canviant • **pp** _sing_ canviat / canviada _plur_ canviats / canviades

capturar /capture/ • **ind** _pre_ capturo, captures, captura, capturem, captureu, capturen _imp_ capturava, capturaves, capturava, capturàvem, capturàveu, capturaven _prt_ capturí, capturares, capturà, capturàrem, capturàreu, capturaren _fut_ capturaré, capturaràs, capturarà, capturarem, capturareu, capturaran _con_ capturaria, capturaries, capturaria, capturaríem, capturaríeu, capturarien • **sub** _pre_ capturi, capturis, capturi,

capturem, captureu, capturin _imp_ capturés, capturessis, capturés, cap-
turéssim, capturéssiu, capturessin • **imp** -, captura, capturi, capturem,
captureu, capturin • **inf** capturar • **ger** capturant • **pp** _sing_ capturat
/ capturada _plur_ capturats / capturades

carregar /load/ • **ind** _pre_ carrego, carregues, carrega, carreguem,
carregueu, carreguen _imp_ carregava, carregaves, carregava, carregàvem,
carregàveu, carregaven _prt_ carreguí, carregares, carregà, carregàrem,
carregàreu, carregaren _fut_ carregaré, carregaràs, carregarà, carregarem,
carregareu, carregaran _con_ carregaria, carregaries, carregaria, carrega-
ríem, carregaríeu, carregarien • **sub** _pre_ carregui, carreguis, carregui,
carreguem, carregueu, carreguin _imp_ carregués, carreguessis, carregués,
carreguéssim, carreguéssiu, carreguessin • **imp** -, carrega, carregui, carreguem, carregueu, carreguin • **inf** carregar • **ger** carregant • **pp** _sing_
carregat / carregada _plur_ carregats / carregades

casar /marry/ • **ind** _pre_ caso, cases, casa, casem, caseu, casen _imp_
casava, casaves, casava, casàvem, casàveu, casaven _prt_ casí, casares, casà,
casàrem, casàreu, casaren _fut_ casaré, casaràs, casarà, casarem, casareu,
casaran _con_ casaria, casaries, casaria, casaríem, casaríeu, casarien • **sub**
pre casi, casis, casi, casem, caseu, casin _imp_ casés, casessis, casés, ca-
séssim, caséssiu, casessin • **imp** -, casa, casi, casem, caseu, casin • **inf**
casar • **ger** casant • **pp** _sing_ casat / casada _plur_ casats / casades

castigar /punish/ • **ind** _pre_ castigo, castigues, castiga, castiguem,
castigueu, castiguen _imp_ castigava, castigaves, castigava, castigàvem, cas-
tigàveu, castigaven _prt_ castiguí, castigares, castigà, castigàrem, castigà-
reu, castigaren _fut_ castigaré, castigaràs, castigarà, castigarem, castigareu,
castigaran _con_ castigaria, castigaries, castigaria, castigaríem, castigaríeu,
castigarien • **sub** _pre_ castigui, castiguis, castigui, castiguem, castigueu,
castiguin _imp_ castigués, castiguessis, castigués, castiguéssim, castiguéssiu,
castiguessin • **imp** -, castiga, castigui, castiguem, castigueu, castiguin •
inf castigar • **ger** castigant • **pp** _sing_ castigat / castigada _plur_ castigats
/ castigades

caure /fall/ • **ind** _pre_ caic, caus, cau, caiem, caieu, cauen _imp_ queia,
queies, queia, quèiem, quèieu, queien _prt_ caiguí, caigueres, caigué, cai-
guérem, caiguéreu, caigueren _fut_ cauré, cauràs, caurà, caurem, caureu,
cauran _con_ cauria, cauries, cauria, cauríem, cauríeu, caurien • **sub** _pre_
caigui, caiguis, caigui, caiguem, caigueu, caiguin _imp_ caigués, caiguessis,
caigués, caiguéssim, caiguéssiu, caiguessin • **imp** -, cau, caigui, caiguem,
caieu, caiguin • **inf** caure • **ger** caient • **pp** _sing_ caigut / caiguda _plur_
caiguts / caigudes

causar /cause/ • **ind** _pre_ causo, causes, causa, causem, causeu, causen _imp_ causava, causaves, causava, causàvem, causàveu, causaven _prt_ causí, causares, causà, causàrem, causàreu, causaren _fut_ causaré, causaràs, causarà, causarem, causareu, causaran _con_ causaria, causaries, causaria, causaríem, causaríeu, causarien • **sub** _pre_ causi, causis, causi, causem, causeu, causin _imp_ causés, causessis, causés, causéssim, causéssiu, causessin • **imp** -, causa, causi, causem, causeu, causin • **inf** causar • **ger** causant • **pp** _sing_ causat / causada _plur_ causats / causades

celebrar /celebrate/ • **ind** _pre_ celebro, celebres, celebra, celebrem, celebreu, celebren _imp_ celebrava, celebraves, celebrava, celebràvem, celebràveu, celebraven _prt_ celebrí, celebrares, celebrà, celebràrem, celebràreu, celebraren _fut_ celebraré, celebraràs, celebrarà, celebrarem, celebrareu, celebraran _con_ celebraria, celebraries, celebraria, celebraríem, celebraríeu, celebrarien • **sub** _pre_ celebri, celebris, celebri, celebrem, celebreu, celebrin _imp_ celebrés, celebressis, celebrés, celebréssim, celebréssiu, celebressin • **imp** -, celebra, celebri, celebrem, celebreu, celebrin • **inf** celebrar • **ger** celebrant • **pp** _sing_ celebrat / celebrada _plur_ celebrats / celebrades

cercar /search/ • **ind** _pre_ cerco, cerques, cerca, cerquem, cerqueu, cerquen _imp_ cercava, cercaves, cercava, cercàvem, cercàveu, cercaven _prt_ cerquí, cercares, cercà, cercàrem, cercàreu, cercaren _fut_ cercaré, cercaràs, cercarà, cercarem, cercareu, cercaran _con_ cercaria, cercaries, cercaria, cercaríem, cercaríeu, cercarien • **sub** _pre_ cerqui, cerquis, cerqui, cerquem, cerqueu, cerquin _imp_ cerqués, cerquessis, cerqués, cerquéssim, cerquéssiu, cerquessin • **imp** -, cerca, cerqui, cerquem, cerqueu, cerquin • **inf** cercar • **ger** cercant • **pp** _sing_ cercat / cercada _plur_ cercats / cercades

clavar /nail/ • **ind** _pre_ clavo, claves, clava, clavem, claveu, claven _imp_ clavava, clavaves, clavava, clavàvem, clavàveu, clavaven _prt_ claví, clavares, clavà, clavàrem, clavàreu, clavaren _fut_ clavaré, clavaràs, clavarà, clavarem, clavareu, clavaran _con_ clavaria, clavaries, clavaria, clavaríem, clavaríeu, clavarien • **sub** _pre_ clavi, clavis, clavi, clavem, claveu, clavin _imp_ clavés, clavessis, clavés, clavéssim, clavéssiu, clavessin • **imp** -, clava, clavi, clavem, claveu, clavin • **inf** clavar • **ger** clavant • **pp** _sing_ clavat / clavada _plur_ clavats / clavades

cobrar /charge/ • **ind** _pre_ cobro, cobres, cobra, cobrem, cobreu, cobren _imp_ cobrava, cobraves, cobrava, cobràvem, cobràveu, cobraven _prt_ cobrí, cobrares, cobrà, cobràrem, cobràreu, cobraren _fut_ cobraré, cobraràs, cobrarà, cobrarem, cobrareu, cobraran _con_ cobraria, cobra-ries, cobraria, cobraríem, cobraríeu, cobrarien • **sub** _pre_ cobri, cobris, cobri, cobrem, cobreu, cobrin _imp_ cobrés, cobressis, cobrés, cobréssim, cobréssiu, cobressin • **imp** -, cobra, cobri, cobrem, cobreu, cobrin • **inf** cobrar • **ger** cobrant • **pp** _sing_ cobrat / cobrada _plur_ cobrats / cobrades

cobrir /cover/ • **ind** _pre_ cobreixo, cobreixes, cobreix, cobrim, cobriu, cobreixen _imp_ cobria, cobries, cobria, cobríem, cobríeu, cobrien _prt_ cobrí, cobrires, cobrí, cobrírem, cobríreu, cobriren _fut_ cobriré, cobrirás, cobrirà, cobrirem, cobrireu, cobriran _con_ cobriria, cobriries, cobriria, cobriríem, cobriríeu, cobririen • **sub** _pre_ cobreixi, cobreixis, cobreixi, cobrim, cobriu, cobreixin _imp_ cobrís, cobrissis, cobrís, cobríssim, cobríssiu, cobrissin • **imp** -, cobreix, cobreixi, cobrim, cobriu, cobreixin • **inf** cobrir • **ger** cobrint • **pp** _sing_ cobert / coberta _plur_ coberts / cobertes

colpejar /hit/ • **ind** _pre_ colpejo, colpeges, colpeja, colpegem, colpegeu, colpegen _imp_ colpejava, colpejaves, colpejava, colpejàvem, colpejàveu, colpejaven _prt_ colpegí, colpejares, colpejà, colpejàrem, colpejàreu, colpejaren _fut_ colpejaré, colpejarás, colpejarà, colpejarem, colpejareu, colpejaran _con_ colpejaria, colpejaries, colpejaria, colpejaríem, colpejaríeu, colpejarien • **sub** _pre_ colpegi, colpegis, colpegi, colpegem, colpegeu, colpegin _imp_ colpegés, colpegessis, colpegés, colpegéssim, colpegéssiu, colpegessin • **imp** -, colpeja, colpegi, colpegem, colpegeu, colpegin • **inf** colpejar • **ger** colpejant • **pp** _sing_ colpejat / colpejada _plur_ colpejats / colpejades

combatre /fight/ • **ind** _pre_ combato, combats, combat, combatem, combateu, combaten _imp_ combatia, combaties, combatia, combatíem, combatíeu, combatien _prt_ combatí, combateres, combaté, combatérem, combatéreu, combateren _fut_ combatré, combatrás, combatrà, combatrem, combatreu, combatran _con_ combatria, combatries, combatria, combatríem, combatríeu, combatrien • **sub** _pre_ combati, combatis, combati, combatem, combateu, combatin _imp_ combatés, combatessis, combatés, combatéssim, combatéssiu, combatessin • **imp** -, combat, combati, combatem, combateu, combatin • **inf** combatre • **ger** combatent • **pp** _sing_ combatut / combatuda _plur_ combatuts / combatudes

comentar /comment/ • **ind** _pre_ comento, comentes, comenta, comentem, comenteu, comenten _imp_ comentava, comentaves, comentava, comentàvem, comentàveu, comentaven _prt_ comentí, comentares, comentà, comentàrem, comentàreu, comentaren _fut_ comentaré, comentaràs, comentarà, comentarem, comentareu, comentaran _con_ comentaria, comentaries, comentaria, comentaríem, comentaríeu, comentarien • **sub** _pre_ comenti, comentis, comenti, comentem, comenteu, comentin _imp_ comentés, comentessis, comentés, comentéssim, comentéssiu, comentessin • **imp** -, comenta, comenti, comentem, comenteu, comentin • **inf** comentar • **ger** comentant • **pp** _sing_ comentat / comentada _plur_ comentats / comentades

cometre /commit/ • **ind** _pre_ cometo, comets, comet, cometem, cometeu, cometen _imp_ cometia, cometies, cometia, cometíem, cometíeu, cometien _prt_ cometí, cometeres, cometé, cometérem, cometéreu, cometeren _fut_ cometré, cometràs, cometrà, cometrem, cometreu, cometran _con_ cometria, cometries, cometria, cometríem, cometríeu, cometrien • **sub** _pre_ cometi, cometis, cometi, cometem, cometeu, cometin _imp_ cometés, cometessis, cometés, cometéssim, cometéssiu, cometessin • **imp** -, comet, cometi, cometem, cometeu, cometin • **inf** cometre • **ger** cometent • **pp** _sing_ comès / comesa _plur_ comesos / comeses

compartir /share/ • **ind** _pre_ comparteixo, comparteixes, comparteix, compartim, compartiu, comparteixen _imp_ compartia, comparties, compartia, compartíem, compartíeu, compartien _prt_ compartí, compartires, compartí, compartírem, compartíreu, compartiren _fut_ compartiré, compartiràs, compartirà, compartirem, compartireu, compartiran _con_ compartiria, compartiries, compartiria, compartiríem, compartiríeu, compartirien • **sub** _pre_ comparteixi, comparteixis, comparteixi, compartim, compartiu, comparteixin _imp_ compartís, compartissis, compartís, compartíssim, compartíssiu, compartissin • **imp** -, comparteix, comparteixi, compartim, compartiu, comparteixin • **inf** compartir • **ger** compartint • **pp** _sing_ compartit / compartida _plur_ compartits / compartides

complaure /please/ • **ind** _pre_ complac, complaus, complau, complaem, complaeu, complauen _imp_ complaïa, complaïes, complaïa, complaíem, complaíeu, complaïen _prt_ complaguí, complagueres, complagué, complaguérem, complaguéreu, complagueren _fut_ complauré, complauràs, complaurà, complaurem, complaureu, complauran _con_ complauria, complauries, complauria, complauríem, complauríeu, complaurien • **sub** _pre_ complagui, complaguis, complagui, complaguem, complagueu, complaguin _imp_ complagués, complaguessis, complagués, complaguéssim, complaguéssiu, complaguessin • **imp** -, complau, complagui, complaguem, complaeu, complaguin • **inf** complaure • **ger** complaent • **pp** _sing_ complagut / complaguda _plur_ complaguts / complagudes

completar /complete/ • **ind** _pre_ completo, completes, completa, completem, completeu, completen _imp_ completava, completaves, completava, completàvem, completàveu, completaven _prt_ completí, completares, completà, completàrem, completàreu, completaren _fut_ completaré, completaràs, completarà, completarem, completareu, completaran _con_ completaria, completaries, completaria, completaríem, completaríeu, completarien • **sub** _pre_ completi, completis, completi, completem, completeu, completin _imp_ completés, completessis, completés, completéssim, completéssiu, completessin • **imp** -, completa, completi, completem, completeu, completin • **inf** completar • **ger** completant • **pp** _sing_ completat / completada _plur_ completats / completades

complir /meet/ • **ind** _pre_ compleixo, compleixes, compleix, complim, compliu, compleixen _imp_ complia, complies, complia, complíem, complíeu, complien _prt_ complí, complires, complí, complírem, complíreu, compliren _fut_ compliré, compliràs, complirà, complirem, complireu, compliran _con_ compliria, compliries, compliria, compliríem, compliríeu, complirien • **sub** _pre_ compleixi, compleixis, compleixi, complim, compliu, compleixin _imp_ complís, complissis, complís, complíssim, complíssiu, complissin • **imp** -, compleix, compleixi, complim, compliu, compleixin • **inf** complir • **ger** complint • **pp** _sing_ complert / complerta _plur_ complerts / complertes

comprar /buy/ • **ind** _pre_ compro, compres, compra, comprem, compreu, compren _imp_ comprava, compraves, comprava, compràvem, compràveu, compraven _prt_ comprí, comprares, comprà, compràrem, compràreu, compraren _fut_ compraré, compraràs, comprarà, comprarem, comprareu, compraran _con_ compraria, compraries, compraria, compraríem, compraríeu, comprarien • **sub** _pre_ compri, compris, compri, comprem, compreu, comprin _imp_ comprés, compressis, comprés, compréssim, compréssiu, compressin • **imp** -, compra, compri, comprem, compreu, comprin • **inf** comprar • **ger** comprant • **pp** _sing_ comprat / comprada _plur_ comprats / comprades

comprendre /understand/ • **ind** _pre_ comprenc, comprens, comprèn, comprenem, compreneu, comprenen _imp_ comprenia, comprenies, comprenia, compreníem, compreníeu, comprenien _prt_ comprenguí, comprengueres, comprengué, comprenguérem, comprenguéreu, comprengueren _fut_ comprendré, comprendràs, comprendrà, comprendrem, comprendreu, comprendran _con_ comprendria, comprendries, comprendria, comprendríem, comprendríeu, comprendrien • **sub** _pre_ comprengui, comprenguis, comprengui, comprenguem, comprengueu, comprenguin _imp_ comprengués, comprenguessis, comprengués, comprengués-

sim, comprenguéssiu, comprenguessin • **imp** -, comprèn, comprengui, comprenguem, compreneu, comprenguin • **inf** comprendre • **ger**
comprenent • **pp** _sing_ comprès / compresa _plur_ compresos / compreses

comprometre /compromise/ • **ind** _pre_ comprometo, compro-
mets, compromet, comprometem, comprometeu, comprometen _imp_
comprometia, comprometies, comprometia, comprometíem, compro-
metíeu, comprometien _prt_ comprometí, comprometeres, comprometé,
comprometérem, comprometéreu, comprometeren _fut_ comprometré,
comprometràs, comprometrà, comprometrem, comprometreu, com-
prometran _con_ comprometria, comprometries, comprometria, com-
prometríem, comprometríeu, comprometrien • **sub** _pre_ comprometi,
comprometis, comprometi, comprometem, comprometeu, comprometin _imp_ comprometés, comprometessis, comprometés, comprometés-
sim, comprometéssiu, comprometessin • **imp** -, compromet, comprometi, comprometem, comprometeu, comprometin • **inf** comprometre
• **ger** comprometent • **pp** _sing_ compromès / compromesa _plur_ com-
promesos / compromeses

comprovar /check/ • **ind** _pre_ comprovo, comproves, comprova,
comprovem, comproveu, comproven _imp_ comprovava, comprovaves,
comprovava, comprovàvem, comprovàveu, comprovaven _prt_ compro-
ví, comprovares, comprovà, comprovàrem, comprovàreu, comprovaren
fut comprovaré, comprovaràs, comprovarà, comprovarem, comprova-
reu, comprovaran _con_ comprovaria, comprovaries, comprovaria, com-
provaríem, comprovaríeu, comprovarien • **sub** _pre_ comprovi, com-
provis, comprovi, comprovem, comproveu, comprovin _imp_ comprovés,
comprovessis, comprovés, comprovéssim, comprovéssiu, comprovessin
• **imp** -, comprova, comprovi, comprovem, comproveu, comprovin •
inf comprovar • **ger** comprovant • **pp** _sing_ comprovat / comprovada
plur comprovats / comprovades

comptar /count/ • **ind** _pre_ compto, comptes, compta, comptem,
compteu, compten _imp_ comptava, comptaves, comptava, comptàvem,
comptàveu, comptaven _prt_ comptí, comptares, comptà, comptàrem,
comptàreu, comptaren _fut_ comptaré, comptaràs, comptarà, comptarem,
comptareu, comptaran _con_ comptaria, comptaries, comptaria, comp-
taríem, comptaríeu, comptarien • **sub** _pre_ compti, comptis, compti,
comptem, compteu, comptin _imp_ comptés, comptessis, comptés, comp-
téssim, comptéssiu, comptessin • **imp** -, compta, compti, comptem,
compteu, comptin • **inf** comptar • **ger** comptant • **pp** _sing_ comptat
/ comptada _plur_ comptats / comptades

comunicar /communicate/ • **ind** _pre_ comunico, comuniques, comunica, comuniquem, comuniqueu, comuniquen _imp_ comunicava, comunicaves, comunicava, comunicàvem, comunicàveu, comunicaven _prt_ comuniquí, comunicares, comunicà, comunicàrem, comunicàreu, comunicaren _fut_ comunicaré, comunicaràs, comunicarà, comunicarem, comunicareu, comunicaran _con_ comunicaria, comunicaries, comunicaria, comunicaríem, comunicaríeu, comunicarien • **sub** _pre_ comuniqui, comuniquis, comuniqui, comuniquem, comuniqueu, comuniquin _imp_ comuniqués, comuniquessis, comuniqués, comuniquéssim, comuniquéssiu, comuniquessin • **imp** -, comunica, comuniqui, comuniquem, comuniqueu, comuniquin • **inf** comunicar • **ger** comunicant • **pp** _sing_ comunicat / comunicada _plur_ comunicats / comunicades

concedir /grant/ • **ind** _pre_ concedeixo, concedeixes, concedeix, concedim, concediu, concedeixen _imp_ concedia, concedies, concedia, concedíem, concedíeu, concedien _prt_ concedí, concedires, concedí, concedírem, concedíreu, concediren _fut_ concediré, concediràs, concedirà, concedirem, concedireu, concediran _con_ concediria, concediries, concediria, concediríem, concediríeu, concedirien • **sub** _pre_ concedeixi, concedeixis, concedeixi, concedim, concediu, concedeixin _imp_ concedís, concedissis, concedís, concedíssim, concedíssiu, concedissin • **imp** -, concedeix, concedeixi, concedim, concediu, concedeixin • **inf** concedir • **ger** concedint • **pp** _sing_ concedit / concedida _plur_ concedits / concedides

condemnar /condemn/ • **ind** _pre_ condemno, condemnes, condemna, condemnem, condemneu, condemnen _imp_ condemnava, condemnaves, condemnava, condemnàvem, condemnàveu, condemnaven _prt_ condemní, condemnares, condemnà, condemnàrem, condemnàreu, condemnaren _fut_ condemnaré, condemnaràs, condemnarà, condemnarem, condemnareu, condemnaran _con_ condemnaria, condemnaries, condemnaria, condemnaríem, condemnaríeu, condemnarien • **sub** _pre_ condemni, condemnis, condemni, condemnem, condemneu, condemnin _imp_ condemnés, condemnessis, condemnés, condemnéssim, condemnéssiu, condemnessin • **imp** -, condemna, condemni, condemnem, condemneu, condemnin • **inf** condemnar • **ger** condemnant • **pp** _sing_ condemnat / condemnada _plur_ condemnats / condemnades

conduir /drive/ • **ind** _pre_ condueixo, condueixes, condueix, conduïm, conduïu, condueixen _imp_ conduïa, conduïes, conduïa, conduíem, conduíeu, conduïen _prt_ conduí, conduïres, conduí, conduírem, conduíreu, conduïren _fut_ conduiré, conduiràs, conduirà, conduirem, conduireu, conduiran _con_ conduiria, conduiries, conduiria, conduiríem, conduiríeu,

conduirien • **sub** _pre_ condueixi, condueixis, condueixi, conduïm, conduïu, condueixin _imp_ conduís, conduïssis, conduís, conduíssim, conduíssiu,
conduïssin • **imp** -, condueix, condueixi, conduïm, conduïu, condueixin • **inf** conduir • **ger** conduint • **pp** _sing_ conduït / conduïda _plur_
conduïts / conduïdes

confessar /confess/ • **ind** _pre_ confesso, confesses, confessa, confessem, confesseu, confessen _imp_ confessava, confessaves, confessava,
confessàvem, confessàveu, confessaven _prt_ confessí, confessares, con-
fessà, confessàrem, confessàreu, confessaren _fut_ confessaré, confessaràs,
confessarà, confessarem, confessareu, confessaran _con_ confessaria, con-
fessaries, confessaria, confessaríem, confessaríeu, confessarien • **sub** _pre_
confessi, confessis, confessi, confessem, confesseu, confessin _imp_ confessés, confessessis, confessés, confesséssim, confesséssiu, confessessin
• **imp** -, confessa, confessi, confessem, confesseu, confessin • **inf** confessar • **ger** confessant • **pp** _sing_ confessat / confessada _plur_ confessats
/ confessades

confiar /trust/ • **ind** _pre_ confio, confies, confia, confiem, confieu,
confien _imp_ confiava, confiaves, confiava, confiàvem, confiàveu, confia-
ven _prt_ confií, confiares, confià, confiàrem, confiàreu, confiaren _fut_ con-
fiaré, confiaràs, confiarà, confiarem, confiareu, confiaran _con_ confiaria,
confiaries, confiaria, confiaríem, confiaríeu, confiarien • **sub** _pre_ confíi,
confíis, confíi, confiem, confieu, confíin _imp_ confiés, confiessis, confiés,
confiéssim, confiéssiu, confiessin • **imp** -, confia, confíi, confiem, confieu, confíin • **inf** confiar • **ger** confiant • **pp** _sing_ confiat / confiada _plur_
confiats / confiades

confirmar /confirm/ • **ind** _pre_ confirmo, confirmes, confirma, confirmem, confirmeu, confirmen _imp_ confirmava, confirmaves, confirmava,
confirmàvem, confirmàveu, confirmaven _prt_ confirmí, confirmares, con-
firmà, confirmàrem, confirmàreu, confirmaren _fut_ confirmaré, confirma-
ràs, confirmarà, confirmarem, confirmareu, confirmaran _con_ confirmaria, confirmaries, confirmaria, confirmaríem, confirmaríeu, confirmarien
• **sub** _pre_ confirmi, confirmis, confirmi, confirmem, confirmeu, confir-
min _imp_ confirmés, confirmessis, confirmés, confirméssim, confirméssiu,
confirmessin • **imp** -, confirma, confirmi, confirmem, confirmeu, confir-
min • **inf** confirmar • **ger** confirmant • **pp** _sing_ confirmat / confirmada
plur confirmats / confirmades

confondre /confuse/ • **ind** _pre_ confonc, confons, confon, confo-
nem, confoneu, confonen _imp_ confonia, confonies, confonia, confoníem,
confoníeu, confonien _prt_ confonguí, confongueres, confongué, confon-

guérem, confonguéreu, confongueren *fut* confondré, confondràs, confondrà, confondrem, confondreu, confondran *con* confondria, confondries, confondria, confondríem, confondríeu, confondrien • **sub** *pre* confongui, confonguis, confongui, confonguem, confongueu, confonguin *imp* confongués, confonguessis, confongués, confonguéssim, confonguéssiu, confonguessin • **imp** -, confon, confongui, confonguem, confoneu, confonguin • **inf** confondre • **ger** confonent • **pp** *sing* confós / confosa *plur* confosos / confoses

connectar /connect/ • **ind** *pre* connecto, connectes, connecta, connectem, connecteu, connecten *imp* connectava, connectaves, connectava, connectàvem, connectàveu, connectaven *prt* connectí, connectares, connectà, connectàrem, connectàreu, connectaren *fut* connectaré, connectaràs, connectarà, connectarem, connectareu, connectaran *con* connectaria, connectaries, connectaria, connectaríem, connectaríeu, connectarien • **sub** *pre* connecti, connectis, connecti, connectem, connecteu, connectin *imp* connectés, connectessis, connectés, connectéssim, connectéssiu, connectessin • **imp** -, connecta, connecti, connectem, connecteu, connectin • **inf** connectar • **ger** connectant • **pp** *sing* connectat / connectada *plur* connectats / connectades

conquerir /conquer/ • **ind** *pre* conquereixo, conquereixes, conquereix, conquerim, conqueriu, conquereixen *imp* conqueria, conqueries, conqueria, conqueríem, conqueríeu, conquerien *prt* conquerí, conquerires, conquerí, conquerírem, conqueríreu, conqueriren *fut* conqueriré, conqueriràs, conquerirà, conquerirem, conquerireu, conqueriran *con* conqueriria, conqueriries, conqueriria, conqueriríem, conqueriríeu, conqueririen • **sub** *pre* conquereixi, conquereixis, conquereixi, conquerim, conqueriu, conquereixin *imp* conquerís, conquerissis, conquerís, conqueríssim, conqueríssiu, conquerissin • **imp** -, conquereix, conquereixi, conquerim, conqueriu, conquereixin • **inf** conquerir • **ger** conquerint • **pp** *sing* conquerit / conquerida *plur* conquerits / conquerides

conrear /cultivate/ • **ind** *pre* conreo, conrees, conrea, conreem, conreeu, conreen *imp* conreava, conreaves, conreava, conreàvem, conreàveu, conreaven *prt* conreí, conreares, conreà, conreàrem, conreàreu, conrearen *fut* conrearé, conrearàs, conrearà, conrearem, conreareu, conrearan *con* conrearia, conrearies, conrearia, conrearíem, conrearíeu, conrearien • **sub** *pre* conreï, conreïs, conreï, conreem, conreeu, conreïn *imp* conreés, conreessis, conreés, conreéssim, conreéssiu, conreessin • **imp** -, conrea, conreï, conreem, conreeu, conreïn • **inf** conrear • **ger** conreant • **pp** *sing* conreat / conreada *plur* conreats / conreades

conservar /preserve/ • **ind** _pre_ conservo, conserves, conserva, conservem, conserveu, conserven _imp_ conservava, conservaves, conservava, conservàvem, conservàveu, conservaven _prt_ conserví, conservares, conservà, conservàrem, conservàreu, conservaren _fut_ conservaré, conservaràs, conservarà, conservarem, conservareu, conservaran _con_ conservaria, conservaries, conservaria, conservaríem, conservaríeu, conservarien • **sub** _pre_ conservi, conservis, conservi, conservem, conserveu, conservin _imp_ conservés, conservessis, conservés, conservéssim, conservéssiu, conservessin • **imp** -, conserva, conservi, conservem, conserveu, conservin • **inf** conservar • **ger** conservant • **pp** _sing_ conservat / conservada _plur_ conservats / conservades

considerar /consider/ • **ind** _pre_ considero, consideres, considera, considerem, considereu, consideren _imp_ considerava, consideraves, considerava, consideràvem, consideràveu, consideraven _prt_ considerí, considerares, considerà, consideràrem, consideràreu, consideraren _fut_ consideraré, consideraràs, considerarà, considerarem, considerareu, consideraran _con_ consideraria, consideraries, consideraria, consideraríem, consideraríeu, considerarien • **sub** _pre_ consideri, consideris, consideri, considerem, considereu, considerin _imp_ considerés, consideressis, considerés, consideréssim, consideréssiu, consideressin • **imp** -, considera, consideri, considerem, considereu, considerin • **inf** considerar • **ger** considerant • **pp** _sing_ considerat / considerada _plur_ considerats / considerades

construir /build, construct/ • **ind** _pre_ construeixo, construeixes, construeix, construïm, construïu, construeixen _imp_ construïa, construïes, construïa, construíem, construíeu, construïen _prt_ construí, construïres, construí, construírem, construíreu, construïren _fut_ construiré, construiràs, construirà, construirem, construireu, construiran _con_ construiria, construiries, construiria, construiríem, construiríeu, construirien • **sub** _pre_ construeixi, construeixis, construeixi, construïm, construïu, construeixin _imp_ construís, construïssis, construís, construíssim, construíssiu, construïssin • **imp** -, construeix, construeixi, construïm, construïu, construeixin • **inf** construir • **ger** construint • **pp** _sing_ construït / construïda _plur_ construïts / construïdes

contactar /contact/ • **ind** _pre_ contacto, contactes, contacta, contactem, contacteu, contacten _imp_ contactava, contactaves, contactava, contactàvem, contactàveu, contactaven _prt_ contactí, contactares, contactà, contactàrem, contactàreu, contactaren _fut_ contactaré, contactaràs, contactarà, contactarem, contactareu, contactaran _con_ contactaria, contactaries, contactaria, contactaríem, contactaríeu, contactarien •

sub _pre_ contacti, contactis, contacti, contactem, contacteu, contactin _imp_ contactés, contactessis, contactés, contactéssim, contactéssiu, contactessin • **imp** -, contacta, contacti, contactem, contacteu, contactin • **inf** contactar • **ger** contactant • **pp** _sing_ contactat / contactada _plur_ contactats / contactades

contar /tell/ • **ind** _pre_ conto, contes, conta, contem, conteu, conten _imp_ contava, contaves, contava, contàvem, contàveu, contaven _prt_ contí, contares, contà, contàrem, contàreu, contaren _fut_ contaré, contaràs, contarà, contarem, contareu, contaran _con_ contaria, contaries, contaria, contaríem, contaríeu, contarien • **sub** _pre_ conti, contis, conti, contem, conteu, contin _imp_ contés, contessis, contés, contéssim, contéssiu, contessin • **imp** -, conta, conti, contem, conteu, contin • **inf** contar • **ger** contant • **pp** _sing_ contat / contada _plur_ contats / contades

contestar /answer/ • **ind** _pre_ contesto, contestes, contesta, contestem, contesteu, contesten _imp_ contestava, contestaves, contestava, contestàvem, contestàveu, contestaven _prt_ contestí, contestares, contestà, contestàrem, contestàreu, contestaren _fut_ contestaré, contestaràs, contestarà, contestarem, contestareu, contestaran _con_ contestaria, contestaries, contestaria, contestaríem, contestaríeu, contestarien • **sub** _pre_ contesti, contestis, contesti, contestem, contesteu, contestin _imp_ contestés, contestessis, contestés, contestéssim, contestéssiu, contestessin • **imp** -, contesta, contesti, contestem, contesteu, contestin • **inf** contestar • **ger** contestant • **pp** _sing_ contestat / contestada _plur_ contestats / contestades

continuar /continue/ • **ind** _pre_ continuo, continues, continua, continuem, continueu, continuen _imp_ continuava, continuaves, continuava, continuàvem, continuàveu, continuaven _prt_ continuí, continuares, continuà, continuàrem, continuàreu, continuaren _fut_ continuaré, continuaràs, continuarà, continuarem, continuareu, continuaran _con_ continuaria, continuaries, continuaria, continuaríem, continuaríeu, continuarien • **sub** _pre_ continuï, continuïs, continuï, continuem, continueu, continuïn _imp_ continués, continuessis, continués, continuéssim, continuéssiu, continuessin • **imp** -, continua, continuï, continuem, continueu, continuïn • **inf** continuar • **ger** continuant • **pp** _sing_ continuat / continuada _plur_ continuats / continuades

contractar /hire/ • **ind** _pre_ contracto, contractes, contracta, contractem, contracteu, contracten _imp_ contractava, contractaves, contractava, contractàvem, contractàveu, contractaven _prt_ contractí, contractares, contractà, contractàrem, contractàreu, contractaren _fut_ contractaré, contractaràs, contractarà, contractarem, contractareu, contractaran _con_ contractaria, contractaries, contractaria, contractaríem, contractaríeu, contractarien • **sub** _pre_ contracti, contractis, contracti, contractem, contracteu, contractin _imp_ contractés, contractessis, contractés, contractéssim, contractéssiu, contractessin • **imp** -, contracta, contracti, contractem, contracteu, contractin • **inf** contractar • **ger** contractant • **pp** _sing_ contractat / contractada _plur_ contractats / contractades

controlar /control/ • **ind** _pre_ controlo, controles, controla, controlem, controleu, controlen _imp_ controlava, controlaves, controlava, controlàvem, controlàveu, controlaven _prt_ controlí, controlares, controlà, controlàrem, controlàreu, controlaren _fut_ controlaré, controlaràs, controlarà, controlarem, controlareu, controlaran _con_ controlaria, controlaries, controlaria, controlaríem, controlaríeu, controlarien • **sub** _pre_ controli, controlis, controli, controlem, controleu, controlin _imp_ controlés, controlessis, controlés, controléssim, controléssiu, controlessin • **imp** -, controla, controli, controlem, controleu, controlin • **inf** controlar • **ger** controlant • **pp** _sing_ controlat / controlada _plur_ controlats / controlades

convertir /convert/ • **ind** _pre_ converteixo, converteixes, converteix, convertim, convertiu, converteixen _imp_ convertia, converties, convertia, convertíem, convertíeu, convertien _prt_ convertí, convertires, convertí, convertírem, convertíreu, convertiren _fut_ convertiré, convertiràs, convertirà, convertirem, convertireu, convertiran _con_ convertiria, convertiries, convertiria, convertiríem, convertiríeu, convertirien • **sub** _pre_ converteixi, converteixis, converteixi, convertim, convertiu, converteixin _imp_ convertís, convertissis, convertís, convertíssim, convertíssiu, convertissin • **imp** -, converteix, converteixi, convertim, convertiu, converteixin • **inf** convertir • **ger** convertint • **pp** _sing_ convertit / convertida _plur_ convertits / convertides

convidar /invite/ • **ind** _pre_ convido, convides, convida, convidem, convideu, conviden _imp_ convidava, convidaves, convidava, convidàvem, convidàveu, convidaven _prt_ convidí, convidares, convidà, convidàrem, convidàreu, convidaren _fut_ convidaré, convidaràs, convidarà, convidarem, convidareu, convidaran _con_ convidaria, convidaries, convidaria, convidaríem, convidaríeu, convidarien • **sub** _pre_ convidi, convidis, convidi, convidem, convideu, convidin _imp_ convidés, convidessis, convidés, convidéssim, convidéssiu, convidessin • **imp** -, convida, convidi, convidem, convideu, convidin • **inf** convidar • **ger** convidant • **pp** _sing_ convidat / convidada _plur_ convidats / convidades

cooperar /cooperate/ • **ind** _pre_ coopero, cooperes, coopera, cooperem, coopereu, cooperen _imp_ cooperava, cooperaves, cooperava, cooperàvem, cooperàveu, cooperaven _prt_ cooperí, cooperares, cooperà, cooperàrem, cooperàreu, cooperaren _fut_ cooperaré, cooperaràs, cooperarà, cooperarem, cooperareu, cooperaran _con_ cooperaria, cooperaries, cooperaria, cooperaríem, cooperaríeu, cooperarien • **sub** _pre_ cooperi, cooperis, cooperi, cooperem, coopereu, cooperin _imp_ cooperés, cooperessis, cooperés, cooperéssim, cooperéssiu, cooperessin • **imp** -, coopera, cooperi, cooperem, coopereu, cooperin • **inf** cooperar • **ger** cooperant • **pp** _sing_ cooperat / cooperada _plur_ cooperats / cooperades

cosir /sew/ • **ind** _pre_ cuso, cuses, cus, cosim, cosiu, cusen _imp_ cosia, cosies, cosia, cosíem, cosíeu, cosien _prt_ cosí, cosires, cosí, cosírem, cosíreu, cosiren _fut_ cosiré, cosiràs, cosirà, cosirem, cosireu, cosiran _con_ cosiria, cosiries, cosiria, cosiríem, cosiríeu, cosirien • **sub** _pre_ cusi, cusis, cusi, cosim, cosiu, cusin _imp_ cosís, cosissis, cosís, cosíssim, cosíssiu, cosissin • **imp** -, cus, cusi, cosim, cosiu, cusin • **inf** cosir • **ger** cosint • **pp** _sing_ cosit / cosida _plur_ cosits / cosides

costar /cost/ • **ind** _pre_ costo, costes, costa, costem, costeu, costen _imp_ costava, costaves, costava, costàvem, costàveu, costaven _prt_ costí, costares, costà, costàrem, costàreu, costaren _fut_ costaré, costaràs, costarà, costarem, costareu, costaran _con_ costaria, costaries, costaria, costaríem, costaríeu, costarien • **sub** _pre_ costi, costis, costi, costem, costeu, costin _imp_ costés, costessis, costés, costéssim, costéssiu, costessin • **imp** -, costa, costi, costem, costeu, costin • **inf** costar • **ger** costant • **pp** _sing_ costat / costada _plur_ costats / costades

crear /create/ • **ind** _pre_ creo, crees, crea, creem, creeu, creen _imp_ creava, creaves, creava, creàvem, creàveu, creaven _prt_ creí, creares, creà, creàrem, creàreu, crearen _fut_ crearé, crearàs, crearà, crearem, creareu, crearan _con_ crearia, crearies, crearia, crearíem, crearíeu, crearien • **sub** _pre_ creï, creïs, creï, creem, creeu, creïn _imp_ creés, creessis, creés, creéssim, creéssiu, creessin • **imp** -, crea, creï, creem, creeu, creïn • **inf** crear • **ger** creant • **pp** _sing_ creat / creada _plur_ creats / creades

cremar /burn/ • **ind** _pre_ cremo, cremes, crema, cremem, cremeu, cremen _imp_ cremava, cremaves, cremava, cremàvem, cremàveu, cremaven _prt_ cremí, cremares, cremà, cremàrem, cremàreu, cremaren _fut_ cremaré, cremaràs, cremarà, cremarem, cremareu, cremaran _con_ cremaria, cremaries, cremaria, cremaríem, cremaríeu, cremarien • **sub** _pre_ cremi, cremis, cremi, cremem, cremeu, cremin _imp_ cremés, cremessis, cremés, creméssim, creméssiu, cremessin • **imp** -, crema, cremi, cremem, cremeu, cremin • **inf** cremar • **ger** cremant • **pp** _sing_ cremat / cremada _plur_ cremats / cremades

creuar /cross/ • **ind** _pre_ creuo, creues, creua, creuem, creueu, creuen _imp_ creuava, creuaves, creuava, creuàvem, creuàveu, creuaven _prt_ creuí, creuares, creuà, creuàrem, creuàreu, creuaren _fut_ creuaré, creuaràs, creuarà, creuarem, creuareu, creuaran _con_ creuaria, creuaries, creuaria, creuaríem, creuaríeu, creuarien • **sub** _pre_ creui, creuis, creui, creuem, creueu, creuin _imp_ creués, creuessis, creués, creuéssim, creuéssiu, creuessin • **imp** -, creua, creui, creuem, creueu, creuin • **inf** creuar • **ger** creuant • **pp** _sing_ creuat / creuada _plur_ creuats / creuades

creure /believe/ • **ind** _pre_ crec, creus, creu, creiem, creieu, creuen _imp_ creia, creies, creia, crèiem, crèieu, creien _prt_ creguí, cregueres, cregué, creguérem, creguéreu, cregueren _fut_ creuré, creuràs, creurà, creurem, creureu, creuran _con_ creuria, creuries, creuria, creuríem, creuríeu, creurien • **sub** _pre_ cregui, creguis, cregui, creguem, cregueu, creguin _imp_ cregués, creguessis, cregués, creguéssim, creguéssiu, creguessin • **imp** -, creu, cregui, creguem, creieu, creguin • **inf** creure • **ger** creient • **pp** _sing_ cregut / creguda _plur_ creguts / cregudes

cridar /shout out/ • **ind** _pre_ crido, crides, crida, cridem, crideu, criden _imp_ cridava, cridaves, cridava, cridàvem, cridàveu, cridaven _prt_ cridí, cridares, cridà, cridàrem, cridàreu, cridaren _fut_ cridaré, cridaràs, cridarà, cridarem, cridareu, cridaran _con_ cridaria, cridaries, cridaria, cridaríem, cridaríeu, cridarien • **sub** _pre_ cridi, cridis, cridi, cridem, crideu, cridin _imp_ cridés, cridessis, cridés, cridéssim, cridéssiu, cridessin • **imp** -, crida, cridi, cridem, crideu, cridin • **inf** cridar • **ger** cridant • **pp** _sing_ cridat / cridada _plur_ cridats / cridades

criticar /criticize/ • **ind** _pre_ critico, critiques, critica, critiquem, critiqueu, critiquen _imp_ criticava, criticaves, criticava, criticàvem, criticàveu, criticaven _prt_ critiquí, criticares, criticà, criticàrem, criticàreu, criticaren _fut_ criticaré, criticaràs, criticarà, criticarem, criticareu, criticaran _con_ criticaria, criticaries, criticaria, criticaríem, criticaríeu, criticarien • **sub** _pre_ critiqui, critiquis, critiqui, critiquem, critiqueu, critiquin _imp_ critiqués, critiquessis, critiqués, critiquéssim, critiquéssiu, critiquessin • **imp** -, critica, critiqui, critiquem, critiqueu, critiquin • **inf** criticar • **ger** criticant • **pp** _sing_ criticat / criticada _plur_ criticats / criticades

cuidar /care/ • **ind** _pre_ cuido, cuides, cuida, cuidem, cuideu, cuiden _imp_ cuidava, cuidaves, cuidava, cuidàvem, cuidàveu, cuidaven _prt_ cuidí, cuidares, cuidà, cuidàrem, cuidàreu, cuidaren *fut* cuidaré, cuidaràs, cuidarà, cuidarem, cuidareu, cuidaran *con* cuidaria, cuidaries, cuidaria, cuidaríem, cuidaríeu, cuidarien • **sub** *pre* cuidi, cuidis, cuidi, cuidem, cuideu, cuidin *imp* cuidés, cuidessis, cuidés, cuidéssim, cuidéssiu, cuidessin • **imp** -, cuida, cuidi, cuidem, cuideu, cuidin • **inf** cuidar • **ger** cuidant • **pp** *sing* cuidat / cuidada *plur* cuidats / cuidades

cuinar /cook/ • **ind** *pre* cuino, cuines, cuina, cuinem, cuineu, cuinen *imp* cuinava, cuinaves, cuinava, cuinàvem, cuinàveu, cuinaven *prt* cuiní, cuinares, cuinà, cuinàrem, cuinàreu, cuinaren *fut* cuinaré, cuinaràs, cuinarà, cuinarem, cuinareu, cuinaran *con* cuinaria, cuinaries, cuinaria, cuinaríem, cuinaríeu, cuinarien • **sub** *pre* cuini, cuinis, cuini, cuinem, cuineu, cuinin *imp* cuinés, cuinessis, cuinés, cuinéssim, cuinéssiu, cuinessin • **imp** -, cuina, cuini, cuinem, cuineu, cuinin • **inf** cuinar • **ger** cuinant • **pp** *sing* cuinat / cuinada *plur* cuinats / cuinades

culpar /blame/ • **ind** *pre* culpo, culpes, culpa, culpem, culpeu, culpen *imp* culpava, culpaves, culpava, culpàvem, culpàveu, culpaven *prt* culpí, culpares, culpà, culpàrem, culpàreu, culparen *fut* culparé, culparàs, culparà, culparem, culpareu, culparan *con* culparia, culparies, culparia, culparíem, culparíeu, culparien • **sub** *pre* culpi, culpis, culpi, culpem, culpeu, culpin *imp* culpés, culpessis, culpés, culpéssim, culpéssiu, culpessin • **imp** -, culpa, culpi, culpem, culpeu, culpin • **inf** culpar • **ger** culpant • **pp** *sing* culpat / culpada *plur* culpats / culpades

curar /cure/ • **ind** *pre* curo, cures, cura, curem, cureu, curen *imp* curava, curaves, curava, curàvem, curàveu, curaven *prt* curí, curares, curà, curàrem, curàreu, curaren *fut* curaré, curaràs, curarà, curarem, curareu, curaran *con* curaria, curaries, curaria, curaríem, curaríeu, curarien • **sub** *pre* curi, curis, curi, curem, cureu, curin *imp* curés, curessis, curés, curéssim, curéssiu, curessin • **imp** -, cura, curi, curem, cureu, curin • **inf** curar • **ger** curant • **pp** *sing* curat / curada *plur* curats / curades

D

decidir /decide/ • **ind** *pre* decideixo, decideixes, decideix, decidim, decidiu, decideixen *imp* decidia, decidies, decidia, decidíem, decidíeu, decidien *prt* decidí, decidires, decidí, decidírem, decidíreu, decidiren *fut*

D

decidiré, decidiràs, decidirà, decidirem, decidireu, decidiran <u>con</u> decidiria, decidiries, decidiria, decidiríem, decidiríeu, decidirien ● **sub** <u>pre</u>
decideixi, decideixis, decideixi, decidim, decidiu, decideixin <u>imp</u> decidís,
decidissis, decidís, decidíssim, decidíssiu, decidissin ● **imp** -, decideix,
decideixi, decidim, decidiu, decideixin ● **inf** decidir ● **ger** decidint ●
pp <u>sing</u> decidit / decidida <u>plur</u> decidits / decidides

declarar /declare/ ● **ind** <u>pre</u> declaro, declares, declara, declarem,
declareu, declaren <u>imp</u> declarava, declaraves, declarava, declaràvem, de-
claràveu, declaraven <u>prt</u> declarí, declarares, declarà, declaràrem, decla-
ràreu, declararen <u>fut</u> declararé, declararàs, declararà, declararem, de-
clarareu, declararan <u>con</u> declararia, declararies, declararia, declararíem,
declararíeu, declararien ● **sub** <u>pre</u> declari, declaris, declari, declarem,
declareu, declarin <u>imp</u> declarés, declaressis, declarés, declaréssim, decla-
réssiu, declaressin ● **imp** -, declara, declari, declarem, declareu, declarin
● **inf** declarar ● **ger** declarant ● **pp** <u>sing</u> declarat / declarada <u>plur</u>
declarats / declarades

dedicar /dedicate/ ● **ind** <u>pre</u> dedico, dediques, dedica, dediquem,
dediqueu, dediquen <u>imp</u> dedicava, dedicaves, dedicava, dedicàvem, de-
dicàveu, dedicaven <u>prt</u> dediquí, dedicares, dedicà, dedicàrem, dedicà-
reu, dedicaren <u>fut</u> dedicaré, dedicaràs, dedicarà, dedicarem, dedicareu,
dedicaran <u>con</u> dedicaria, dedicaries, dedicaria, dedicaríem, dedicaríeu,
dedicarien ● **sub** <u>pre</u> dediqui, dediquis, dediqui, dediquem, dediqueu,
dediquin <u>imp</u> dediqués, dediquessis, dediqués, dediquéssim, dediqués-
siu, dediquessin ● **imp** -, dedica, dediqui, dediquem, dediqueu, dediquin
● **inf** dedicar ● **ger** dedicant ● **pp** <u>sing</u> dedicat / dedicada <u>plur</u> dedicats
/ dedicades

defensar /stand up for/ ● **ind** <u>pre</u> defenso, defenses, defensa, defensem, defenseu, defensen <u>imp</u> defensava, defensaves, defensava, de-
fensàvem, defensàveu, defensaven <u>prt</u> defensí, defensares, defensà, de-
fensàrem, defensàreu, defensaren <u>fut</u> defensaré, defensaràs, defensarà,
defensarem, defensareu, defensaran <u>con</u> defensaria, defensaries, defensaria, defensaríem, defensaríeu, defensarien ● **sub** <u>pre</u> defensi, defensis,
defensi, defensem, defenseu, defensin <u>imp</u> defensés, defensessis, defensés, defenséssim, defenséssiu, defensessin ● **imp** -, defensa, defensi, defensem, defenseu, defensin ● **inf** defensar ● **ger** defensant ● **pp** <u>sing</u>
defensat / defensada <u>plur</u> defensats / defensades

deixar /leave/ ● **ind** <u>pre</u> deixo, deixes, deixa, deixem, deixeu, deixen
<u>imp</u> deixava, deixaves, deixava, deixàvem, deixàveu, deixaven <u>prt</u> dei-
xí, deixares, deixà, deixàrem, deixàreu, deixaren <u>fut</u> deixaré, deixaràs,

deixarà, deixarem, deixareu, deixaran _con_ deixaria, deixaries, deixaria, deixaríem, deixaríeu, deixarien • **sub** _pre_ deixi, deixis, deixi, deixem, deixeu, deixin _imp_ deixés, deixessis, deixés, deixéssim, deixéssiu, deixessin • **imp** -, deixa, deixi, deixem, deixeu, deixin • **inf** deixar • **ger** deixant • **pp** _sing_ deixat / deixada _plur_ deixats / deixades

demanar /ask, require/ • **ind** _pre_ demano, demanes, demana, demanem, demaneu, demanen _imp_ demanava, demanaves, demanava, demanàvem, demanàveu, demanaven _prt_ demaní, demanares, demanà, demanàrem, demanàreu, demanaren _fut_ demanaré, demanaràs, demanarà, demanarem, demanareu, demanaran _con_ demanaria, demanaries, demanaria, demanaríem, demanaríeu, demanarien • **sub** _pre_ demani, demanis, demani, demanem, demaneu, demanin _imp_ demanés, demanessis, demanés, demanéssim, demanéssiu, demanessin • **imp** -, demana, demani, demanem, demaneu, demanin • **inf** demanar • **ger** demanant • **pp** _sing_ demanat / demanada _plur_ demanats / demanades

demostrar /demonstrate/ • **ind** _pre_ demostro, demostres, demostra, demostrem, demostreu, demostren _imp_ demostrava, demostraves, demostrava, demostràvem, demostràveu, demostraven _prt_ demostrí, demostrares, demostrà, demostràrem, demostràreu, demostraren _fut_ demostraré, demostraràs, demostrarà, demostrarem, demostrareu, demostraran _con_ demostraria, demostraries, demostraria, demostraríem, demostraríeu, demostrarien • **sub** _pre_ demostri, demostris, demostri, demostrem, demostreu, demostrin _imp_ demostrés, demostressis, demostrés, demostréssim, demostréssiu, demostressin • **imp** -, demostra, demostri, demostrem, demostreu, demostrin • **inf** demostrar • **ger** demostrant • **pp** _sing_ demostrat / demostrada _plur_ demostrats / demostrades

denunciar /denounce/ • **ind** _pre_ denuncio, denuncies, denuncia, denunciem, denuncieu, denuncien _imp_ denunciava, denunciaves, denunciava, denunciàvem, denunciàveu, denunciaven _prt_ denuncií, denunciares, denuncià, denunciàrem, denunciàreu, denunciaren _fut_ denunciaré, denunciaràs, denunciarà, denunciarem, denunciareu, denunciaran _con_ denunciaria, denunciaries, denunciaria, denunciaríem, denunciaríeu, denunciarien • **sub** _pre_ denunciï, denunciïs, denunciï, denunciem, denuncieu, denunciïn _imp_ denunciés, denunciessis, denunciés, denunciéssim, denunciéssiu, denunciessin • **imp** -, denuncia, denunciï, denunciem, denuncieu, denunciïn • **inf** denunciar • **ger** denunciant • **pp** _sing_ denunciat / denunciada _plur_ denunciats / denunciades

derrotar /defeat/ • **ind** _pre_ derroto, derrotes, derrota, derrotem, derroteu, derroten *imp* derrotava, derrotaves, derrotava, derrotàvem, derrotàveu, derrotaven *prt* derrotí, derrotares, derrotà, derrotàrem, derrotàreu, derrotaren *fut* derrotaré, derrotaràs, derrotarà, derrotarem, derrotareu, derrotaran *con* derrotaria, derrotaries, derrotaria, derrotaríem, derrotaríeu, derrotarien • **sub** *pre* derroti, derrotis, derroti, derrotem, derroteu, derrotin *imp* derrotés, derrotessis, derrotés, derrotéssim, derrotéssiu, derrotessin • **imp** -, derrota, derroti, derrotem, derroteu, derrotin • **inf** derrotar • **ger** derrotant • **pp** *sing* derrotat / derrotada *plur* derrotats / derrotades

descansar /rest/ • **ind** *pre* descanso, descanses, descansa, descansem, descanseu, descansen *imp* descansava, descansaves, descansava, descansàvem, descansàveu, descansaven *prt* descansí, descansares, descansà, descansàrem, descansàreu, descansaren *fut* descansaré, descansaràs, descansarà, descansarem, descansareu, descansaran *con* descansaria, descansaries, descansaria, descansaríem, descansaríeu, descansarien • **sub** *pre* descansi, descansis, descansi, descansem, descanseu, descansin *imp* descansés, descansessis, descansés, descanséssim, descanséssiu, descansessin • **imp** -, descansa, descansi, descansem, descanseu, descansin • **inf** descansar • **ger** descansant • **pp** *sing* descansat / descansada *plur* descansats / descansades

descobrir /discover/ • **ind** *pre* descobreixo, descobreixes, descobreix, descobrim, descobriu, descobreixen *imp* descobria, descobries, descobria, descobríem, descobríeu, descobrien *prt* descobrí, descobrires, descobrí, descobrírem, descobríreu, descobriren *fut* descobriré, descobriràs, descobrirà, descobrirem, descobrireu, descobriran *con* descobriria, descobriries, descobriria, descobriríem, descobriríeu, descobririen • **sub** *pre* descobreixi, descobreixis, descobreixi, descobrim, descobriu, descobreixin *imp* descobrís, descobrissis, descobrís, descobríssim, descobríssiu, descobrissin • **imp** -, descobreix, descobreixi, descobrim, descobriu, descobreixin • **inf** descobrir • **ger** descobrint • **pp** *sing* descobert / — *plur* — / —

descriure /describe/ • **ind** *pre* descric, descrius, descriu, descrivim, descriviu, descriuen *imp* descrivia, descrivies, descrivia, descrivíem, descrivíeu, descrivien *prt* descriguí, descrigueres, descrigué, descriguérem, descriguéreu, descrigueren *fut* descriuré, descriuràs, descriurà, descriurem, descriureu, descriuran *con* descriuria, descriuries, descriuria, descriuríem, descriuríeu, descriurien • **sub** *pre* descrigui, descriguis, descrigui, descriguem, descrigueu, descriguin *imp* descrigués, descriguessis, descrigués, descriguéssim, descriguéssiu, descriguessin • **imp** -, descriu, descrigui, descriguem, descriviu, descriguin • **inf** descriure • **ger** des-

crivint • **pp** _sing_ descrit / descrita _plur_ descrits / descrites

desenvolupar /develop/ • **ind** _pre_ desenvolupo, desenvolupes, desenvolupa, desenvolupem, desenvolupeu, desenvolupen _imp_ desenvolupava, desenvolupaves, desenvolupava, desenvolupàvem, desenvolupàveu, desenvolupaven _prt_ desenvolupí, desenvolupares, desenvolupà, desenvolupàrem, desenvolupàreu, desenvoluparen _fut_ desenvoluparé, desenvoluparàs, desenvoluparà, desenvoluparem, desenvolupareu, desenvoluparan _con_ desenvoluparia, desenvoluparies, desenvoluparia, desenvoluparíem, desenvoluparíeu, desenvoluparien • **sub** _pre_ desenvolupi, desenvolupis, desenvolupi, desenvolupem, desenvolupeu, desenvolupin _imp_ desenvolupés, desenvolupessis, desenvolupés, desenvolupéssim, desenvolupéssiu, desenvolupessin • **imp** -, desenvolupa, desenvolupi, desenvolupem, desenvolupeu, desenvolupin • **inf** desenvolupar • **ger** desenvolupant • **pp** _sing_ desenvolupat / desenvolupada _plur_ desenvolupats / desenvolupades

desfer /undo/ • **ind** _pre_ desfaig, desfàs, desfà, desfem, desfeu, desfan _imp_ desfeia, desfeies, desfeia, desfèiem, desfèieu, desfeien _prt_ desfiu, desferes, desféu, desférem, desféreu, desferen _fut_ desfaré, desfaràs, desfarà, desfarem, desfareu, desfaran _con_ desfaria, desfaries, desfaria, desfariem, desfarieu, desfarien • **sub** _pre_ desfaci, desfacis, desfaci, desfem, desfeu, desfacin _imp_ desfés, desfessis, desfés, desféssim, desféssiu, desfessin • **imp** -, desfés, desfaci, desfem, desfeu, desfacin • **inf** desfer • **ger** desfent • **pp** _sing_ desfet / desfeta _plur_ desfets / desfetes

desitjar /wish/ • **ind** _pre_ desitjo, desitges, desitja, desitgem, desitgeu, desitgen _imp_ desitjava, desitjaves, desitjava, desitjàvem, desitjàveu, desitjaven _prt_ desitgí, desitjares, desitjà, desitjàrem, desitjàreu, desitjaren _fut_ desitjaré, desitjaràs, desitjarà, desitjarem, desitjareu, desitjaran _con_ desitjaria, desitjaries, desitjaria, desitjaríem, desitjaríeu, desitjarien • **sub** _pre_ desitgi, desitgis, desitgi, desitgem, desitgeu, desitgin _imp_ desitgés, desitgessis, desitgés, desitgéssim, desitgéssiu, desitgessin • **imp** -, desitja, desitgi, desitgem, desitgeu, desitgin • **inf** desitjar • **ger** desitjant • **pp** _sing_ desitjat / desitjada _plur_ desitjats / desitjades

despertar /wake up/ • **ind** _pre_ desperto, despertes, desperta, despertem, desperteu, desperten _imp_ despertava, despertaves, despertava, despertàvem, despertàveu, despertaven _prt_ despertí, despertares, despertà, despertàrem, despertàreu, despertaren _fut_ despertaré, despertaràs, despertarà, despertarem, despertareu, despertaran _con_ despertaria, despertaries, despertaria, despertaríem, despertaríeu, despertarien • **sub** _pre_ desperti, despertis, desperti, despertem, desperteu, despertin _imp_ despertés, despertessis, despertés, despertéssim, despertéssiu, despertessin • **imp** -, desperta, desperti, despertem, desperteu, despertin • **inf** despertar • **ger** despertant • **pp** _sing_ despertat / despertada _plur_ despertats / despertades

destrossar /wreck/ • **ind** _pre_ destrosso, destrosses, destrossa, destrossem, destrosseu, destrossen _imp_ destrossava, destrossaves, destrossava, destrossàvem, destrossàveu, destrossaven _prt_ destrossí, destrossares, destrossà, destrossàrem, destrossàreu, destrossaren _fut_ destrossaré, destrossaràs, destrossarà, destrossarem, destrossareu, destrossaran _con_ destrossaria, destrossaries, destrossaria, destrossaríem, destrossaríeu, destrossarien • **sub** _pre_ destrossi, destrossis, destrossi, destrossem, destrosseu, destrossin _imp_ destrossés, destrossessis, destrossés, destrosséssim, destrosséssiu, destrossessin • **imp** -, destrossa, destrossi, destrossem, destrosseu, destrossin • **inf** destrossar • **ger** destrossant • **pp** _sing_ destrossat / destrossada _plur_ destrossats / destrossades

destruir /destroy/ • **ind** _pre_ destrueixo, destrueixes, destrueix, destruïm, destruïu, destrueixen _imp_ destruïa, destruïes, destruïa, destruíem, destruíeu, destruïen _prt_ destruí, destruïres, destruí, destruírem, destruíreu, destruïren _fut_ destruiré, destruiràs, destruirà, destruirem, destruireu, destruiran _con_ destruiria, destruiries, destruiria, destruiríem, destruiríeu, destruirien • **sub** _pre_ destrueixi, destrueixis, destrueixi, destruïm, destruïu, destrueixin _imp_ destruís, destruïssis, destruís, destruíssim, destruíssiu, destruïssin • **imp** -, destrueix, destrueixi, destruïm, destruïu, destrueixin • **inf** destruir • **ger** destruint • **pp** _sing_ destruït / destruïda _plur_ destruïts / destruïdes

detenir /stop, detain/ • **ind** _pre_ detinc, detens, deté, detenim, deteniu, detenen _imp_ detenia, detenies, detenia, deteníem, deteníeu, detenien _prt_ detinguí, detingueres, detingué, detinguérem, detinguéreu, detingueren _fut_ detindré, detindràs, detindrà, detindrem, detindreu, detindran _con_ detindria, detindries, detindria, detindríem, detindríeu, detindrien • **sub** _pre_ detingui, detinguis, detingui, detinguem, detingueu, detinguin _imp_ detingués, detinguessis, detingués, detinguéssim, detinguéssiu, detinguessin • **imp** -, deté, detingui, detinguem, deteniu, detinguin • **inf** detenir • **ger** detenint • **pp** _sing_ detingut / detinguda _plur_ detinguts / detingudes

determinar /determine/ • **ind** _pre_ determino, determines, determina, determinem, determineu, determinen _imp_ determinava, determinaves, determinava, determinàvem, determinàveu, determinaven _prt_

determiní, determinares, determinà, determinàrem, determinàreu, de-
terminaren _fut_ determinaré, determinaràs, determinarà, determinarem,
determinareu, determinaran _con_ determinaria, determinaries, determinaria, determinaríem, determinaríeu, determinarien • **sub** _pre_ determini, determinis, determini, determinem, determineu, determinin _imp_
determinés, determinessis, determinés, determinéssim, determinéssiu,
determinessin • **imp** -, determina, determini, determinem, determineu,
determinin • **inf** determinar • **ger** determinant • **pp** _sing_ determinat
/ determinada _plur_ determinats / determinades

deure /owe/ • **ind** _pre_ dec, deus, deu, devem, deveu, deuen _imp_
devia, devies, devia, devíem, devíeu, devien _prt_ deguí, degueres, degué,
deguérem, deguéreu, degueren _fut_ deuré, deuràs, deurà, deurem, deu-
reu, deuran _con_ deuria, deuries, deuria, deuríem, deuríeu, deurien • **sub**
pre degui, deguis, degui, deguem, degueu, deguin _imp_ degués, deguessis,
degués, deguéssim, deguéssiu, deguessin • **imp** -, deu, degui, deguem,
deveu, deguin • **inf** deure • **ger** devent • **pp** _sing_ degut / deguda _plur_
deguts / degudes

dibuixar /draw/ • **ind** _pre_ dibuixo, dibuixes, dibuixa, dibuixem, dibuixeu, dibuixen _imp_ dibuixava, dibuixaves, dibuixava, dibuixàvem, di-
buixàveu, dibuixaven _prt_ dibuixí, dibuixares, dibuixà, dibuixàrem, dibui-
xàreu, dibuixaren _fut_ dibuixaré, dibuixaràs, dibuixarà, dibuixarem, di-
buixareu, dibuixaran _con_ dibuixaria, dibuixaries, dibuixaria, dibuixaríem,
dibuixaríeu, dibuixarien • **sub** _pre_ dibuixi, dibuixis, dibuixi, dibuixem,
dibuixeu, dibuixin _imp_ dibuixés, dibuixessis, dibuixés, dibuixéssim, dibui-
xéssiu, dibuixessin • **imp** -, dibuixa, dibuixi, dibuixem, dibuixeu, dibuixin
• **inf** dibuixar • **ger** dibuixant • **pp** _sing_ dibuixat / dibuixada _plur_
dibuixats / dibuixades

dir /say/ • **ind** _pre_ dic, dius, diu, diem, dieu, diuen _imp_ deia, deies,
deia, dèiem, dèieu, deien _prt_ diguí, digueres, digué, diguérem, diguéreu,
digueren _fut_ diré, diràs, dirà, direm, direu, diran _con_ diria, diries, diria,
diríem, diríeu, dirien • **sub** _pre_ digui, diguis, digui, diguem, digueu, diguin
imp digués, diguessis, digués, diguéssim, diguéssiu, diguessin • **imp** -,
digues, digui, diguem, digueu, diguin • **inf** dir • **ger** dient • **pp** _sing_ dit
/ dita _plur_ dits / dites

dirigir /direct/ • **ind** _pre_ dirigeixo, dirigeixes, dirigeix, dirigim, dirigiu,
dirigeixen _imp_ dirigia, dirigies, dirigia, dirigíem, dirigíeu, dirigien _prt_ dirigí,
dirigires, dirigí, dirigírem, dirigíreu, dirigiren _fut_ dirigiré, dirigiràs, dirigirà,
dirigirem, dirigireu, dirigiran _con_ dirigiria, dirigiries, dirigiria, dirigiríem,
dirigiríeu, dirigirien • **sub** _pre_ dirigeixi, dirigeixis, dirigeixi, dirigim, diri-

giu, dirigeixin _imp_ dirigís, dirigissis, dirigís, dirigíssim, dirigíssiu, dirigissin • **imp** -, dirigeix, dirigeixi, dirigim, dirigiu, dirigeixin • **inf** dirigir • **ger** dirigint • **pp** _sing_ dirigit / dirigida _plur_ dirigits / dirigides

disculpar /apologize/ • **ind** _pre_ disculpo, disculpes, disculpa, disculpem, disculpeu, disculpen _imp_ disculpava, disculpaves, disculpava, disculpàvem, disculpàveu, disculpaven _prt_ disculpí, disculpares, disculpà, disculpàrem, disculpàreu, disculparen _fut_ disculparé, disculparàs, disculparà, disculparem, disculpareu, disculparan _con_ disculparia, disculparies, disculparia, disculparíem, disculparíeu, disculparien • **sub** _pre_ disculpi, disculpis, disculpi, disculpem, disculpeu, disculpin _imp_ disculpés, disculpessis, disculpés, disculpéssim, disculpéssiu, disculpessin • **imp** -, disculpa, disculpi, disculpem, disculpeu, disculpin • **inf** disculpar • **ger** disculpant • **pp** _sing_ disculpat / disculpada _plur_ disculpats / disculpades

discutir /argue/ • **ind** _pre_ discuteixo, discuteixes, discuteix, discutim, discutiu, discuteixen _imp_ discutia, discuties, discutia, discutíem, discutíeu, discutien _prt_ discutí, discutires, discutí, discutírem, discutíreu, discutiren _fut_ discutiré, discutiràs, discutirà, discutirem, discutireu, discutiran _con_ discutiria, discutiries, discutiria, discutiríem, discutiríeu, discutirien • **sub** _pre_ discuteixi, discuteixis, discuteixi, discutim, discutiu, discuteixin _imp_ discutís, discutissis, discutís, discutíssim, discutíssiu, discutissin • **imp** -, discuteix, discuteixi, discutim, discutiu, discuteixin • **inf** discutir • **ger** discutint • **pp** _sing_ discutit / discutida _plur_ discutits / discutides

disparar /shoot/ • **ind** _pre_ disparo, dispares, dispara, disparem, dispareu, disparen _imp_ disparava, disparaves, disparava, disparàvem, disparàveu, disparaven _prt_ disparí, disparares, disparà, disparàrem, disparàreu, dispararen _fut_ dispararé, dispararàs, dispararà, dispararem, disparareu, dispararan _con_ dispararia, dispararies, dispararia, dispararíem, dispararíeu, dispararien • **sub** _pre_ dispari, disparis, dispari, disparem, dispareu, disparin _imp_ disparés, disparessis, disparés, disparéssim, disparéssiu, disparessin • **imp** -, dispara, dispari, disparem, dispareu, disparin • **inf** disparar • **ger** disparant • **pp** _sing_ disparat / disparada _plur_ disparats / disparades

dissenyar /design/ • **ind** _pre_ dissenyo, dissenyes, dissenya, dissenyem, dissenyeu, dissenyen _imp_ dissenyava, dissenyaves, dissenyava, dissenyàvem, dissenyàveu, dissenyaven _prt_ dissenyí, dissenyares, dissenyà, dissenyàrem, dissenyàreu, dissenyaren _fut_ dissenyaré, dissenyaràs, dissenyarà, dissenyarem, dissenyareu, dissenyaran _con_ dissenyaria, dissenyaries, dissenyaria, dissenyaríem, dissenyaríeu, dissenyarien • **sub** _pre_

dissenyi, dissenyis, dissenyi, dissenyem, dissenyeu, dissenyin _imp_ dissenyés, dissenyessis, dissenyés, dissenyéssim, dissenyéssiu, dissenyessin •
imp -, dissenya, dissenyi, dissenyem, dissenyeu, dissenyin • **inf** dissenyar • **ger** dissenyant • **pp** _sing_ dissenyat / dissenyada _plur_ dissenyats
/ dissenyades

distingir /distinguish/ • **ind** _pre_ distingeixo, distingeixes, distingeix,
distingim, distingiu, distingeixen _imp_ distingia, distingies, distingia, distin-
gíem, distingíeu, distingien _prt_ distingí, distingires, distingí, distingírem,
distingíreu, distingiren _fut_ distingiré, distingiràs, distingirà, distingirem,
distingireu, distingiran _con_ distingiria, distingiries, distingiria, distingirí-
em, distingiríeu, distingirien • **sub** _pre_ distingeixi, distingeixis, distingeixi, distingim, distingiu, distingeixin _imp_ distingís, distingissis, distingís,
distingíssim, distingíssiu, distingissin • **imp** -, distingeix, distingeixi, distingim, distingiu, distingeixin • **inf** distingir • **ger** distingint • **pp** _sing_
distingit / distingida _plur_ distingits / distingides

distreure /distract/ • **ind** _pre_ distrec, distreus, distreu, distraiem,
distraieu, distreuen _imp_ distreia, distreies, distreia, distrèiem, distrèieu,
distreien _prt_ distraguí, distragueres, distragué, distraguérem, distragué-
reu, distragueren _fut_ distrauré, distrauràs, distraurà, distraurem, dis-
traureu, distrauran _con_ distrauria, distrauries, distrauria, distrauríem,
distrauríeu, distraurien • **sub** _pre_ distregui, distreguis, distregui, distraguem, distragueu, distreguin _imp_ distragués, distraguessis, distragués,
distraguéssim, distraguéssiu, distraguessin • **imp** -, distreu, distregui,
distraguem, distraieu, distreguin • **inf** distreure • **ger** distraient • **pp**
sing distret / distreta _plur_ distrets / distretes

dominar /master/ • **ind** _pre_ domino, domines, domina, dominem,
domineu, dominen _imp_ dominava, dominaves, dominava, dominàvem,
dominàveu, dominaven _prt_ dominí, dominares, dominà, dominàrem, do-
minàreu, dominaren _fut_ dominaré, dominaràs, dominarà, dominarem,
dominareu, dominaran _con_ dominaria, dominaries, dominaria, dominarí-
em, dominaríeu, dominarien • **sub** _pre_ domini, dominis, domini, dominem, domineu, dominin _imp_ dominés, dominessis, dominés, dominéssim,
dominéssiu, dominessin • **imp** -, domina, domini, dominem, domineu,
dominin • **inf** dominar • **ger** dominant • **pp** _sing_ dominat / dominada
plur dominats / dominades

donar /give/ • **ind** _pre_ dono, dónes, dóna, donem, doneu, donen
imp donava, donaves, donava, donàvem, donàveu, donaven _prt_ doní,
donares, donà, donàrem, donàreu, donaren _fut_ donaré, donaràs, donarà,
donarem, donareu, donaran _con_ donaria, donaries, donaria, donaríem,

donaríeu, donarien • **sub** _pre_ doni, donis, doni, donem, doneu, donin _imp_ donés, donessis, donés, donéssim, donéssiu, donessin • **imp** -, dóna, doni, donem, doneu, donin • **inf** donar • **ger** donant • **pp** _sing_ donat / donada _plur_ donats / donades

dormir /sleep/ • **ind** _pre_ dormo, dorms, dorm, dormim, dormiu, dormen _imp_ dormia, dormies, dormia, dormíem, dormíeu, dormien _prt_ dormí, dormires, dormí, dormírem, dormíreu, dormiren _fut_ dormiré, dormiràs, dormirà, dormirem, dormireu, dormiran _con_ dormiria, dormiries, dormiria, dormiríem, dormiríeu, dormirien • **sub** _pre_ dormi, dormis, dormi, dormim, dormiu, dormin _imp_ dormís, dormissis, dormís, dormíssim, dormíssiu, dormissin • **imp** -, dorm, dormi, dormim, dormiu, dormin • **inf** dormir • **ger** dormint • **pp** _sing_ dormit / dormida _plur_ dormits / dormides

dubtar /doubt/ • **ind** _pre_ dubto, dubtes, dubta, dubtem, dubteu, dubten _imp_ dubtava, dubtaves, dubtava, dubtàvem, dubtàveu, dubtaven _prt_ dubtí, dubtares, dubtà, dubtàrem, dubtàreu, dubtaren _fut_ dubtaré, dubtaràs, dubtarà, dubtarem, dubtareu, dubtaran _con_ dubtaria, dubtaries, dubtaria, dubtaríem, dubtaríeu, dubtarien • **sub** _pre_ dubti, dubtis, dubti, dubtem, dubteu, dubtin _imp_ dubtés, dubtessis, dubtés, dubtéssim, dubtéssiu, dubtessin • **imp** -, dubta, dubti, dubtem, dubteu, dubtin • **inf** dubtar • **ger** dubtant • **pp** _sing_ dubtat / dubtada _plur_ dubtats / dubtades

durar /last/ • **ind** _pre_ duro, dures, dura, durem, dureu, duren _imp_ durava, duraves, durava, duràvem, duràveu, duraven _prt_ durí, durares, durà, duràrem, duràreu, duraren _fut_ duraré, duraràs, durarà, durarem, durareu, duraran _con_ duraria, duraries, duraria, duraríem, duraríeu, durarien • **sub** _pre_ duri, duris, duri, durem, dureu, durin _imp_ durés, duressis, durés, duréssim, duréssiu, duressin • **imp** -, dura, duri, durem, dureu, durin • **inf** durar • **ger** durant • **pp** _sing_ durat / durada _plur_ durats / durades

E

eixir /emerge/ • **ind** _pre_ ixo, ixes, ix, eixim, eixiu, ixen _imp_ eixia, eixies, eixia, eixíem, eixíeu, eixien _prt_ eixí, eixires, eixí, eixírem, eixíreu, eixiren _fut_ eixiré, eixiràs, eixirà, eixirem, eixireu, eixiran _con_ eixiria, eixiries, eixiria, eixiríem, eixiríeu, eixirien • **sub** _pre_ ixi, ixis, ixi, eixim, eixiu, ixin _imp_ eixís, eixissis, eixís, eixíssim, eixíssiu, eixissin • **imp** -, ix, ixi, eixim, eixiu, ixin • **inf** eixir • **ger** eixint • **pp** _sing_ eixit / eixida _plur_ eixits / eixides

elegir /choose/ • **ind** _pre_ elegeixo, elegeixes, elegeix, elegim, elegiu, elegeixen _imp_ elegia, elegies, elegia, elegíem, elegíeu, elegien _prt_ elegí, elegires, elegí, elegírem, elegíreu, elegiren _fut_ elegiré, elegiràs, elegirà, elegirem, elegireu, elegiran _con_ elegiria, elegiries, elegiria, elegiríem, elegiríeu, elegirien • **sub** _pre_ elegeixi, elegeixis, elegeixi, elegim, elegiu, elegeixin _imp_ elegís, elegissis, elegís, elegíssim, elegíssiu, elegissin • **imp** -, elegeix, elegeixi, elegim, elegiu, elegeixin • **inf** elegir • **ger** elegint • **pp** _sing_ elegit / elegida _plur_ elegits / elegides

eliminar /remove, eliminate/ • **ind** _pre_ elimino, elimines, elimina, eliminem, elimineu, eliminen _imp_ eliminava, eliminaves, eliminava, eliminàvem, eliminàveu, eliminaven _prt_ eliminí, eliminares, eliminà, eliminàrem, eliminàreu, eliminaren _fut_ eliminaré, eliminaràs, eliminarà, eliminarem, eliminareu, eliminaran _con_ eliminaria, eliminaries, eliminaria, eliminaríem, eliminaríeu, eliminarien • **sub** _pre_ elimini, eliminis, elimini, eliminem, elimineu, eliminin _imp_ eliminés, eliminessis, eliminés, eliminéssim, eliminéssiu, eliminessin • **imp** -, elimina, elimini, eliminem, elimineu, eliminin • **inf** eliminar • **ger** eliminant • **pp** _sing_ eliminat / eliminada _plur_ eliminats / eliminades

emetre /emit/ • **ind** _pre_ emeto, emets, emet, emetem, emeteu, emeten _imp_ emetia, emeties, emetia, emetíem, emetíeu, emetien _prt_ emetí, emeteres, emeté, emetérem, emetéreu, emeteren _fut_ emetré, emetràs, emetrà, emetrem, emetreu, emetran _con_ emetria, emetries, emetria, emetríem, emetríeu, emetrien • **sub** _pre_ emeti, emetis, emeti, emetem, emeteu, emetin _imp_ emetés, emetessis, emetés, emetéssim, emetéssiu, emetessin • **imp** -, emet, emeti, emetem, emeteu, emetin • **inf** emetre • **ger** emetent • **pp** _sing_ emès / emesa _plur_ emesos / emeses

emprar /use/ • **ind** _pre_ empro, empres, empra, emprem, empreu, empren _imp_ emprava, empraves, emprava, empràvem, empràveu, empraven _prt_ emprí, emprares, emprà, empràrem, empràreu, empraren _fut_ empraré, empraràs, emprarà, emprarem, emprareu, empraran _con_ empraria, empraries, empraria, empraríem, empraríeu, emprarien • **sub** _pre_ empri, empris, empri, emprem, empreu, emprin _imp_ emprés, empressis, emprés, empréssim, empréssiu, empressin • **imp** -, empra, empri, emprem, empreu, emprin • **inf** emprar • **ger** emprant • **pp** _sing_ emprat / emprada _plur_ emprats / emprades

enamorar /fall in love/ • **ind** _pre_ enamoro, enamores, enamora, enamorem, enamoreu, enamoren _imp_ enamorava, enamoraves, enamorava, enamoràvem, enamoràveu, enamoraven _prt_ enamorí, enamorares, enamorà, enamoràrem, enamoràreu, enamoraren _fut_ enamoraré, enamoraràs, enamorarà, enamorarem, enamorareu, enamoraran _con_ enamoraria, enamoraries, enamoraria, enamoraríem, enamoraríeu, enamorarien • **sub** _pre_ enamori, enamoris, enamori, enamorem, enamoreu, enamorin _imp_ enamorés, enamoressis, enamorés, enamoréssim, enamoréssiu, enamoressin • **imp** -, enamora, enamori, enamorem, enamoreu, enamorin • **inf** enamorar • **ger** enamorant • **pp** _sing_ enamorat / enamorada _plur_ enamorats / enamorades

encaixar /fit in/ • **ind** _pre_ encaixo, encaixes, encaixa, encaixem, encaixeu, encaixen _imp_ encaixava, encaixaves, encaixava, encaixàvem, encaixàveu, encaixaven _prt_ encaixí, encaixares, encaixà, encaixàrem, encaixàreu, encaixaren _fut_ encaixaré, encaixaràs, encaixarà, encaixarem, encaixareu, encaixaran _con_ encaixaria, encaixaries, encaixaria, encaixaríem, encaixaríeu, encaixarien • **sub** _pre_ encaixi, encaixis, encaixi, encaixem, encaixeu, encaixin _imp_ encaixés, encaixessis, encaixés, encaixéssim, encaixéssiu, encaixessin • **imp** -, encaixa, encaixi, encaixem, encaixeu, encaixin • **inf** encaixar • **ger** encaixant • **pp** _sing_ encaixat / encaixada _plur_ encaixats / encaixades

encantar /love it/ • **ind** _pre_ encanto, encantes, encanta, encantem, encanteu, encanten _imp_ encantava, encantaves, encantava, encantàvem, encantàveu, encantaven _prt_ encantí, encantares, encantà, encantàrem, encantàreu, encantaren _fut_ encantaré, encantaràs, encantarà, encantarem, encantareu, encantaran _con_ encantaria, encantaries, encantaria, encantaríem, encantaríeu, encantarien • **sub** _pre_ encanti, encantis, encanti, encantem, encanteu, encantin _imp_ encantés, encantessis, encantés, encantéssim, encantéssiu, encantessin • **imp** -, encanta, encanti, encantem, encanteu, encantin • **inf** encantar • **ger** encantant • **pp** _sing_ encantat / encantada _plur_ encantats / encantades

encarregar /order/ • **ind** _pre_ encarrego, encarregues, encarrega, encarreguem, encarregueu, encarreguen _imp_ encarregava, encarregaves, encarregava, encarregàvem, encarregàveu, encarregaven _prt_ encarreguí, encarregares, encarregà, encarregàrem, encarregàreu, encarregaren _fut_ encarregaré, encarregaràs, encarregarà, encarregarem, encarregareu, encarregaran _con_ encarregaria, encarregaries, encarregaria, encarregaríem, encarregaríeu, encarregarien • **sub** _pre_ encarregui, encarreguis, encarregui, encarreguem, encarregueu, encarreguin _imp_ encarregués, encarreguessis, encarregués, encarreguéssim, encarreguéssiu, encarreguessin • **imp** -, encarrega, encarregui, encarreguem, encarregueu, encarreguin • **inf** encarregar • **ger** encarregant • **pp** _sing_ encarregat / encarregada _plur_ encarregats / encarregades

encendre /switch on/ • **ind** _pre_ encenc, encens, encén, encenem, enceneu, encenen _imp_ encenia, encenies, encenia, enceníem, enceníeu, encenien _prt_ encenguí, encengueres, encengué, encenguérem, encenguéreu, encengueren _fut_ encendré, encendràs, encendrà, encendrem, encendreu, encendran _con_ encendria, encendries, encendria, encendríem, encendríeu, encendrien • **sub** _pre_ encengui, encenguis, encengui, encenguem, encengueu, encenguin _imp_ encengués, encenguessis, encengués, encenguéssim, encenguéssiu, encenguessin • **imp** -, encén, encengui, encenguem, enceneu, encenguin • **inf** encendre • **ger** encenent • **pp** _sing_ encès / encesa _plur_ encesos / enceses

endevinar /guess/ • **ind** _pre_ endevino, endevines, endevina, endevinem, endevineu, endevinen _imp_ endevinava, endevinaves, endevinava, endevinàvem, endevinàveu, endevinaven _prt_ endeviní, endevinares, endevinà, endevinàrem, endevinàreu, endevinaren _fut_ endevinaré, endevinaràs, endevinarà, endevinarem, endevinareu, endevinaran _con_ endevinaria, endevinaries, endevinaria, endevinaríem, endevinaríeu, endevinarien • **sub** _pre_ endevini, endevinis, endevini, endevinem, endevineu, endevinin _imp_ endevinés, endevinessis, endevinés, endevinéssim, endevinéssiu, endevinessin • **imp** -, endevina, endevini, endevinem, endevineu, endevinin • **inf** endevinar • **ger** endevinant • **pp** _sing_ endevinat / endevinada _plur_ endevinats / endevinades

enfadar /angry/ • **ind** _pre_ enfado, enfades, enfada, enfadem, enfadeu, enfaden _imp_ enfadava, enfadaves, enfadava, enfadàvem, enfadàveu, enfadaven _prt_ enfadí, enfadares, enfadà, enfadàrem, enfadàreu, enfadaren _fut_ enfadaré, enfadaràs, enfadarà, enfadarem, enfadareu, enfadaran _con_ enfadaria, enfadaries, enfadaria, enfadaríem, enfadaríeu, enfadarien • **sub** _pre_ enfadi, enfadis, enfadi, enfadem, enfadeu, enfadin _imp_ enfadés, enfadessis, enfadés, enfadéssim, enfadéssiu, enfadessin • **imp** -, enfada, enfadi, enfadem, enfadeu, enfadin • **inf** enfadar • **ger** enfadant • **pp** _sing_ enfadat / enfadada _plur_ enfadats / enfadades

enfonsar /sink down/ • **ind** _pre_ enfonso, enfonses, enfonsa, enfonsem, enfonseu, enfonsen _imp_ enfonsava, enfonsaves, enfonsava, enfonsàvem, enfonsàveu, enfonsaven _prt_ enfonsí, enfonsares, enfonsà, enfonsàrem, enfonsàreu, enfonsaren _fut_ enfonsaré, enfonsaràs, enfonsarà, enfonsarem, enfonsareu, enfonsaran _con_ enfonsaria, enfonsaries, enfonsaria, enfonsaríem, enfonsaríeu, enfonsarien • **sub** _pre_ enfonsi, enfonsis,

enfonsi, enfonsem, enfonseu, enfonsin _imp_ enfonsés, enfonsessis, enfonsés, enfonséssim, enfonséssiu, enfonsessin • **imp** -, enfonsa, enfonsi,
enfonsem, enfonseu, enfonsin • **inf** enfonsar • **ger** enfonsant • **pp**
sing enfonsat / enfonsada _plur_ enfonsats / enfonsades

enfrontar /face it/ • **ind** _pre_ enfronto, enfrontes, enfronta, enfrontem, enfronteu, enfronten _imp_ enfrontava, enfrontaves, enfrontava, en-
frontàvem, enfrontàveu, enfrontaven _prt_ enfrontí, enfrontares, enfron-
tà, enfrontàrem, enfrontàreu, enfrontaren _fut_ enfrontaré, enfrontaràs,
enfrontarà, enfrontarem, enfrontareu, enfrontaran _con_ enfrontaria, en-
frontaries, enfrontaria, enfrontaríem, enfrontaríeu, enfrontarien • **sub**
pre enfronti, enfrontis, enfronti, enfrontem, enfronteu, enfrontin _imp_
enfrontés, enfrontessis, enfrontés, enfrontéssim, enfrontéssiu, enfron-
tessin • **imp** -, enfronta, enfronti, enfrontem, enfronteu, enfrontin •
inf enfrontar • **ger** enfrontant • **pp** _sing_ enfrontat / enfrontada _plur_
enfrontats / enfrontades

enganxar /paste/ • **ind** _pre_ enganxo, enganxes, enganxa, enganxem, enganxeu, enganxen _imp_ enganxava, enganxaves, enganxava, en-
ganxàvem, enganxàveu, enganxaven _prt_ enganxí, enganxares, enganxà,
enganxàrem, enganxàreu, enganxaren _fut_ enganxaré, enganxaràs, engan-
xarà, enganxarem, enganxareu, enganxaran _con_ enganxaria, enganxaries,
enganxaria, enganxaríem, enganxaríeu, enganxarien • **sub** _pre_ enganxi,
enganxis, enganxi, enganxem, enganxeu, enganxin _imp_ enganxés, engan-
xessis, enganxés, enganxéssim, enganxéssiu, enganxessin • **imp** -, enganxa, enganxi, enganxem, enganxeu, enganxin • **inf** enganxar • **ger**
enganxant • **pp** _sing_ enganxat / enganxada _plur_ enganxats / enganxades

enganyar /cheat on/ • **ind** _pre_ enganyo, enganyes, enganya, enganyem, enganyeu, enganyen _imp_ enganyava, enganyaves, enganyava, enga-
nyàvem, enganyàveu, enganyaven _prt_ enganyí, enganyares, enganyà, enga-
nyàrem, enganyàreu, enganyaren _fut_ enganyaré, enganyaràs, enganyarà,
enganyarem, enganyareu, enganyaran _con_ enganyaria, enganyaries, enganyaria, enganyaríem, enganyaríeu, enganyarien • **sub** _pre_ enganyi, enga-
nyis, enganyi, enganyem, enganyeu, enganyin _imp_ enganyés, enganyessis,
enganyés, enganyéssim, enganyéssiu, enganyessin • **imp** -, enganya, enganyi, enganyem, enganyeu, enganyin • **inf** enganyar • **ger** enganyant
• **pp** _sing_ enganyat / enganyada _plur_ enganyats / enganyades

ensenyar /teach/ • **ind** _pre_ ensenyo, ensenyes, ensenya, ensenyem,
ensenyeu, ensenyen _imp_ ensenyava, ensenyaves, ensenyava, ensenyàvem,
ensenyàveu, ensenyaven _prt_ ensenyí, ensenyares, ensenyà, ensenyàrem,

ensenyàreu, ensenyaren _fut_ ensenyaré, ensenyaràs, ensenyarà, ensenya-
rem, ensenyareu, ensenyaran _con_ ensenyaria, ensenyaries, ensenyaria,
ensenyaríem, ensenyaríeu, ensenyarien • **sub** _pre_ ensenyi, ensenyis, ensenyi, ensenyem, ensenyeu, ensenyin _imp_ ensenyés, ensenyessis, ensenyés, ensenyéssim, ensenyéssiu, ensenyessin • **imp** -, ensenya, ensenyi,
ensenyem, ensenyeu, ensenyin • **inf** ensenyar • **ger** ensenyant • **pp**
sing ensenyat / ensenyada _plur_ ensenyats / ensenyades

entendre /understand/ • **ind** _pre_ entenc, entens, entén, entenem,
enteneu, entenen _imp_ entenia, entenies, entenia, enteníem, enteníeu,
entenien _prt_ entenguí, entengueres, entengué, entenguérem, entengué-
reu, entengueren _fut_ entendré, entendràs, entendrà, entendrem, en-
tendreu, entendran _con_ entendria, entendries, entendria, entendríem,
entendríeu, entendrien • **sub** _pre_ entengui, entenguis, entengui, enten-
guem, entengueu, entenguin _imp_ entengués, entenguessis, entengués,
entenguéssim, entenguéssiu, entenguessin • **imp** -, entén, entengui, en-
tenguem, enteneu, entenguin • **inf** entendre • **ger** entenent • **pp** _sing_
entès / entesa _plur_ entesos / enteses

enterrar /bury/ • **ind** _pre_ enterro, enterres, enterra, enterrem,
enterreu, enterren _imp_ enterrava, enterraves, enterrava, enterràvem,
enterràveu, enterraven _prt_ enterrí, enterrares, enterrà, enterràrem, en-
terràreu, enterraren _fut_ enterraré, enterraràs, enterrarà, enterrarem,
enterrareu, enterraran _con_ enterraria, enterraries, enterraria, enter-
raríem, enterraríeu, enterrarien • **sub** _pre_ enterri, enterris, enterri,
enterrem, enterreu, enterrin _imp_ enterrés, enterressis, enterrés, en-
terréssim, enterréssiu, enterressin • **imp** -, enterra, enterri, enterrem,
enterreu, enterrin • **inf** enterrar • **ger** enterrant • **pp** _sing_ enterrat
/ enterrada _plur_ enterrats / enterrades

entrar /enter/ • **ind** _pre_ entro, entres, entra, entrem, entreu, entren
imp entrava, entraves, entrava, entràvem, entràveu, entraven _prt_ en-
trí, entrares, entrà, entràrem, entràreu, entraren _fut_ entraré, entraràs,
entrarà, entrarem, entrareu, entraran _con_ entraria, entraries, entraria,
entraríem, entraríeu, entrarien • **sub** _pre_ entri, entris, entri, entrem,
entreu, entrin _imp_ entrés, entressis, entrés, entréssim, entréssiu, en-
tressin • **imp** -, entra, entri, entrem, entreu, entrin • **inf** entrar • **ger**
entrant • **pp** _sing_ entrat / entrada _plur_ entrats / entrades

entregar /deliver/ • **ind** _pre_ entrego, entregues, entrega, entreguem, entregueu, entreguen _imp_ entregava, entregaves, entregava, en-
tregàvem, entregàveu, entregaven _prt_ entreguí, entregares, entregà, en-
tregàrem, entregàreu, entregaren _fut_ entregaré, entregaràs, entregarà,

entregarem, entregareu, entregaran _con_ entregaria, entregaries, entrega-ria, entregaríem, entregaríeu, entregarien • **sub** _pre_ entregui, entreguis, entregui, entreguem, entregueu, entreguin _imp_ entregués, entreguessis, entregués, entreguéssim, entreguéssiu, entreguessin • **imp** -, entrega, entregui, entreguem, entregueu, entreguin • **inf** entregar • **ger** entre-gant • **pp** _sing_ entregat / entregada _plur_ entregats / entregades

entrenar /train/ • **ind** _pre_ entreno, entrenes, entrena, entrenem, entreneu, entrenen _imp_ entrenava, entrenaves, entrenava, entrenàvem, entrenàveu, entrenaven _prt_ entrení, entrenares, entrenà, entrenàrem, entrenàreu, entrenaren _fut_ entrenaré, entrenaràs, entrenarà, entrena-rem, entrenareu, entrenaran _con_ entrenaria, entrenaries, entrenaria, en-trenaríem, entrenaríeu, entrenarien • **sub** _pre_ entreni, entrenis, entreni, entrenem, entreneu, entrenin _imp_ entrenés, entrenessis, entrenés, en-trenéssim, entrenéssiu, entrenessin • **imp** -, entrena, entreni, entrenem, entreneu, entrenin • **inf** entrenar • **ger** entrenant • **pp** _sing_ entrenat / entrenada _plur_ entrenats / entrenades

enverinar /poisoning/ • **ind** _pre_ enverino, enverines, enverina, en-verinem, enverineu, enverinen _imp_ enverinava, enverinaves, enverinava, enverinàvem, enverinàveu, enverinaven _prt_ enveriní, enverinares, enve-rinà, enverinàrem, enverinàreu, enverinaren _fut_ enverinaré, enverinaràs, enverinarà, enverinarem, enverinareu, enverinaran _con_ enverinaria, en-verinaries, enverinaria, enverinaríem, enverinaríeu, enverinarien • **sub** _pre_ enverini, enverinis, enverini, enverinem, enverineu, enverinin _imp_ enverinés, enverinessis, enverinés, enverinéssim, enverinéssiu, enveri-nessin • **imp** -, enverina, enverini, enverinem, enverineu, enverinin • **inf** enverinar • **ger** enverinant • **pp** _sing_ enverinat / enverinada _plur_ enverinats / enverinades

enviar /send/ • **ind** _pre_ envio, envies, envia, enviem, envieu, envien _imp_ enviava, enviaves, enviava, enviàvem, enviàveu, enviaven _prt_ en-vií, enviares, envià, enviàrem, enviàreu, enviaren _fut_ enviaré, enviaràs, enviarà, enviarem, enviareu, enviaran _con_ enviaria, enviaries, enviaria, enviaríem, enviaríeu, enviarien • **sub** _pre_ envïi, envïis, envïi, enviem, en-vieu, envïin _imp_ enviés, enviessis, enviés, enviéssim, enviéssiu, enviessin • **imp** -, envia, envïi, enviem, envieu, envïin • **inf** enviar • **ger** enviant • **pp** _sing_ enviat / enviada _plur_ enviats / enviades

enxampar /catch/ • **ind** _pre_ enxampo, enxampes, enxampa, en-xampem, enxampeu, enxampen _imp_ enxampava, enxampaves, enxam-pava, enxampàvem, enxampàveu, enxampaven _prt_ enxampí, enxampa-res, enxampà, enxampàrem, enxampàreu, enxamparen _fut_ enxampa-

ré, enxamparàs, enxamparà, enxamparem, enxampareu, enxamparan _con_
enxamparia, enxamparies, enxamparia, enxamparíem, enxamparíeu, en-
xamparien • **sub** _pre_ enxampi, enxampis, enxampi, enxampem, enxampeu, enxampin _imp_ enxampés, enxampessis, enxampés, enxampéssim,
enxampéssiu, enxampessin • **imp** -, enxampa, enxampi, enxampem, enxampeu, enxampin • **inf** enxampar • **ger** enxampant • **pp** _sing_ en-
xampat / enxampada _plur_ enxampats / enxampades

E

equivocar /make mistakes/ • **ind** _pre_ equivoco, equivoques, equivoca, equivoquem, equivoqueu, equivoquen _imp_ equivocava, equivocaves,
equivocava, equivocàvem, equivocàveu, equivocaven _prt_ equivoquí, equi-
vocares, equivocà, equivocàrem, equivocàreu, equivocaren _fut_ equivoca-
ré, equivocaràs, equivocarà, equivocarem, equivocareu, equivocaran _con_
equivocaria, equivocaries, equivocaria, equivocaríem, equivocaríeu, equi-
vocarien • **sub** _pre_ equivoqui, equivoquis, equivoqui, equivoquem, equivoqueu, equivoquin _imp_ equivoqués, equivoquessis, equivoqués, equi-
voquéssim, equivoquéssiu, equivoquessin • **imp** -, equivoca, equivoqui,
equivoquem, equivoqueu, equivoquin • **inf** equivocar • **ger** equivocant
• **pp** _sing_ equivocat / equivocada _plur_ equivocats / equivocades

esborrar /erase/ • **ind** _pre_ esborro, esborres, esborra, esborrem,
esborreu, esborren _imp_ esborrava, esborraves, esborrava, esborràvem,
esborràveu, esborraven _prt_ esborrí, esborrares, esborrà, esborràrem,
esborràreu, esborraren _fut_ esborraré, esborraràs, esborrarà, esborra-
rem, esborrareu, esborraran _con_ esborraria, esborraries, esborraria,
esborraríem, esborraríeu, esborrarien • **sub** _pre_ esborri, esborris, esborri, esborrem, esborreu, esborrin _imp_ esborrés, esborressis, esborrés, esborréssim, esborréssiu, esborressin • **imp** -, esborra, esborri,
esborrem, esborreu, esborrin • **inf** esborrar • **ger** esborrant • **pp**
sing esborrat / esborrada _plur_ esborrats / esborrades

esbrinar /find out/ • **ind** _pre_ esbrino, esbrines, esbrina, esbrinem,
esbrineu, esbrinen _imp_ esbrinava, esbrinaves, esbrinava, esbrinàvem, es-
brinàveu, esbrinaven _prt_ esbriní, esbrinares, esbrinà, esbrinàrem, esbri-
nàreu, esbrinaren _fut_ esbrinaré, esbrinaràs, esbrinarà, esbrinarem, es-
brinareu, esbrinaran _con_ esbrinaria, esbrinaries, esbrinaria, esbrinaríem,
esbrinaríeu, esbrinarien • **sub** _pre_ esbrini, esbrinis, esbrini, esbrinem,
esbrineu, esbrinin _imp_ esbrinés, esbrinessis, esbrinés, esbrinéssim, es-
brinéssiu, esbrinessin • **imp** -, esbrina, esbrini, esbrinem, esbrineu, esbrinin • **inf** esbrinar • **ger** esbrinant • **pp** _sing_ esbrinat / esbrinada
plur esbrinats / esbrinades

escalar /climb/ • **ind** _pre_ escalo, escales, escala, escalem, escaleu, escalen _imp_ escalava, escalaves, escalava, escalàvem, escalàveu, escalaven _prt_ escalí, escalares, escalà, escalàrem, escalàreu, escalaren _fut_ escalaré, escalaràs, escalarà, escalarem, escalareu, escalaran _con_ escalaria, escalaries, escalaria, escalaríem, escalaríeu, escalarien ● **sub** _pre_ escali, escalis, escali, escalem, escaleu, escalin _imp_ escalés, escalessis, escalés, escaléssim, escaléssiu, escalessin ● **imp** -, escala, escali, escalem, escaleu, escalin ● **inf** escalar ● **ger** escalant ● **pp** _sing_ escalat / escalada _plur_ escalats / escalades

escampar /scatter/ ● **ind** _pre_ escampo, escampes, escampa, escampem, escampeu, escampen _imp_ escampava, escampaves, escampava, escampàvem, escampàveu, escampaven _prt_ escampí, escampares, escampà, escampàrem, escampàreu, escamparen _fut_ escamparé, escamparàs, escamparà, escamparem, escampareu, escamparan _con_ escamparia, escamparies, escamparia, escamparíem, escamparíeu, escamparien ● **sub** _pre_ escampi, escampis, escampi, escampem, escampeu, escampin _imp_ escampés, escampessis, escampés, escampéssim, escampéssiu, escampessin ● **imp** -, escampa, escampi, escampem, escampeu, escampin ● **inf** escampar ● **ger** escampant ● **pp** _sing_ escampat / escampada _plur_ escampats / escampades

escapar /escape/ ● **ind** _pre_ escapo, escapes, escapa, escapem, escapeu, escapen _imp_ escapava, escapaves, escapava, escapàvem, escapàveu, escapaven _prt_ escapí, escapares, escapà, escapàrem, escapàreu, escaparen _fut_ escaparé, escaparàs, escaparà, escaparem, escapareu, escaparan _con_ escaparia, escaparies, escaparia, escaparíem, escaparíeu, escaparien ● **sub** _pre_ escapi, escapis, escapi, escapem, escapeu, escapin _imp_ escapés, escapessis, escapés, escapéssim, escapéssiu, escapessin ● **imp** -, escapa, escapi, escapem, escapeu, escapin ● **inf** escapar ● **ger** escapant ● **pp** _sing_ escapat / escapada _plur_ escapats / escapades

esclatar /burst/ ● **ind** _pre_ esclato, esclates, esclata, esclatem, esclateu, esclaten _imp_ esclatava, esclataves, esclatava, esclatàvem, esclatàveu, esclataven _prt_ esclatí, esclatares, esclatà, esclatàrem, esclatàreu, esclataren _fut_ esclataré, esclataràs, esclatarà, esclatarem, esclatareu, esclataran _con_ esclataria, esclataries, esclataria, esclataríem, esclataríeu, esclatarien ● **sub** _pre_ esclati, esclatis, esclati, esclatem, esclateu, esclatin _imp_ esclatés, esclatessis, esclatés, esclatéssim, esclatéssiu, esclatessin ● **imp** -, esclata, esclati, esclatem, esclateu, esclatin ● **inf** esclatar ● **ger** esclatant ● **pp** _sing_ esclatat / esclatada _plur_ esclatats / esclatades

escollir /choose/ ● **ind** _pre_ escullo, esculls, escull, escollim, escolliu, escullen _imp_ escollia, escollies, escollia, escollíem, escollíeu, escollien *prt* escollí, escollires, escollí, escollírem, escollíreu, escolliren *fut* escolliré, escolliràs, escollirà, escollirem, escollireu, escolliran *con* escolliria, escolliries, escolliria, escolliríem, escolliríeu, escollirien • **sub** *pre* esculli, escullis, esculli, escollim, escolliu, escullin *imp* escollís, escollissis, escollís, escollíssim, escollíssiu, escollissin • **imp** -, escull, esculli, escollim, escolliu, escullin • **inf** escollir • **ger** escollint • **pp** *sing* escollit / escollida *plur* escollits / escollides

escoltar /listen/ • **ind** *pre* escolto, escoltes, escolta, escoltem, escolteu, escolten *imp* escoltava, escoltaves, escoltava, escoltàvem, escoltàveu, escoltaven *prt* escoltí, escoltares, escoltà, escoltàrem, escoltàreu, escoltaren *fut* escoltaré, escoltaràs, escoltarà, escoltarem, escoltareu, escoltaran *con* escoltaria, escoltaries, escoltaria, escoltaríem, escoltaríeu, escoltarien • **sub** *pre* escolti, escoltis, escolti, escoltem, escolteu, escoltin *imp* escoltés, escoltessis, escoltés, escoltéssim, escoltéssiu, escoltessin • **imp** -, escolta, escolti, escoltem, escolteu, escoltin • **inf** escoltar • **ger** escoltant • **pp** *sing* escoltat / escoltada *plur* escoltats / escoltades

escriure /write/ • **ind** *pre* escric, escrius, escriu, escrivim, escriviu, escriuen *imp* escrivia, escrivies, escrivia, escrivíem, escrivíeu, escrivien *prt* escriguí, escrigueres, escrigué, escriguérem, escriguéreu, escrigueren *fut* escriuré, escriuràs, escriurà, escriurem, escriureu, escriuran *con* escriuria, escriuries, escriuria, escriuríem, escriuríeu, escriurien • **sub** *pre* escrigui, escriguis, escrigui, escriguem, escrigueu, escriguin *imp* escrigués, escriguessis, escrigués, escriguéssim, escriguéssiu, escriguessin • **imp** -, escriu, escrigui, escriguem, escriviu, escriguin • **inf** escriure • **ger** escrivint • **pp** *sing* escrit / escrita *plur* escrits / escrites

esdevenir /become/ • **ind** *pre* esdevinc, esdevens, esdevé, esdevenim, esdeveniu, esdevenen *imp* esdevenia, esdevenies, esdevenia, esdeveníem, esdeveníeu, esdevenien *prt* esdevinguí, esdevingueres, esdevingué, esdevinguérem, esdevinguéreu, esdevingueren *fut* esdevindré, esdevindràs, esdevindrà, esdevindrem, esdevindreu, esdevindran *con* esdevindria, esdevindries, esdevindria, esdevindríem, esdevindríeu, esdevindrien • **sub** *pre* esdevingui, esdevinguis, esdevingui, esdevinguem, esdevingueu, esdevinguin *imp* esdevingués, esdevinguessis, esdevingués, esdevinguéssim, esdevinguéssiu, esdevinguessin • **imp** -, esdevén, esdevingui, esdevinguem, esdeveniu, esdevinguin • **inf** esdevenir • **ger** esdevenint • **pp** *sing* esdevingut / esdevinguda *plur* esdevinguts / esdevingudes

esmentar /mention/ • **ind** *pre* esmento, esmentes, esmenta, esmentem, esmenteu, esmenten _imp_ esmentava, esmentaves, esmentava, esmentàvem, esmentàveu, esmentaven _prt_ esmentí, esmentares, esmentà, esmentàrem, esmentàreu, esmentaren _fut_ esmentaré, esmentaràs, esmentarà, esmentarem, esmentareu, esmentaran _con_ esmentaria, esmentaries, esmentaria, esmentaríem, esmentaríeu, esmentarien • **sub** _pre_ esmenti, esmentis, esmenti, esmentem, esmenteu, esmentin _imp_ esmentés, esmentessis, esmentés, esmentéssim, esmentéssiu, esmentessin • **imp** -, esmenta, esmenti, esmentem, esmenteu, esmentin • **inf** esmentar • **ger** esmentant • **pp** _sing_ esmentat / esmentada _plur_ esmentats / esmentades

esmorzar /breakfast/ • **ind** _pre_ esmorzo, esmorzes, esmorza, esmorzem, esmorzeu, esmorzen _imp_ esmorzava, esmorzaves, esmorzava, esmorzàvem, esmorzàveu, esmorzaven _prt_ esmorzí, esmorzares, esmorzà, esmorzàrem, esmorzàreu, esmorzaren _fut_ esmorzaré, esmorzaràs, esmorzarà, esmorzarem, esmorzareu, esmorzaran _con_ esmorzaria, esmorzaries, esmorzaria, esmorzaríem, esmorzaríeu, esmorzarien • **sub** _pre_ esmorzi, esmorzis, esmorzi, esmorzem, esmorzeu, esmorzin _imp_ esmorzés, esmorzessis, esmorzés, esmorzéssim, esmorzéssiu, esmorzessin • **imp** -, esmorza, esmorzi, esmorzem, esmorzeu, esmorzin • **inf** esmorzar • **ger** esmorzant • **pp** _sing_ esmorzat / esmorzada _plur_ esmorzats / esmorzades

espantar /scare/ • **ind** _pre_ espanto, espantes, espanta, espantem, espanteu, espanten _imp_ espantava, espantaves, espantava, espantàvem, espantàveu, espantaven _prt_ espantí, espantares, espantà, espantàrem, espantàreu, espantaren _fut_ espantaré, espantaràs, espantarà, espantarem, espantareu, espantaran _con_ espantaria, espantaries, espantaria, espantaríem, espantaríeu, espantarien • **sub** _pre_ espanti, espantis, espanti, espantem, espanteu, espantin _imp_ espantés, espantessis, espantés, espantéssim, espantéssiu, espantessin • **imp** -, espanta, espanti, espantem, espanteu, espantin • **inf** espantar • **ger** espantant • **pp** _sing_ espantat / espantada _plur_ espantats / espantades

esperar /wait, hope, expect/ • **ind** _pre_ espero, esperes, espera, esperem, espereu, esperen _imp_ esperava, esperaves, esperava, esperàvem, esperàveu, esperaven _prt_ esperí, esperares, esperà, esperàrem, esperàreu, esperaren _fut_ esperaré, esperaràs, esperarà, esperarem, esperareu, esperaran _con_ esperaria, esperaries, esperaria, esperaríem, esperaríeu, esperarien • **sub** _pre_ esperi, esperis, esperi, esperem, espereu, esperin _imp_ esperés, esperessis, esperés, esperéssim, esperéssiu, esperessin • **imp** -, espera, esperi, esperem, espereu, esperin • **inf** esperar • **ger** esperant • **pp** _sing_ esperat / esperada _plur_ esperats / esperades

establir /set, establish/ • **ind** _pre_ estableixo, estableixes, estableix, establim, establiu, estableixen _imp_ establia, establies, establia, establíem, establíeu, establien _prt_ establí, establires, establí, establírem, establíreu, establiren _fut_ establiré, establiràs, establirà, establirem, establireu, establiran _con_ establiria, establiries, establiria, establiríem, establiríeu, establirien • **sub** _pre_ estableixi, estableixis, estableixi, establim, establiu, estableixin _imp_ establís, establissis, establís, establíssim, establíssiu, establissin • **imp** -, estableix, estableixi, establim, establiu, estableixin • **inf** establir • **ger** establint • **pp** _sing_ establert / establerta _plur_ establerts / establertes

estalviar /save/ • **ind** _pre_ estalvio, estalvies, estalvia, estalviem, estalvieu, estalvien _imp_ estalviava, estalviaves, estalviava, estalviàvem, estalviàveu, estalviaven _prt_ estalvií, estalviares, estalvià, estalviàrem, estalviàreu, estalviaren _fut_ estalviaré, estalviaràs, estalviarà, estalviarem, estalviareu, estalviaran _con_ estalviaria, estalviaries, estalviaria, estalviaríem, estalviaríeu, estalviarien • **sub** _pre_ estalviï, estalviïs, estalviï, estalviem, estalvieu, estalviïn _imp_ estalviés, estalviessis, estalviés, estalviéssim, estalviéssiu, estalviessin • **imp** -, estalvia, estalviï, estalviem, estalvieu, estalviïn • **inf** estalviar • **ger** estalviant • **pp** _sing_ estalviat / estalviada _plur_ estalviats / estalviades

estar /be/ • **ind** _pre_ estic, estàs, està, estem, esteu, estan _imp_ estava, estaves, estava, estàvem, estàveu, estaven _prt_ estiguí, estigueres, estigué, estiguérem, estiguéreu, estigueren _fut_ estaré, estaràs, estarà, estarem, estareu, estaran _con_ estaria, estaries, estaria, estaríem, estaríeu, estarien • **sub** _pre_ estigui, estiguis, estigui, estiguem, estigueu, estiguin _imp_ estigués, estiguessis, estigués, estiguéssim, estiguéssiu, estiguessin • **imp** -, estigues, estigui, estiguem, estigueu, estiguin • **inf** estar • **ger** estant • **pp** _sing_ estat / estada _plur_ estats / estades

estendre /extend/ • **ind** _pre_ estenc, estens, estén, estenem, esteneu, estenen _imp_ estenia, estenies, estenia, esteníem, esteníeu, estenien _prt_ estenguí, estengueres, estengué, estenguérem, estenguéreu, estengueren _fut_ estendré, estendràs, estendrà, estendrem, estendreu, estendran _con_ estendria, estendries, estendria, estendríem, estendríeu, estendrien • **sub** _pre_ estengui, estenguis, estengui, estenguem, estengueu, estenguin _imp_ estengués, estenguessis, estengués, estenguéssim, estenguéssiu, estenguessin • **imp** -, estén, estengui, estenguem, esteneu, estenguin • **inf** estendre • **ger** estenent • **pp** _sing_ estès / estesa _plur_ estesos / esteses

estimar /love/ • **ind** _pre_ estimo, estimes, estima, estimem, estimeu, estimen _imp_ estimava, estimaves, estimava, estimàvem, estimàveu, esti-maven _prt_ estimí, estimares, estimà, estimàrem, estimàreu, estimaren _fut_ estimaré, estimaràs, estimarà, estimarem, estimareu, estimaran _con_ es-timaria, estimaries, estimaria, estimaríem, estimaríeu, estimarien • **sub** _pre_ estimi, estimis, estimi, estimem, estimeu, estimin _imp_ estimés, es-timessis, estimés, estiméssim, estiméssiu, estimessin • **imp** -, estima, estimi, estimem, estimeu, estimin • **inf** estimar • **ger** estimant • **pp** _sing_ estimat / estimada _plur_ estimats / estimades

estirar /lay back/ • **ind** _pre_ estiro, estires, estira, estirem, estireu, estiren _imp_ estirava, estiraves, estirava, estiràvem, estiràveu, estiraven _prt_ estirí, estirares, estirà, estiràrem, estiràreu, estiraren _fut_ estiraré, estiraràs, estirarà, estirarem, estirareu, estiraran _con_ estiraria, estirari-es, estiraria, estiraríem, estiraríeu, estirarien • **sub** _pre_ estiri, estiris, estiri, estirem, estireu, estirin _imp_ estirés, estiressis, estirés, estiréssim, estiréssiu, estiressin • **imp** -, estira, estiri, estirem, estireu, estirin • **inf** estirar • **ger** estirant • **pp** _sing_ estirat / estirada _plur_ estirats / estirades

estudiar /study/ • **ind** _pre_ estudio, estudies, estudia, estudiem, estu-dieu, estudien _imp_ estudiava, estudiaves, estudiava, estudiàvem, estudi-àveu, estudiaven _prt_ estudií, estudiares, estudià, estudiàrem, estudiàreu, estudiaren _fut_ estudiaré, estudiaràs, estudiarà, estudiarem, estudiareu, estudiaran _con_ estudiaria, estudiaries, estudiaria, estudiaríem, estudiarí-eu, estudiarien • **sub** _pre_ estudiï, estudiïs, estudiï, estudiem, estudieu, estudiïn _imp_ estudiés, estudiessis, estudiés, estudiéssim, estudiéssiu, es-tudiessin • **imp** -, estudia, estudiï, estudiem, estudieu, estudiïn • **inf** estudiar • **ger** estudiant • **pp** _sing_ estudiat / estudiada _plur_ estudiats / estudiades

evacuar /evacuate/ • **ind** _pre_ evacuo, evacues, evacua, evacuem, evacueu, evacuen _imp_ evacuava, evacuaves, evacuava, evacuàvem, eva-cuàveu, evacuaven _prt_ evacuí, evacuares, evacuà, evacuàrem, evacuà-reu, evacuaren _fut_ evacuaré, evacuaràs, evacuarà, evacuarem, evacuareu, evacuaran _con_ evacuaria, evacuaries, evacuaria, evacuaríem, evacuaríeu, evacuarien • **sub** _pre_ evacuï, evacuïs, evacuï, evacuem, evacueu, evacuïn _imp_ evacués, evacuessis, evacués, evacuéssim, evacuéssiu, evacuessin • **imp** -, evacua, evacuï, evacuem, evacueu, evacuïn • **inf** evacuar • **ger** evacuant • **pp** _sing_ evacuat / evacuada _plur_ evacuats / evacuades

evitar /avoid/ • **ind** _pre_ evito, evites, evita, evitem, eviteu, eviten _imp_ evitava, evitaves, evitava, evitàvem, evitàveu, evitaven _prt_ evití, evitares, evità, evitàrem, evitàreu, evitaren _fut_ evitaré, evitaràs, evitarà, evitarem, evitareu, evitaran _con_ evitaria, evitaries, evitaria, evitaríem, evitaríeu, evitarien • **sub** _pre_ eviti, evitis, eviti, evitem, eviteu, evitin _imp_ evités, evitessis, evités, evitéssim, evitéssiu, evitessin • **imp** -, evita, eviti, evitem, eviteu, evitin • **inf** evitar • **ger** evitant • **pp** _sing_ evitat / evitada _plur_ evitats / evitades

examinar /examine/ • **ind** _pre_ examino, examines, examina, examinem, examineu, examinen _imp_ examinava, examinaves, examinava, examinàvem, examinàveu, examinaven _prt_ examiní, examinares, examinà, examinàrem, examinàreu, examinaren _fut_ examinaré, examinaràs, examinarà, examinarem, examinareu, examinaran _con_ examinaria, examinaries, examinaria, examinaríem, examinaríeu, examinarien • **sub** _pre_ examini, examinis, examini, examinem, examineu, examinin _imp_ examinés, examinessis, examinés, examinéssim, examinéssiu, examinessin • **imp** -, examina, examini, examinem, examineu, examinin • **inf** examinar • **ger** examinant • **pp** _sing_ examinat / examinada _plur_ examinats / examinades

executar /run/ • **ind** _pre_ executo, executes, executa, executem, executeu, executen _imp_ executava, executaves, executava, executàvem, executàveu, executaven _prt_ executí, executares, executà, executàrem, executàreu, executaren _fut_ executaré, executaràs, executarà, executarem, executareu, executaran _con_ executaria, executaries, executaria, executaríem, executaríeu, executarien • **sub** _pre_ executi, executis, executi, executem, executeu, executin _imp_ executés, executessis, executés, executéssim, executéssiu, executessin • **imp** -, executa, executi, executem, executeu, executin • **inf** executar • **ger** executant • **pp** _sing_ executat / executada _plur_ executats / executades

existir /exist/ • **ind** _pre_ existeixo, existeixes, existeix, existim, existiu, existeixen _imp_ existia, existies, existia, existíem, existíeu, existien _prt_ existí, existires, existí, existírem, existíreu, existiren _fut_ existiré, existiràs, existirà, existirem, existireu, existiran _con_ existiria, existiries, existiria, existiríem, existiríeu, existirien • **sub** _pre_ existeixi, existeixis, existeixi, existim, existiu, existeixin _imp_ existís, existissis, existís, existíssim, existíssiu, existissin • **imp** -, existeix, existeixi, existim, existiu, existeixin • **inf** existir • **ger** existint • **pp** _sing_ existit / existida _plur_ existits / existides

experimentar /experience/ • **ind** _pre_ experimento, experimentes, experimenta, experimentem, experimenteu, experimenten _imp_ experimentava, experimentaves, experimentava, experimentàvem, experimentàveu, experimentaven _prt_ experimentí, experimentares, experimentà, experimentàrem, experimentàreu, experimentaren _fut_ experimentaré, experimentaràs, experimentarà, experimentarem, experimentareu, experimentaran _con_ experimentaria, experimentaries, experimentaria, experimentaríem, experimentaríeu, experimentarien • **sub** _pre_ experimenti, experimentis, experimenti, experimentem, experimenteu, experimentin _imp_ experimentés, experimentessis, experimentés, experimentéssim, experimentéssiu, experimentessin • **imp** -, experimenta, experimenti, experimentem, experimenteu, experimentin • **inf** experimentar • **ger** experimentant • **pp** _sing_ experimentat / experimentada _plur_ experimentats / experimentades

explicar /explain/ • **ind** _pre_ explico, expliques, explica, expliquem, expliqueu, expliquen _imp_ explicava, explicaves, explicava, explicàvem, explicàveu, explicaven _prt_ expliquí, explicares, explicà, explicàrem, explicàreu, explicaren _fut_ explicaré, explicaràs, explicarà, explicarem, explicareu, explicaran _con_ explicaria, explicaries, explicaria, explicaríem, explicaríeu, explicarien • **sub** _pre_ expliqui, expliquis, expliqui, expliquem, expliqueu, expliquin _imp_ expliqués, expliquessis, expliqués, expliquéssim, expliquéssiu, expliquessin • **imp** -, explica, expliqui, expliquem, expliqueu, expliquin • **inf** explicar • **ger** explicant • **pp** _sing_ explicat / explicada _plur_ explicats / explicades

explorar /explore/ • **ind** _pre_ exploro, explores, explora, explorem, exploreu, exploren _imp_ explorava, exploraves, explorava, exploràvem, exploràveu, exploraven _prt_ explorí, explorares, explorà, exploràrem, exploràreu, exploraren _fut_ exploraré, exploraràs, explorarà, explorarem, explorareu, exploraran _con_ exploraria, explorararies, exploraria, exploraríem, exploraríeu, explorarien • **sub** _pre_ explori, exploris, explori, explorem, exploreu, explorin _imp_ explorés, exploressis, explorés, exploréssim, exploréssiu, exploressin • **imp** -, explora, explori, explorem, exploreu, explorin • **inf** explorar • **ger** explorant • **pp** _sing_ explorat / explorada _plur_ explorats / explorades

explotar /explode/ • **ind** _pre_ exploto, explotes, explota, explotem, exploteu, exploten _imp_ explotava, explotaves, explotava, explotàvem, explotàveu, explotaven _prt_ explotí, explotares, explotà, explotàrem, explotàreu, explotaren _fut_ explotaré, explotaràs, explotarà, explotarem, explotareu, explotaran _con_ explotaria, explotaries, explotaria, explotaríem, explotaríeu, explotarien • **sub** _pre_ exploti, explotis, exploti, explotem, exploteu, explotin _imp_ explotés, explotessis, explotés, explotéssim, explotéssiu, explotessin • **imp** -, explota, exploti, explotem, exploteu, explotin • **inf** explotar • **ger** explotant • **pp** _sing_ explotat / explotada _plur_ explotats / explotades

expressar /express/ • **ind** _pre_ expresso, expresses, expressa, expressem, expresseu, expressen _imp_ expressava, expressaves, expressava, expressàvem, expressàveu, expressaven _prt_ expressí, expressares, expressà, expressàrem, expressàreu, expressaren _fut_ expressaré, expressaràs, expressarà, expressarem, expressareu, expressaran _con_ expressaria, expressaries, expressaria, expressaríem, expressaríeu, expressarien • **sub** _pre_ expressi, expressis, expressi, expressem, expresseu, expressin _imp_ expressés, expressessis, expressés, expresséssim, expresséssiu, expressessin • **imp** -, expressa, expressi, expressem, expresseu, expressin • **inf** expressar • **ger** expressant • **pp** _sing_ expressat / expressada _plur_ expressats / expressades

expulsar /kick out/ • **ind** _pre_ expulso, expulses, expulsa, expulsem, expulseu, expulsen _imp_ expulsava, expulsaves, expulsava, expulsàvem, expulsàveu, expulsaven _prt_ expulsí, expulsares, expulsà, expulsàrem, expulsàreu, expulsaren _fut_ expulsaré, expulsaràs, expulsarà, expulsarem, expulsareu, expulsaran _con_ expulsaria, expulsaries, expulsaria, expulsaríem, expulsaríeu, expulsarien • **sub** _pre_ expulsi, expulsis, expulsi, expulsem, expulseu, expulsin _imp_ expulsés, expulsessis, expulsés, expulséssim, expulséssiu, expulsessin • **imp** -, expulsa, expulsi, expulsem, expulseu, expulsin • **inf** expulsar • **ger** expulsant • **pp** _sing_ expulsat / expulsada _plur_ expulsats / expulsades

exterminar /exterminate/ • **ind** _pre_ extermino, extermines, extermina, exterminem, extermineu, exterminen _imp_ exterminava, exterminaves, exterminava, exterminàvem, exterminàveu, exterminaven _prt_ exterminí, exterminares, exterminà, exterminàrem, exterminàreu, exterminaren _fut_ exterminaré, exterminaràs, exterminarà, exterminarem, exterminareu, exterminaran _con_ exterminaria, exterminaries, exterminaria, exterminaríem, exterminaríeu, exterminarien • **sub** _pre_ extermini, exterminis, extermini, exterminem, extermineu, exterminin _imp_ exterminés, exterminessis, exterminés, exterminéssim, exterminéssiu, exterminessin • **imp** -, extermina, extermini, exterminem, extermineu, exterminin • **inf** exterminar • **ger** exterminant • **pp** _sing_ exterminat / exterminada _plur_ exterminats / exterminades

extreure /extract/ • **ind** _pre_ extrec, extreus, extreu, extraiem, extraieu, extreuen _imp_ extreia, extreies, extreia, extrèiem, extrèieu, extreien _prt_ extraguí, extragueres, extragué, extraguérem, extraguéreu, extragueren _fut_ extrauré, extrauràs, extraurà, extraurem, extraureu, extrauran _con_ extrauria, extrauries, extrauria, extrauríem, extrauríeu, extraurien • **sub** _pre_ extregui, extreguis, extregui, extraguem, extragueu, extreguin _imp_ extragués, extraguessis, extragués, extraguéssim, extraguéssiu, extraguessin • **imp** -, extreu, extregui, extraguem, extra-ieu, extreguin • **inf** extreure • **ger** extraient • **pp** *sing* extret / extreta *plur* extrets / extretes

F

fabricar /make/ • **ind** *pre* fabrico, fabriques, fabrica, fabriquem, fa-briqueu, fabriquen *imp* fabricava, fabricaves, fabricava, fabricàvem, fabri-càveu, fabricaven *prt* fabriquí, fabricares, fabricà, fabricàrem, fabricàreu, fabricaren *fut* fabricaré, fabricaràs, fabricarà, fabricarem, fabricareu, fa-bricaran *con* fabricaria, fabricaries, fabricaria, fabricaríem, fabricaríeu, fabricarien • **sub** *pre* fabriqui, fabriquis, fabriqui, fabriquem, fabriqueu, fabriquin *imp* fabriqués, fabriquessis, fabriqués, fabriquéssim, fabriqués-siu, fabriquessin • **imp** -, fabrica, fabriqui, fabriquem, fabriqueu, fabriquin • **inf** fabricar • **ger** fabricant • **pp** *sing* fabricat / fabricada *plur* fabricats / fabricades

faltar /miss/ • **ind** *pre* falto, faltes, falta, faltem, falteu, falten *imp* fal-tava, faltaves, faltava, faltàvem, faltàveu, faltaven *prt* faltí, faltares, faltà, faltàrem, faltàreu, faltaren *fut* faltaré, faltaràs, faltarà, faltarem, faltareu, faltaran *con* faltaria, faltaries, faltaria, faltaríem, faltaríeu, faltarien • **sub** *pre* falti, faltis, falti, faltem, falteu, faltin *imp* faltés, faltessis, faltés, fal-téssim, faltéssiu, faltessin • **imp** -, falta, falti, faltem, falteu, faltin • **inf** faltar • **ger** faltant • **pp** *sing* faltat / faltada *plur* faltats / faltades

ferir /hurt/ • **ind** *pre* fereixo, fereixes, fereix, ferim, feriu, fereixen *imp* feria, feries, feria, feríem, feríeu, ferien *prt* ferí, ferires, ferí, ferí-rem, feríreu, feriren *fut* feriré, feriràs, ferirà, ferirem, ferireu, feriran *con* feriria, feriries, feriria, feriríem, feriríeu, feririen • **sub** *pre* fereixi, fereixis, fereixi, ferim, feriu, fereixin *imp* ferís, ferissis, ferís, feríssim, feríssiu, ferissin • **imp** -, fereix, fereixi, ferim, feriu, fereixin • **inf** ferir • **ger** ferint • **pp** *sing* ferit / ferida *plur* ferits / ferides

fiar /trust/ • **ind** *pre* fio, fies, fia, fiem, fieu, fien *imp* fiava, fiaves, fiava, fiàvem, fiàveu, fiaven *prt* fií, fiares, fià, fiàrem, fiàreu, fiaren *fut* fiaré, fiaràs, fiarà, fiarem, fiareu, fiaran *con* fiaria, fiaries, fiaria, fiaríem, fiaríeu, fiarien • **sub** *pre* fiï, fiïs, fiï, fiem, fieu, fiïn *imp* fiés, fiessis, fiés, fiéssim, fiéssiu, fiessin • **imp** -, fia, fiï, fiem, fieu, fiïn • **inf** fiar • **ger** fiant • **pp** *sing* fiat / fiada *plur* fiats / fiades

ficar /put/ • **ind** _pre_ fico, fiques, fica, fiquem, fiqueu, fiquen _imp_ ficava, ficaves, ficava, ficàvem, ficàveu, ficaven _prt_ fiquí, ficares, ficà, ficàrem, ficàreu, ficaren _fut_ ficaré, ficaràs, ficarà, ficarem, ficareu, ficaran _con_ ficaria, ficaries, ficaria, ficaríem, ficaríeu, ficarien • **sub** _pre_ fiqui, fiquis, fiqui, fiquem, fiqueu, fiquin _imp_ fiqués, fiquessis, fiqués, fiquéssim, fiquéssiu, fiquessin • **imp** -, fica, fiqui, fiquem, fiqueu, fiquin • **inf** ficar • **ger** ficant • **pp** _sing_ ficat / ficada _plur_ ficats / ficades

filmar /film/ • **ind** _pre_ filmo, filmes, filma, filmem, filmeu, filmen _imp_ filmava, filmaves, filmava, filmàvem, filmàveu, filmaven _prt_ filmí, filmares, filmà, filmàrem, filmàreu, filmaren _fut_ filmaré, filmaràs, filmarà, filmarem, filmareu, filmaran _con_ filmaria, filmaries, filmaria, filmaríem, filmaríeu, filmarien • **sub** _pre_ filmi, filmis, filmi, filmem, filmeu, filmin _imp_ filmés, filmessis, filmés, filméssim, filméssiu, filmessin • **imp** -, filma, filmi, filmem, filmeu, filmin • **inf** filmar • **ger** filmant • **pp** _sing_ filmat / filmada _plur_ filmats / filmades

firmar /sign/ • **ind** _pre_ firmo, firmes, firma, firmem, firmeu, firmen _imp_ firmava, firmaves, firmava, firmàvem, firmàveu, firmaven _prt_ firmí, firmares, firmà, firmàrem, firmàreu, firmaren _fut_ firmaré, firmaràs, firmarà, firmarem, firmareu, firmaran _con_ firmaria, firmaries, firmaria, firmaríem, firmaríeu, firmarien • **sub** _pre_ firmi, firmis, firmi, firmem, firmeu, firmin _imp_ firmés, firmessis, firmés, firméssim, firméssiu, firmessin • **imp** -, firma, firmi, firmem, firmeu, firmin • **inf** firmar • **ger** firmant • **pp** _sing_ firmat / firmada _plur_ firmats / firmades

follar /fuck/ • **ind** _pre_ follo, folles, folla, follem, folleu, follen _imp_ follava, follaves, follava, follàvem, follàveu, follaven _prt_ follí, follares, follà, follàrem, follàreu, follaren _fut_ follaré, follaràs, follarà, follarem, follareu, follaran _con_ follaria, follaries, follaria, follaríem, follaríeu, follarien • **sub** _pre_ folli, follis, folli, follem, folleu, follin _imp_ follés, follessis, follés, folléssim, folléssiu, follessin • **imp** -, folla, folli, follem, folleu, follin • **inf** follar • **ger** follant • **pp** _sing_ follat / follada _plur_ follats / follades

forjar /forge/ • **ind** _pre_ forjo, forges, forja, forgem, forgeu, forgen _imp_ forjava, forjaves, forjava, forjàvem, forjàveu, forjaven _prt_ forgí, forjares, forjà, forjàrem, forjàreu, forjaren _fut_ forjaré, forjaràs, forjarà, forjarem, forjareu, forjaran _con_ forjaria, forjaries, forjaria, forjaríem, forjaríeu, forjarien • **sub** _pre_ forgi, forgis, forgi, forgem, forgeu, forgin _imp_ forgés, forgessis, forgés, forgéssim, forgéssiu, forgessin • **imp** -, forja, forgi, forgem, forgeu, forgin • **inf** forjar • **ger** forjant • **pp** _sing_ forjat / forjada _plur_ forjats / forjades

formar /form/ • **ind** _pre_ formo, formes, forma, formem, formeu, formen _imp_ formava, formaves, formava, formàvem, formàveu, formaven _prt_ formí, formares, formà, formàrem, formàreu, formaren _fut_ formaré, formaràs, formarà, formarem, formareu, formaran _con_ formaria, formaries, formaria, formaríem, formaríeu, formarien • **sub** _pre_ formi, formis, formi, formem, formeu, formin _imp_ formés, formessis, formés, forméssim, forméssiu, formessin • **imp** -, forma, formi, formem, formeu, formin • **inf** formar • **ger** formant • **pp** _sing_ format / formada _plur_ formats / formades

fotre /fuck/ • **ind** _pre_ foto, fots, fot, fotem, foteu, foten _imp_ fotia, foties, fotia, fotíem, fotíeu, fotien _prt_ fotí, foteres, foté, fotérem, fotéreu, foteren _fut_ fotré, fotràs, fotrà, fotrem, fotreu, fotran _con_ fotria, fotries, fotria, fotríem, fotríeu, fotrien • **sub** _pre_ foti, fotis, foti, fotem, foteu, fotin _imp_ fotés, fotessis, fotés, fotéssim, fotéssiu, fotessin • **imp** -, fot, foti, fotem, foteu, fotin • **inf** fotre • **ger** fotent • **pp** _sing_ fotut / fotuda _plur_ fotuts / fotudes

fugir /flee/ • **ind** _pre_ fujo, fuges, fuig, fugim, fugiu, fugen _imp_ fugia, fugies, fugia, fugíem, fugíeu, fugien _prt_ fugí, fugires, fugí, fugírem, fugíreu, fugiren _fut_ fugiré, fugiràs, fugirà, fugirem, fugireu, fugiran _con_ fugiria, fugiries, fugiria, fugiríem, fugiríeu, fugirien • **sub** _pre_ fugi, fugis, fugi, fugim, fugiu, fugin _imp_ fugís, fugissis, fugís, fugíssim, fugíssiu, fugissin • **imp** -, fuig, fugi, fugim, fugiu, fugin • **inf** fugir • **ger** fugint • **pp** _sing_ fugit / fugida _plur_ fugits / fugides

fumar /smoke/ • **ind** _pre_ fumo, fumes, fuma, fumem, fumeu, fumen _imp_ fumava, fumaves, fumava, fumàvem, fumàveu, fumaven _prt_ fumí, fumares, fumà, fumàrem, fumàreu, fumaren _fut_ fumaré, fumaràs, fumarà, fumarem, fumareu, fumaran _con_ fumaria, fumaries, fumaria, fumaríem, fumaríeu, fumarien • **sub** _pre_ fumi, fumis, fumi, fumem, fumeu, fumin _imp_ fumés, fumessis, fumés, fuméssim, fuméssiu, fumessin • **imp** -, fuma, fumi, fumem, fumeu, fumin • **inf** fumar • **ger** fumant • **pp** _sing_ fumat / fumada _plur_ fumats / fumades

funcionar /work, function/ • **ind** _pre_ funciono, funciones, funciona, funcionem, funcioneu, funcionen _imp_ funcionava, funcionaves, funcionava, funcionàvem, funcionàveu, funcionaven _prt_ funcioní, funcionares, funcionà, funcionàrem, funcionàreu, funcionaren _fut_ funcionaré, funcionaràs, funcionarà, funcionarem, funcionareu, funcionaran _con_ funcionaria, funcionaries, funcionaria, funcionaríem, funcionaríeu, funcionarien • **sub** _pre_ funcioni, funcionis, funcioni, funcionem, funcioneu, funcionin _imp_ funcionés, funcionessis, funcionés, funcionéssim, funcionéssiu, fun-

cionessin • **imp** -, funciona, funcioni, funcionem, funcioneu, funcionin •
inf funcionar • **ger** funcionant • **pp** _sing_ funcionat / funcionada _plur_
funcionats / funcionades

G

garantir /guarantee/ • **ind** _pre_ garanteixo, garanteixes, garanteix,
garantim, garantiu, garanteixen _imp_ garantia, garanties, garantia, garantí-
em, garantíeu, garantien _prt_ garantí, garantires, garantí, garantírem, ga-
rantíreu, garantiren _fut_ garantiré, garantiràs, garantirà, garantirem, ga-
rantireu, garantiran _con_ garantiria, garantiries, garantiria, garantiríem,
garantiríeu, garantirien • **sub** _pre_ garanteixi, garanteixis, garanteixi, garantim, garantiu, garanteixin _imp_ garantís, garantissis, garantís, garan-
tíssim, garantíssiu, garantissin • **imp** -, garanteix, garanteixi, garantim,
garantiu, garanteixin • **inf** garantir • **ger** garantint • **pp** _sing_ garantit
/ garantida _plur_ garantits / garantides

gaudir /enjoy/ • **ind** _pre_ gaudeixo, gaudeixes, gaudeix, gaudim, gaudiu, gaudeixen _imp_ gaudia, gaudies, gaudia, gaudíem, gaudíeu, gaudien _prt_
gaudí, gaudires, gaudí, gaudírem, gaudíreu, gaudiren _fut_ gaudiré, gaudiràs,
gaudirà, gaudirem, gaudireu, gaudiran _con_ gaudiria, gaudiries, gaudiria,
gaudiríem, gaudiríeu, gaudirien • **sub** _pre_ gaudeixi, gaudeixis, gaudeixi,
gaudim, gaudiu, gaudeixin _imp_ gaudís, gaudissis, gaudís, gaudíssim, gau-
díssiu, gaudissin • **imp** -, gaudeix, gaudeixi, gaudim, gaudiu, gaudeixin
• **inf** gaudir • **ger** gaudint • **pp** _sing_ gaudit / gaudida _plur_ gaudits /
gaudides

girar /turn/ • **ind** _pre_ giro, gires, gira, girem, gireu, giren _imp_ girava,
giraves, girava, giràvem, giràveu, giraven _prt_ girí, girares, girà, giràrem,
giràreu, giraren _fut_ giraré, giraràs, girarà, girarem, girareu, giraran _con_
giraria, giraries, giraria, giraríem, giraríeu, girarien • **sub** _pre_ giri, giris,
giri, girem, gireu, girin _imp_ girés, giressis, girés, giréssim, giréssiu, giressin
• **imp** -, gira, giri, girem, gireu, girin • **inf** girar • **ger** girant • **pp** _sing_
girat / girada _plur_ girats / girades

governar /govern/ • **ind** _pre_ governo, governes, governa, governem, governeu, governen _imp_ governava, governaves, governava, go-
vernàvem, governàveu, governaven _prt_ governí, governares, governà,
governàrem, governàreu, governaren _fut_ governaré, governaràs, gover-
narà, governarem, governareu, governaran _con_ governaria, governaries,

governaria, governaríem, governaríeu, governarien • **sub** _pre_ governi, governis, governi, governem, governeu, governin _imp_ governés, governessis, governés, governéssim, governéssiu, governessin • **imp** -, governa, governi, governem, governeu, governin • **inf** governar • **ger** governant • **pp** _sing_ governat / governada _plur_ governats / governades

gravar /record/ • **ind** _pre_ gravo, graves, grava, gravem, graveu, graven _imp_ gravava, gravaves, gravava, gravàvem, gravàveu, gravaven _prt_ graví, gravares, gravà, gravàrem, gravàreu, gravaren _fut_ gravaré, gravaràs, gravarà, gravarem, gravareu, gravaran _con_ gravaria, gravaries, gravaria, gravaríem, gravaríeu, gravarien • **sub** _pre_ gravi, gravis, gravi, gravem, graveu, gravin _imp_ gravés, gravessis, gravés, gravéssim, gravéssiu, gravessin • **imp** -, grava, gravi, gravem, graveu, gravin • **inf** gravar • **ger** gravant • **pp** _sing_ gravat / gravada _plur_ gravats / gravades

guanyar /win/ • **ind** _pre_ guanyo, guanyes, guanya, guanyem, guanyeu, guanyen _imp_ guanyava, guanyaves, guanyava, guanyàvem, guanyàveu, guanyaven _prt_ guanyí, guanyares, guanyà, guanyàrem, guanyàreu, guanyaren _fut_ guanyaré, guanyaràs, guanyarà, guanyarem, guanyareu, guanyaran _con_ guanyaria, guanyaries, guanyaria, guanyaríem, guanyaríeu, guanyarien • **sub** _pre_ guanyi, guanyis, guanyi, guanyem, guanyeu, guanyin _imp_ guanyés, guanyessis, guanyés, guanyéssim, guanyéssiu, guanyessin • **imp** -, guanya, guanyi, guanyem, guanyeu, guanyin • **inf** guanyar • **ger** guanyant • **pp** _sing_ guanyat / guanyada _plur_ guanyats / guanyades

guardar /save/ • **ind** _pre_ guardo, guardes, guarda, guardem, guardeu, guarden _imp_ guardava, guardaves, guardava, guardàvem, guardàveu, guardaven _prt_ guardí, guardares, guardà, guardàrem, guardàreu, guardaren _fut_ guardaré, guardaràs, guardarà, guardarem, guardareu, guardaran _con_ guardaria, guardaries, guardaria, guardaríem, guardaríeu, guardarien • **sub** _pre_ guardi, guardis, guardi, guardem, guardeu, guardin _imp_ guardés, guardessis, guardés, guardéssim, guardéssiu, guardessin • **imp** -, guarda, guardi, guardem, guardeu, guardin • **inf** guardar • **ger** guardant • **pp** _sing_ guardat / guardada _plur_ guardats / guardades

guiar /guide/ • **ind** _pre_ guio, guies, guia, guiem, guieu, guien _imp_ guiava, guiaves, guiava, guiàvem, guiàveu, guiaven _prt_ guií, guiares, guià, guiàrem, guiàreu, guiaren _fut_ guiaré, guiaràs, guiarà, guiarem, guiareu, guiaran _con_ guiaria, guiaries, guiaria, guiaríem, guiaríeu, guiarien • **sub** _pre_ guiï, guiïs, guiï, guiem, guieu, guiïn _imp_ guiés, guiessis, guiés, guiéssim, guiéssiu, guiessin • **imp** -, guia, guiï, guiem, guieu, guiïn • **inf** guiar • **ger** guiant • **pp** _sing_ guiat / guiada _plur_ guiats / guiades

G

H

haver /have/ • **ind** _pre_ he, has, ha, hem, heu, han _imp_ havia, havíes, havia, havíem, havíeu, havien _prt_ haguí, hagueres, hagué, haguérem, haguéreu, hagueren _fut_ hauré, hauràs, haurà, haurem, haureu, hauran _con_ hauria, hauries, hauria, hauríem, hauríeu, haurien • **sub** _pre_ hagi, hagis, hagi, hàgim, hàgiu, hagin _imp_ hagués, haguessis, hagués, haguéssim, haguéssiu, haguessin • **imp** -, –, –, –, –, – • **inf** haver • **ger** havent • **pp** _sing_ hagut / haguda _plur_ haguts / hagudes

honrar /honor/ • **ind** _pre_ honro, honres, honra, honrem, honreu, honren _imp_ honrava, honraves, honrava, honràvem, honràveu, honraven _prt_ honrí, honrares, honrà, honràrem, honràreu, honraren _fut_ honraré, honraràs, honrarà, honrarem, honrareu, honraran _con_ honraria, honraries, honraria, honraríem, honraríeu, honrarien • **sub** _pre_ honri, honris, honri, honrem, honreu, honrin _imp_ honrés, honressis, honrés, honréssim, honréssiu, honressin • **imp** -, honra, honri, honrem, honreu, honrin • **inf** honrar • **ger** honrant • **pp** _sing_ honrat / honrada _plur_ honrats / honrades

I

identificar /identify/ • **ind** _pre_ identifico, identifiques, identifica, identifiquem, identifiqueu, identifiquen _imp_ identificava, identificaves, identificava, identificàvem, identificàveu, identificaven _prt_ identifiquí, identificares, identificà, identificàrem, identificàreu, identificaren _fut_ identificaré, identificaràs, identificarà, identificarem, identificareu, identificaran _con_ identificaria, identificaries, identificaria, identificaríem, identificaríeu, identificarien • **sub** _pre_ identifiqui, identifiquis, identifiqui, identifiquem, identifiqueu, identifiquin _imp_ identifiqués, identifiquessis, identifiqués, identifiquéssim, identifiquéssiu, identifiquessin • **imp** -, identifica, identifiqui, identifiquem, identifiqueu, identifiquin • **inf** identificar • **ger** identificant • **pp** _sing_ identificat / identificada _plur_ identificats / identificades

ignorar /ignore/ • **ind** _pre_ ignoro, ignores, ignora, ignorem, ignoreu, ignoren _imp_ ignorava, ignoraves, ignorava, ignoràvem, ignoràveu, ignoraven _prt_ ignorí, ignorares, ignorà, ignoràrem, ignoràreu, ignoraren _fut_ ignoraré, ignoraràs, ignorarà, ignorarem, ignorareu, ignoraran _con_ ignoraria, ignoraries, ignoraria, ignoraríem, ignoraríeu, ignorarien • **sub** _pre_ ignori, ignoris, ignori, ignorem, ignoreu, ignorin _imp_ ignorés, ignoressis, ignorés, ignoréssim, ignoréssiu, ignoressin • **imp** -, ignora, ignori, ignorem, ignoreu, ignorin • **inf** ignorar • **ger** ignorant • **pp** _sing_ ignorat / ignorada _plur_ ignorats / ignorades

imaginar /imagine/ • **ind** _pre_ imagino, imagines, imagina, imaginem, imagineu, imaginen _imp_ imaginava, imaginaves, imaginava, imaginàvem, imaginàveu, imaginaven _prt_ imaginí, imaginares, imaginà, imaginàrem, imaginàreu, imaginaren _fut_ imaginaré, imaginaràs, imaginarà, imaginarem, imaginareu, imaginaran _con_ imaginaria, imaginaries, imaginaria, imaginaríem, imaginaríeu, imaginarien • **sub** _pre_ imagini, imaginis, imagini, imaginem, imagineu, imaginin _imp_ imaginés, imaginessis, imaginés, imaginéssim, imaginéssiu, imaginessin • **imp** -, imagina, imagini, imaginem, imagineu, imaginin • **inf** imaginar • **ger** imaginant • **pp** _sing_ imaginat / imaginada _plur_ imaginats / imaginades

impedir /prevent/ • **ind** _pre_ impedeixo, impedeixes, impedeix, impedim, impediu, impedeixen _imp_ impedia, impedies, impedia, impedíem, impedíeu, impedien _prt_ impedí, impedires, impedí, impedírem, impedíreu, impediren _fut_ impediré, impediràs, impedirà, impedirem, impedireu, impediran _con_ impediria, impediries, impediria, impediríem, impediríeu, impedirien • **sub** _pre_ impedeixi, impedeixis, impedeixi, impedim, impediu, impedeixin _imp_ impedís, impedissis, impedís, impedíssim, impedíssiu, impedissin • **imp** -, impedeix, impedeixi, impedim, impediu, impedeixin • **inf** impedir • **ger** impedint • **pp** _sing_ impedit / impedida _plur_ impedits / impedides

importar /import/ • **ind** _pre_ importo, importes, importa, importem, importeu, importen _imp_ importava, importaves, importava, importàvem, importàveu, importaven _prt_ importí, importares, importà, importàrem, importàreu, importaren _fut_ importaré, importaràs, importarà, importarem, importareu, importaran _con_ importaria, importaries, importaria, importaríem, importaríeu, importarien • **sub** _pre_ importi, importis, importi, importem, importeu, importin _imp_ importés, importessis, importés, importéssim, importéssiu, importessin • **imp** -, importa, importi, importem, importeu, importin • **inf** importar • **ger** important • **pp** _sing_ importat / importada _plur_ importats / importades

indicar /indicate/ • **ind** <u>pre</u> indico, indiques, indica, indiquem, indiqueu, indiquen <u>imp</u> indicava, indicaves, indicava, indicàvem, indicàveu, indicaven <u>prt</u> indiquí, indicares, indicà, indicàrem, indicàreu, indicaren <u>fut</u> indicaré, indicaràs, indicarà, indicarem, indicareu, indicaran <u>con</u> indicaria, indicaries, indicaria, indicaríem, indicaríeu, indicarien • **sub** <u>pre</u> indiqui, indiquis, indiqui, indiquem, indiqueu, indiquin <u>imp</u> indiqués, indiquessis, indiqués, indiquéssim, indiquéssiu, indiquessin • **imp** -, indica, indiqui, indiquem, indiqueu, indiquin • **inf** indicar • **ger** indicant • **pp** <u>sing</u> indicat / indicada <u>plur</u> indicats / indicades

informar /inform/ • **ind** <u>pre</u> informo, informes, informa, informem, informeu, informen <u>imp</u> informava, informaves, informava, informàvem, informàveu, informaven <u>prt</u> informí, informares, informà, informàrem, informàreu, informaren <u>fut</u> informaré, informaràs, informarà, informarem, informareu, informaran <u>con</u> informaria, informaries, informaria, informaríem, informaríeu, informarien • **sub** <u>pre</u> informi, informis, informi, informem, informeu, informin <u>imp</u> informés, informessis, informés, informéssim, informéssiu, informessin • **imp** -, informa, informi, informem, informeu, informin • **inf** informar • **ger** informant • **pp** <u>sing</u> informat / informada <u>plur</u> informats / informades

iniciar /start/ • **ind** <u>pre</u> inicio, inicies, inicia, iniciem, inicieu, inicien <u>imp</u> iniciava, iniciaves, iniciava, iniciàvem, iniciàveu, iniciaven <u>prt</u> inicií, iniciares, inicià, iniciàrem, iniciàreu, iniciaren <u>fut</u> iniciaré, iniciaràs, iniciarà, iniciarem, iniciareu, iniciaran <u>con</u> iniciaria, iniciaries, iniciaria, iniciaríem, iniciaríeu, iniciarien • **sub** <u>pre</u> inicïi, inicïis, inicïi, iniciem, inicieu, inicïin <u>imp</u> iniciés, iniciessis, iniciés, iniciéssim, iniciéssiu, iniciessin • **imp** -, inicia, inicïi, iniciem, inicieu, inicïin • **inf** iniciar • **ger** iniciant • **pp** <u>sing</u> iniciat / iniciada <u>plur</u> iniciats / iniciades

insistir /insist on/ • **ind** <u>pre</u> insisteixo, insisteixes, insisteix, insistim, insistiu, insisteixen <u>imp</u> insistia, insisties, insistia, insistíem, insistíeu, insistien <u>prt</u> insistí, insistires, insistí, insistírem, insistíreu, insistiren <u>fut</u> insistiré, insistiràs, insistirà, insistirem, insistireu, insistiran <u>con</u> insistiria, insistiries, insistiria, insistiríem, insistiríeu, insistirien • **sub** <u>pre</u> insisteixi, insisteixis, insisteixi, insistim, insistiu, insisteixin <u>imp</u> insistís, insistissis, insistís, insistíssim, insistíssiu, insistissin • **imp** -, insisteix, insisteixi, insistim, insistiu, insisteixin • **inf** insistir • **ger** insistint • **pp** <u>sing</u> insistit / insistida <u>plur</u> insistits / insistides

intentar /try/ • **ind** <u>pre</u> intento, intentes, intenta, intentem, intenteu, intenten <u>imp</u> intentava, intentaves, intentava, intentàvem, intentàveu, intentaven <u>prt</u> intentí, intentares, intentà, intentàrem, intentàreu, intentaren _fut_ intentaré, intentaràs, intentarà, intentarem, intentareu, intentaran _con_ intentaria, intentaries, intentaria, intentaríem, intentaríeu, intentarien • **sub** _pre_ intenti, intentis, intenti, intentem, intenteu, intentin _imp_ intentés, intentessis, intentés, intentéssim, intentéssiu, intentessin • **imp** -, intenta, intenti, intentem, intenteu, intentin • **inf** intentar • **ger** intentant • **pp** _sing_ intentat / intentada _plur_ intentats / intentades

interessar /interest/ • **ind** _pre_ interesso, interesses, interessa, interessem, interesseu, interessen _imp_ interessava, interessaves, interessava, interessàvem, interessàveu, interessaven _prt_ interessí, interessares, interessà, interessàrem, interessàreu, interessaren _fut_ interessaré, interessaràs, interessarà, interessarem, interessareu, interessaran _con_ interessaria, interessaries, interessaria, interessaríem, interessaríeu, interessarien • **sub** _pre_ interessi, interessis, interessi, interessem, interesseu, interessin _imp_ interessés, interessessis, interessés, interesséssim, interesséssiu, interessessin • **imp** -, interessa, interessi, interessem, interesseu, interessin • **inf** interessar • **ger** interessant • **pp** _sing_ interessat / interessada _plur_ interessats / interessades

interpretar /interpret/ • **ind** _pre_ interpreto, interpretes, interpreta, interpretem, interpreteu, interpreten _imp_ interpretava, interpretaves, interpretava, interpretàvem, interpretàveu, interpretaven _prt_ interpretí, interpretares, interpretà, interpretàrem, interpretàreu, interpretaren _fut_ interpretaré, interpretaràs, interpretarà, interpretarem, interpretareu, interpretaran _con_ interpretaria, interpretaries, interpretaria, interpretaríem, interpretaríeu, interpretarien • **sub** _pre_ interpreti, interpretis, interpreti, interpretem, interpreteu, interpretin _imp_ interpretés, interpretessis, interpretés, interpretéssim, interpretéssiu, interpretessin • **imp** -, interpreta, interpreti, interpretem, interpreteu, interpretin • **inf** interpretar • **ger** interpretant • **pp** _sing_ interpretat / interpretada _plur_ interpretats / interpretades

interrogar /interrogate/ • **ind** _pre_ interrogo, interrogues, interroga, interroguem, interrogueu, interroguen _imp_ interrogava, interrogaves, interrogava, interrogàvem, interrogàveu, interrogaven _prt_ interroguí, interrogares, interrogà, interrogàrem, interrogàreu, interrogaren _fut_ interrogaré, interrogaràs, interrogarà, interrogarem, interrogareu, interrogaran _con_ interrogaria, interrogaries, interrogaria, interrogaríem, interrogaríeu, interrogarien • **sub** _pre_ interrogui, interroguis, interrogui, interroguem, interrogueu, interroguin _imp_ interrogués, interroguessis, interrogués, interroguéssim, interroguéssiu, interroguessin • **imp** -, interroga, interrogui, interroguem, interrogueu, interroguin • **inf** interrogar • **ger** interrogant • **pp** _sing_ interrogat / interrogada _plur_ interrogats / interrogades

interrompre /interrupt/ • **ind** _pre_ interrompo, interromps, interromp, interrompem, interrompeu, interrompen _imp_ interrompia, interrompies, interrompia, interrompíem, interrompíeu, interrompien _prt_ interrompí, interromperes, interrompé, interrompérem, interrompéreu, interromperen _fut_ interrompré, interrompràs, interromprà, interromprem, interrompreu, interrompran _con_ interrompria, interrompries, interrompria, interrompríem, interrompríeu, interromprien • **sub** _pre_ interrompi, interrompis, interrompi, interrompem, interrompeu, interrompin _imp_ interrompés, interrompessis, interrompés, interrompéssim, interrompéssiu, interrompessin • **imp** -, interromp, interrompi, interrompem, interrompeu, interrompin • **inf** interrompre • **ger** interrompent • **pp** _sing_ interromput / interrompuda _plur_ interromputs / interrompudes

intervenir /intervene/ • **ind** _pre_ intervinc, intervens, intervé, intervenim, interveniu, intervenen _imp_ intervenia, intervenies, intervenia, interveníem, interveníeu, intervenien _prt_ intervinguí, intervingueres, intervingué, intervinguérem, intervinguéreu, intervingueren _fut_ intervindré, intervindràs, intervindrà, intervindrem, intervindreu, intervindran _con_ intervindria, intervindries, intervindria, intervindríem, intervindríeu, intervindrien • **sub** _pre_ intervingui, intervinguis, intervingui, intervinguem, intervingueu, intervinguin _imp_ intervingués, intervinguessis, intervingués, intervinguéssim, intervinguéssiu, intervinguessin • **imp** -, intervén, intervingui, intervinguem, interveniu, intervinguin • **inf** intervenir • **ger** intervenint • **pp** _sing_ intervingut / intervinguda _plur_ intervinguts / intervingudes

inventar /invent/ • **ind** _pre_ invento, inventes, inventa, inventem, inventeu, inventen _imp_ inventava, inventaves, inventava, inventàvem, inventàveu, inventaven _prt_ inventí, inventares, inventà, inventàrem, inventàreu, inventaren _fut_ inventaré, inventaràs, inventarà, inventarem, inventareu, inventaran _con_ inventaria, inventaries, inventaria, inventaríem, inventaríeu, inventarien • **sub** _pre_ inventi, inventis, inventi, inventem, inventeu, inventin _imp_ inventés, inventessis, inventés, inventéssim, inventéssiu, inventessin • **imp** -, inventa, inventi, inventem, inventeu, inventin • **inf** inventar • **ger** inventant • **pp** _sing_ inventat / inventada _plur_ inventats / inventades

invertir /invest/ • **ind** _pre_ inverteixo, inverteixes, inverteix, invertim, invertiu, inverteixen _imp_ invertia, inverties, invertia, invertíem, invertíeu, invertien _prt_ invertí, invertires, invertí, invertírem, invertíreu, invertiren _fut_ invertiré, invertiràs, invertirà, invertirem, invertireu, invertiran _con_ invertiria, invertiries, invertiria, invertiríem, invertiríeu, invertirien • **sub** _pre_ inverteixi, inverteixis, inverteixi, invertim, invertiu, inverteixin _imp_ invertís, invertissis, invertís, invertíssim, invertíssiu, invertissin • **imp** -, inverteix, inverteixi, invertim, invertiu, inverteixin • **inf** invertir • **ger** invertint • **pp** _sing_ invertit / invertida _plur_ invertits / invertides

investigar /research/ • **ind** _pre_ investigo, investigues, investiga, investiguem, investigueu, investiguen _imp_ investigava, investigaves, investigava, investigàvem, investigàveu, investigaven _prt_ investiguí, investigares, investigà, investigàrem, investigàreu, investigaren _fut_ investigaré, investigaràs, investigarà, investigarem, investigareu, investigaran _con_ investigaria, investigaries, investigaria, investigaríem, investigaríeu, investigarien • **sub** _pre_ investigui, investiguis, investigui, investiguem, investigueu, investiguin _imp_ investigués, investiguessis, investigués, investiguéssim, investiguéssiu, investiguessin • **imp** -, investiga, investigui, investiguem, investigueu, investiguin • **inf** investigar • **ger** investigant • **pp** _sing_ investigat / investigada _plur_ investigats / investigades

involucrar /involve/ • **ind** _pre_ involucro, involucres, involucra, involucrem, involucreu, involucren _imp_ involucrava, involucraves, involucrava, involucràvem, involucràveu, involucraven _prt_ involucrí, involucrares, involucrà, involucràrem, involucràreu, involucraren _fut_ involucraré, involucraràs, involucrarà, involucrarem, involucrareu, involucraran _con_ involucraria, involucraries, involucraria, involucraríem, involucraríeu, involucrarien • **sub** _pre_ involucri, involucris, involucri, involucrem, involucreu, involucrin _imp_ involucrés, involucressis, involucrés, involucréssim, involucréssiu, involucressin • **imp** -, involucra, involucri, involucrem, involucreu, involucrin • **inf** involucrar • **ger** involucrant • **pp** _sing_ involucrat / involucrada _plur_ involucrats / involucrades

J

jugar /play/ • **ind** _pre_ jugo, jugues, juga, juguem, jugueu, juguen _imp_ jugava, jugaves, jugava, jugàvem, jugàveu, jugaven _prt_ juguí, jugares, jugà, jugàrem, jugàreu, jugaren _fut_ jugaré, jugaràs, jugarà, jugarem, jugareu, jugaran _con_ jugaria, jugaries, jugaria, jugaríem, jugaríeu, jugarien • **sub** _pre_ jugui, juguis, jugui, juguem, jugueu, juguin _imp_ jugués, juguessis, jugués, juguéssim, juguéssiu, juguessin • **imp** -, juga, jugui, juguem, jugueu, juguin • **inf** jugar • **ger** jugant • **pp** _sing_ jugat / jugada _plur_ jugats / jugades

jurar /swear, promise/ • **ind** _pre_ juro, jures, jura, jurem, jureu, juren _imp_ jurava, juraves, jurava, juràvem, juràveu, juraven _prt_ jurí, jurares, jurà, juràrem, juràreu, juraren _fut_ juraré, juraràs, jurarà, jurarem, jurareu, juraran _con_ juraria, juraries, juraria, juraríem, juraríeu, jurarien • **sub** _pre_ juri, juris, juri, jurem, jureu, jurin _imp_ jurés, juressis, jurés, juréssim, juréssiu, juressin • **imp** -, jura, juri, jurem, jureu, jurin • **inf** jurar • **ger** jurant • **pp** _sing_ jurat / jurada _plur_ jurats / jurades

jutjar /judge/ • **ind** _pre_ jutjo, jutges, jutja, jutgem, jutgeu, jutgen _imp_ jutjava, jutjaves, jutjava, jutjàvem, jutjàveu, jutjaven _prt_ jutgí, jutjares, jutjà, jutjàrem, jutjàreu, jutjaren _fut_ jutjaré, jutjaràs, jutjarà, jutjarem, jutjareu, jutjaran _con_ jutjaria, jutjaries, jutjaria, jutjaríem, jutjaríeu, jutjarien • **sub** _pre_ jutgi, jutgis, jutgi, jutgem, jutgeu, jutgin _imp_ jutgés, jutgessis, jutgés, jutgéssim, jutgéssiu, jutgessin • **imp** -, jutja, jutgi, jutgem, jutgeu, jutgin • **inf** jutjar • **ger** jutjant • **pp** _sing_ jutjat / jutjada _plur_ jutjats / jutjades

L

liderar /lead/ • **ind** _pre_ lidero, lideres, lidera, liderem, lidereu, lideren _imp_ liderava, lideraves, liderava, lideràvem, lideràveu, lideraven _prt_ liderí, liderares, liderà, lideràrem, lideràreu, lideraren _fut_ lideraré, lideraràs, liderarà, liderarem, liderareu, lideraran _con_ lideraria, lideraries, lideraria, lideraríem, lideraríeu, liderarien • **sub** _pre_ lideri, lideris, lideri, liderem, lidereu, liderin _imp_ liderés, lideressis, liderés, lideréssim, lideréssiu, lideressin • **imp** -, lidera, lideri, liderem, lidereu, liderin • **inf** liderar • **ger** liderant • **pp** _sing_ liderat / liderada _plur_ liderats / liderades

llegir /read/ • **ind** _pre_ llegeixo, llegeixes, llegeix, llegim, llegiu, llegeixen _imp_ llegia, llegies, llegia, llegíem, llegíeu, llegien _prt_ llegí, llegires, llegí, llegírem, llegíreu, llegiren _fut_ llegiré, llegiràs, llegirà, llegirem, llegireu, llegiran _con_ llegiria, llegiries, llegiria, llegiríem, llegiríeu, llegirien • **sub** _pre_ llegeixi, llegeixis, llegeixi, llegim, llegiu, llegeixin _imp_ llegís, llegissis, llegís, llegíssim, llegíssiu, llegissin • **imp** -, llegeix, llegeixi, llegim, llegiu, llegeixin • **inf** llegir • **ger** llegint • **pp** _sing_ llegit / llegida _plur_ llegits / llegides

llevar /remove, take out/ • **ind** <u>pre</u> llevo, lleves, lleva, llevem, lleveu, lleven <u>imp</u> llevava, llevaves, llevava, llevàvem, llevàveu, llevaven <u>prt</u> lleví, llevares, llevà, llevàrem, llevàreu, llevaren <u>fut</u> llevaré, llevaràs, llevarà, llevarem, llevareu, llevaran <u>con</u> llevaria, llevaries, llevaria, llevaríem, llevaríeu, llevarien • **sub** <u>pre</u> llevi, llevis, llevi, llevem, lleveu, llevin <u>imp</u> llevés, llevessis, llevés, llevéssim, llevéssiu, llevessin • **imp** -, lleva, llevi, llevem, lleveu, llevin • **inf** llevar • **ger** llevant • **pp** <u>sing</u> llevat / llevada <u>plur</u> llevats / llevades

lligar /tie up/ • **ind** <u>pre</u> lligo, lligues, lliga, lliguem, lligueu, lliguen <u>imp</u> lligava, lligaves, lligava, lligàvem, lligàveu, lligaven <u>prt</u> lliguí, lligares, lligà, lligàrem, lligàreu, lligaren <u>fut</u> lligaré, lligaràs, lligarà, lligarem, lligareu, lligaran <u>con</u> lligaria, lligaries, lligaria, lligaríem, lligaríeu, lligarien • **sub** <u>pre</u> lligui, lliguis, lligui, lliguem, lligueu, lliguin <u>imp</u> lligués, lliguessis, lligués, lliguéssim, lliguéssiu, lliguessin • **imp** -, lliga, lligui, lliguem, lligueu, lliguin • **inf** lligar • **ger** lligant • **pp** <u>sing</u> lligat / lligada <u>plur</u> lligats / lligades

lliurar /deliver/ • **ind** <u>pre</u> lliuro, lliures, lliura, lliurem, lliureu, lliuren <u>imp</u> lliurava, lliuraves, lliurava, lliuràvem, lliuràveu, lliuraven <u>prt</u> lliurí, lliurares, lliurà, lliuràrem, lliuràreu, lliuraren <u>fut</u> lliuraré, lliuraràs, lliurarà, lliurarem, lliurareu, lliuraran <u>con</u> lliuraria, lliuraries, lliuraria, lliuraríem, lliuraríeu, lliurarien • **sub** <u>pre</u> lliuri, lliuris, lliuri, lliurem, lliureu, lliurin <u>imp</u> lliurés, lliuressis, lliurés, lliuréssim, lliuréssiu, lliuressin • **imp** -, lliura, lliuri, lliurem, lliureu, lliurin • **inf** lliurar • **ger** lliurant • **pp** <u>sing</u> lliurat / lliurada <u>plur</u> lliurats / lliurades

llogar /rent/ • **ind** <u>pre</u> llogo, llogues, lloga, lloguem, llogueu, lloguen <u>imp</u> llogava, llogaves, llogava, llogàvem, llogàveu, llogaven <u>prt</u> lloguí, llogares, llogà, llogàrem, llogàreu, llogaren <u>fut</u> llogaré, llogaràs, llogarà, llogarem, llogareu, llogaran <u>con</u> llogaria, llogaries, llogaria, llogaríem, llogaríeu, llogarien • **sub** <u>pre</u> llogui, lloguis, llogui, lloguem, llogueu, lloguin <u>imp</u> llogués, lloguessis, llogués, lloguéssim, lloguéssiu, lloguessin • **imp** -, lloga, llogui, lloguem, llogueu, lloguin • **inf** llogar • **ger** llogant • **pp** <u>sing</u> llogat / llogada <u>plur</u> llogats / llogades

lluitar /fight/ • **ind** <u>pre</u> lluito, lluites, lluita, lluitem, lluiteu, lluiten <u>imp</u> lluitava, lluitaves, lluitava, lluitàvem, lluitàveu, lluitaven <u>prt</u> lluití, lluitares, lluità, lluitàrem, lluitàreu, lluitaren <u>fut</u> lluitaré, lluitaràs, lluitarà, lluitarem, lluitareu, lluitaran <u>con</u> lluitaria, lluitaries, lluitaria, lluitaríem, lluitaríeu, lluitarien • **sub** <u>pre</u> lluiti, lluitis, lluiti, lluitem, lluiteu, lluitin <u>imp</u> lluités, lluitessis, lluités, lluitéssim, lluitéssiu, lluitessin • **imp** -, lluita, lluiti, lluitem, lluiteu, lluitin • **inf** lluitar • **ger** lluitant • **pp** <u>sing</u> lluitat / lluitada <u>plur</u> lluitats / lluitades

localitzar /locate/ • **ind** _pre_ localitzo, localitzes, localitza, localitzem, localitzeu, localitzen _imp_ localitzava, localitzaves, localitzava, lo-
calitzàvem, localitzàveu, localitzaven _prt_ localitzí, localitzares, localitzà,
localitzàrem, localitzàreu, localitzaren _fut_ localitzaré, localitzaràs, localit-
zarà, localitzarem, localitzareu, localitzaran _con_ localitzaria, localitzaries,
localitzaria, localitzaríem, localitzaríeu, localitzarien • **sub** _pre_ localitzi,
localitzis, localitzi, localitzem, localitzeu, localitzin _imp_ localitzés, loca-
litzessis, localitzés, localitzéssim, localitzéssiu, localitzessin • **imp** -, localitza, localitzi, localitzem, localitzeu, localitzin • **inf** localitzar • **ger**
localitzant • **pp** _sing_ localitzat / localitzada _plur_ localitzats / localitzades

M

manar /order/ • **ind** _pre_ mano, manes, mana, manem, maneu, manen
imp manava, manaves, manava, manàvem, manàveu, manaven _prt_ ma-
ní, manares, manà, manàrem, manàreu, manaren _fut_ manaré, manaràs,
manarà, manarem, manareu, manaran _con_ manaria, manaries, manaria,
manaríem, manaríeu, manarien • **sub** _pre_ mani, manis, mani, manem,
maneu, manin _imp_ manés, manessis, manés, manéssim, manéssiu, ma-
nessin • **imp** -, mana, mani, manem, maneu, manin • **inf** manar • **ger**
manant • **pp** _sing_ manat / manada _plur_ manats / manades

manipular /manipulate/ • **ind** _pre_ manipulo, manipules, manipula,
manipulem, manipuleu, manipulen _imp_ manipulava, manipulaves, manipulava, manipulàvem, manipulàveu, manipulaven _prt_ manipulí, manipulares,
manipulà, manipulàrem, manipulàreu, manipularen _fut_ manipularé, mani-
pularàs, manipularà, manipularem, manipulareu, manipularan _con_ manipularia, manipularies, manipularia, manipularíem, manipularíeu, manipu-
larien • **sub** _pre_ manipuli, manipulis, manipuli, manipulem, manipuleu,
manipulin _imp_ manipulés, manipulessis, manipulés, manipuléssim, mani-
puléssiu, manipulessin • **imp** -, manipula, manipuli, manipulem, manipuleu, manipulin • **inf** manipular • **ger** manipulant • **pp** _sing_ manipulat
/ manipulada _plur_ manipulats / manipulades

mantenir /keep/ • **ind** _pre_ mantinc, mantens, manté, mantenim,
manteniu, mantenen _imp_ mantenia, mantenies, mantenia, manteníem,
manteníeu, mantenien _prt_ mantinguí, mantingueres, mantingué, mantin-
guérem, mantinguéreu, mantingueren _fut_ mantindré, mantindràs, man-
tindrà, mantindrem, mantindreu, mantindran _con_ mantindria, mantindri-
es, mantindria, mantindríem, mantindríeu, mantindrien • **sub** _pre_ man-

tingui, mantinguis, mantingui, mantinguem, mantingueu, mantinguin _imp_ mantingués, mantinguessis, mantingués, mantinguéssim, mantinguéssiu, mantinguessin • **imp** -, manté, mantingui, mantinguem, manteniu, mantinguin • **inf** mantenir • **ger** mantenint • **pp** _sing_ mantingut / mantinguda _plur_ mantinguts / mantingudes

marcar /mark, brand, dial/ • **ind** _pre_ marco, marques, marca, marquem, marqueu, marquen _imp_ marcava, marcaves, marcava, marcàvem, marcàveu, marcaven _prt_ marquí, marcares, marcà, marcàrem, marcàreu, marcaren _fut_ marcaré, marcaràs, marcarà, marcarem, marcareu, marcaran _con_ marcaria, marcaries, marcaria, marcaríem, marcaríeu, marcarien • **sub** _pre_ marqui, marquis, marqui, marquem, marqueu, marquin _imp_ marqués, marquessis, marqués, marquéssim, marquéssiu, marquessin • **imp** -, marca, marqui, marquem, marqueu, marquin • **inf** marcar • **ger** marcant • **pp** _sing_ marcat / marcada _plur_ marcats / marcades

marxar /leave/ • **ind** _pre_ marxo, marxes, marxa, marxem, marxeu, marxen _imp_ marxava, marxaves, marxava, marxàvem, marxàveu, marxaven _prt_ marxí, marxares, marxà, marxàrem, marxàreu, marxaren _fut_ marxaré, marxaràs, marxarà, marxarem, marxareu, marxaran _con_ marxaria, marxaries, marxaria, marxaríem, marxaríeu, marxarien • **sub** _pre_ marxi, marxis, marxi, marxem, marxeu, marxin _imp_ marxés, marxessis, marxés, marxéssim, marxéssiu, marxessin • **imp** -, marxa, marxi, marxem, marxeu, marxin • **inf** marxar • **ger** marxant • **pp** _sing_ marxat / marxada _plur_ marxats / marxades

M

matar /kill/ • **ind** _pre_ mato, mates, mata, matem, mateu, maten _imp_ matava, mataves, matava, matàvem, matàveu, mataven _prt_ matí, matares, matà, matàrem, matàreu, mataren _fut_ mataré, mataràs, matarà, matarem, matareu, mataran _con_ mataria, mataries, mataria, mataríem, mataríeu, matarien • **sub** _pre_ mati, matis, mati, matem, mateu, matin _imp_ matés, matessis, matés, matéssim, matéssiu, matessin • **imp** -, mata, mati, matem, mateu, matin • **inf** matar • **ger** matant • **pp** _sing_ matat / matada _plur_ matats / matades

menjar /eat/ • **ind** _pre_ menjo, menges, menja, mengem, mengeu, mengen _imp_ menjava, menjaves, menjava, menjàvem, menjàveu, menjaven _prt_ mengí, menjares, menjà, menjàrem, menjàreu, menjaren _fut_ menjaré, menjaràs, menjarà, menjarem, menjareu, menjaran _con_ menjaria, menjaries, menjaria, menjaríem, menjaríeu, menjarien • **sub** _pre_ mengi, mengis, mengi, mengem, mengeu, mengin _imp_ mengés, mengessis, mengés, mengéssim, mengéssiu, mengessin • **imp** -, menja, mengi, mengem, mengeu, mengin • **inf** menjar • **ger** menjant • **pp** _sing_ menjat

/ menjada *plur* menjats / menjades

mentir /lie/ • **ind** *pre* menteixo, menteixes, menteix, mentim, mentiu, menteixen *imp* mentia, menties, mentia, mentíem, mentíeu, mentien *prt* mentí, mentires, mentí, mentírem, mentíreu, mentiren *fut* mentiré, mentiràs, mentirà, mentirem, mentireu, mentiran *con* mentiria, mentiries, mentiria, mentiríem, mentiríeu, mentirien • **sub** *pre* menteixi, menteixis, menteixi, mentim, mentiu, menteixin *imp* mentís, mentissis, mentís, mentíssim, mentíssiu, mentissin • **imp** -, menteix, menteixi, mentim, mentiu, menteixin • **inf** mentir • **ger** mentint • **pp** *sing* mentit / mentida *plur* mentits / mentides

millorar /improve/ • **ind** *pre* milloro, millores, millora, millorem, milloreu, milloren *imp* millorava, milloraves, millorava, milloràvem, milloràveu, milloraven *prt* millorí, millorares, millorà, milloràrem, milloràreu, milloraren *fut* milloraré, milloraràs, millorarà, millorarem, millorareu, milloraran *con* milloraria, milloraries, milloraria, milloraríem, milloraríeu, millorarien • **sub** *pre* millori, milloris, millori, millorem, milloreu, millorin *imp* millorés, milloressis, millorés, milloréssim, milloréssiu, milloressin • **imp** -, millora, millori, millorem, milloreu, millorin • **inf** millorar • **ger** millorant • **pp** *sing* millorat / millorada *plur* millorats / millorades

mirar /watch/ • **ind** *pre* miro, mires, mira, mirem, mireu, miren *imp* mirava, miraves, mirava, miràvem, miràveu, miraven *prt* mirí, mirares, mirà, miràrem, miràreu, miraren *fut* miraré, miraràs, mirarà, mirarem, mirareu, miraran *con* miraria, miraries, miraria, miraríem, miraríeu, mirarien • **sub** *pre* miri, miris, miri, mirem, mireu, mirin *imp* mirés, miressis, mirés, miréssim, miréssiu, miressin • **imp** -, mira, miri, mirem, mireu, mirin • **inf** mirar • **ger** mirant • **pp** *sing* mirat / mirada *plur* mirats / mirades

molestar /disturb/ • **ind** *pre* molesto, molestes, molesta, molestem, molesteu, molesten *imp* molestava, molestaves, molestava, molestàvem, molestàveu, molestaven *prt* molestí, molestares, molestà, molestàrem, molestàreu, molestaren *fut* molestaré, molestaràs, molestarà, molestarem, molestareu, molestaran *con* molestaria, molestaries, molestaria, molestaríem, molestaríeu, molestarien • **sub** *pre* molesti, molestis, molesti, molestem, molesteu, molestin *imp* molestés, molestessis, molestés, molestéssim, molestéssiu, molestessin • **imp** -, molesta, molesti, molestem, molesteu, molestin • **inf** molestar • **ger** molestant • **pp** *sing* molestat / molestada *plur* molestats / molestades

morir /die/ • **ind** _pre_ moro, mors, mor, morim, moriu, moren _imp_ moria, mories, moria, moríem, moríeu, morien _prt_ morí, morires, morí, morírem, moríreu, moriren _fut_ moriré, moriràs, morirà, morirem, morireu, moriran _con_ moriria, moriries, moriria, moriríem, moriríeu, moririen • **sub** _pre_ mori, moris, mori, morim, moriu, morin _imp_ morís, morissis, morís, moríssim, moríssiu, morissin • **imp** -, mor, mori, morim, moriu, morin • **inf** morir • **ger** morint • **pp** _sing_ mort / — _plur_ — / —

mossegar /bite/ • **ind** _pre_ mossego, mossegues, mossega, mosseguem, mossegueu, mosseguen _imp_ mossegava, mossegaves, mossegava, mossegàvem, mossegàveu, mossegaven _prt_ mosseguí, mossegares, mossegà, mossegàrem, mossegàreu, mossegaren _fut_ mossegaré, mossegaràs, mossegarà, mossegarem, mossegareu, mossegaran _con_ mossegaria, mossegaries, mossegaria, mossegaríem, mossegaríeu, mossegarien • **sub** _pre_ mossegui, mosseguis, mossegui, mosseguem, mossegueu, mosseguin _imp_ mossegués, mosseguessis, mossegués, mosseguéssim, mosseguéssiu, mosseguessin • **imp** -, mossega, mossegui, mosseguem, mossegueu, mosseguin • **inf** mossegar • **ger** mossegant • **pp** _sing_ mossegat / mossegada _plur_ mossegats / mossegades

mostrar /show/ • **ind** _pre_ mostro, mostres, mostra, mostrem, mostreu, mostren _imp_ mostrava, mostraves, mostrava, mostràvem, mostràveu, mostraven _prt_ mostrí, mostrares, mostrà, mostràrem, mostràreu, mostraren _fut_ mostraré, mostraràs, mostrarà, mostrarem, mostrareu, mostraran _con_ mostraria, mostraries, mostraria, mostraríem, mostraríeu, mostrarien • **sub** _pre_ mostri, mostris, mostri, mostrem, mostreu, mostrin _imp_ mostrés, mostressis, mostrés, mostréssim, mostréssiu, mostressin • **imp** -, mostra, mostri, mostrem, mostreu, mostrin • **inf** mostrar • **ger** mostrant • **pp** _sing_ mostrat / mostrada _plur_ mostrats / mostrades

moure /move/ • **ind** _pre_ moc, mous, mou, movem, moveu, mouen _imp_ movia, movies, movia, movíem, movíeu, movien _prt_ moguí, mogueres, mogué, moguérem, moguéreu, mogueren _fut_ mouré, mouràs, mourà, mourem, moureu, mouran _con_ mouria, mouries, mouria, mouríem, mouríeu, mourien • **sub** _pre_ mogui, moguis, mogui, moguem, mogueu, moguin _imp_ mogués, moguessis, mogués, moguéssim, moguéssiu, moguessin • **imp** -, mou, mogui, moguem, moveu, moguin • **inf** moure • **ger** movent • **pp** _sing_ mogut / moguda _plur_ moguts / mogudes

mudar /change, move/ • **ind** _pre_ mudo, mudes, muda, mudem, mudeu, muden _imp_ mudava, mudaves, mudava, mudàvem, mudàveu, mudaven _prt_ mudí, mudares, mudà, mudàrem, mudàreu, mudaren _fut_ mudaré, mudaràs, mudarà, mudarem, mudareu, mudaran _con_ mudaria, mudaries, mudaria, mudaríem, mudaríeu, mudarien • **sub** _pre_ mudi, mudis, mudi, mudem, mudeu, mudin _imp_ mudés, mudessis, mudés, mudéssim, mudéssiu, mudessin • **imp** -, muda, mudi, mudem, mudeu, mudin • **inf** mudar • **ger** mudant • **pp** _sing_ mudat / mudada _plur_ mudats / mudades

N

necessitar /need/ • **ind** _pre_ necessito, necessites, necessita, necessitem, necessiteu, necessiten _imp_ necessitava, necessitaves, necessitava, necessitàvem, necessitàveu, necessitaven _prt_ necessití, necessitares, necessità, necessitàrem, necessitàreu, necessitaren _fut_ necessitaré, necessitaràs, necessitarà, necessitarem, necessitareu, necessitaran _con_ necessitaria, necessitaries, necessitaria, necessitaríem, necessitaríeu, necessitarien • **sub** _pre_ necessiti, necessitis, necessiti, necessitem, necessiteu, necessitin _imp_ necessités, necessitessis, necessités, necessitéssim, necessitéssiu, necessitessin • **imp** -, necessita, necessiti, necessitem, necessiteu, necessitin • **inf** necessitar • **ger** necessitant • **pp** _sing_ necessitat / necessitada _plur_ necessitats / necessitades

nedar /swim/ • **ind** _pre_ nedo, nedes, neda, nedem, nedeu, neden _imp_ nedava, nedaves, nedava, nedàvem, nedàveu, nedaven _prt_ nedí, nedares, nedà, nedàrem, nedàreu, nedaren _fut_ nedaré, nedaràs, nedarà, nedarem, nedareu, nedaran _con_ nedaria, nedaries, nedaria, nedaríem, nedaríeu, nedarien • **sub** _pre_ nedi, nedis, nedi, nedem, nedeu, nedin _imp_ nedés, nedessis, nedés, nedéssim, nedéssiu, nedessin • **imp** -, neda, nedi, nedem, nedeu, nedin • **inf** nedar • **ger** nedant • **pp** _sing_ nedat / nedada _plur_ nedats / nedades

negociar /negotiate/ • **ind** _pre_ negocio, negocies, negocia, negociem, negocieu, negocien _imp_ negociava, negociaves, negociava, negociàvem, negociàveu, negociaven _prt_ negocií, negociares, negocià, negociàrem, negociàreu, negociaren _fut_ negociaré, negociaràs, negociarà, negociarem, negociareu, negociaran _con_ negociaria, negociaries, negociaria, negociaríem, negociaríeu, negociarien • **sub** _pre_ negociï, negociïs, negociï, negociem, negocieu, negociïn _imp_ negociés, negociessis, negociés, negociéssim, negociéssiu, negociessin • **imp** -, negocia, negociï, negociem, negocieu, negociïn • **inf** negociar • **ger** negociant • **pp** _sing_ negociat / negociada _plur_ negociats / negociades

netejar /clean up/ • **ind** _pre_ netejo, neteges, neteja, netegem, netegeu, netegen _imp_ netejava, netejaves, netejava, netejàvem, netejàveu, netejaven _prt_ netegí, netejares, netejà, netejàrem, netejàreu, netejaren _fut_ netejaré, netejaràs, netejarà, netejarem, netejareu, netejaran _con_ netejaria, netejaries, netejaria, netejaríem, netejaríeu, netejarien • **sub** _pre_ netegi, netegis, netegi, netegem, netegeu, netegin _imp_ netegés, netegessis, netegés, netegéssim, netegéssiu, netegessin • **imp** -, neteja, netegi, netegem, netegeu, netegin • **inf** netejar • **ger** netejant • **pp** _sing_ netejat / netejada _plur_ netejats / netejades

nomenar /appoint/ • **ind** _pre_ nomeno, nomenes, nomena, nomenem, nomeneu, nomenen _imp_ nomenava, nomenaves, nomenava, nomenàvem, nomenàveu, nomenaven _prt_ nomení, nomenares, nomenà, nomenàrem, nomenàreu, nomenaren _fut_ nomenaré, nomenaràs, nomenarà, nomenarem, nomenareu, nomenaran _con_ nomenaria, nomenaries, nomenaria, nomenaríem, nomenaríeu, nomenarien • **sub** _pre_ nomeni, nomenis, nomeni, nomenem, nomeneu, nomenin _imp_ nomenés, nomenessis, nomenés, nomenéssim, nomenéssiu, nomenessin • **imp** -, nomena, nomeni, nomenem, nomeneu, nomenin • **inf** nomenar • **ger** nomenant • **pp** _sing_ nomenat / nomenada _plur_ nomenats / nomenades

notar /note, make a note/ • **ind** _pre_ noto, notes, nota, notem, noteu, noten _imp_ notava, notaves, notava, notàvem, notàveu, notaven _prt_ notí, notares, notà, notàrem, notàreu, notaren _fut_ notaré, notaràs, notarà, notarem, notareu, notaran _con_ notaria, notaries, notaria, notaríem, notaríeu, notarien • **sub** _pre_ noti, notis, noti, notem, noteu, notin _imp_ notés, notessis, notés, notéssim, notéssiu, notessin • **imp** -, nota, noti, notem, noteu, notin • **inf** notar • **ger** notant • **pp** _sing_ notat / notada _plur_ notats / notades

O

obeir /obey/ • **ind** _pre_ obeeixo, obeeixes, obeeix, obeïm, obeïu, obeeixen _imp_ obeïa, obeïes, obeïa, obeíem, obeíeu, obeïen _prt_ obeí, obeïres, obeí, obeírem, obeíreu, obeïren _fut_ obeiré, obeiràs, obeirà, obeirem, obeireu, obeiran _con_ obeiria, obeiries, obeiria, obeiríem, obeiríeu, obeirien • **sub** _pre_ obeeixi, obeeixis, obeeixi, obeïm, obeïu, obeeixin _imp_ obeís, obeïssis, obeís, obeíssim, obeíssiu, obeïssin • **imp** -, obeeix, obeeixi, obeïm, obeïu, obeeixin • **inf** obeir • **ger** obeint • **pp** _sing_ obeït / obeïda _plur_ obeïts / obeïdes

oblidar /forget/ • **ind** _pre_ oblido, oblides, oblida, oblidem, oblideu, obliden _imp_ oblidava, oblidaves, oblidava, oblidàvem, oblidàveu, oblidaven _prt_ oblidí, oblidares, oblidà, oblidàrem, oblidàreu, oblidaren _fut_ oblidaré, oblidaràs, oblidarà, oblidarem, oblidareu, oblidaran _con_ oblidaria, oblidaries, oblidaria, oblidaríem, oblidaríeu, oblidarien • **sub** _pre_ oblidi, oblidis, oblidi, oblidem, oblideu, oblidin _imp_ oblidés, oblidessis, oblidés, oblidéssim, oblidéssiu, oblidessin • **imp** -, oblida, oblidi, oblidem, oblideu, oblidin • **inf** oblidar • **ger** oblidant • **pp** _sing_ oblidat / oblidada _plur_ oblidats / oblidades

obligar /obligate/ • **ind** _pre_ obligo, obligues, obliga, obliguem, obligueu, obliguen _imp_ obligava, obligaves, obligava, obligàvem, obligàveu, obligaven _prt_ obliguí, obligares, obligà, obligàrem, obligàreu, obligaren _fut_ obligaré, obligaràs, obligarà, obligarem, obligareu, obligaran _con_ obligaria, obligaries, obligaria, obligaríem, obligaríeu, obligarien • **sub** _pre_ obligui, obliguis, obligui, obliguem, obligueu, obliguin _imp_ obligués, obliguessis, obligués, obliguéssim, obliguéssiu, obliguessin • **imp** -, obliga, obligui, obliguem, obligueu, obliguin • **inf** obligar • **ger** obligant • **pp** _sing_ obligat / obligada _plur_ obligats / obligades

obrir /open/ • **ind** _pre_ obro, obres, obre, obrim, obriu, obren _imp_ obria, obries, obria, obríem, obríeu, obrien _prt_ obrí, obrires, obrí, obrírem, obríreu, obriren _fut_ obriré, obriràs, obrirà, obrirem, obrireu, obriran _con_ obriria, obriries, obriria, obriríem, obriríeu, obririen • **sub** _pre_ obri, obris, obri, obrim, obriu, obrin _imp_ obrís, obrissis, obrís, obríssim, obríssiu, obrissin • **imp** -, obre, obri, obrim, obriu, obrin • **inf** obrir • **ger** obrint • **pp** _sing_ obert / oberta _plur_ oberts / obertes

observar /observe/ • **ind** _pre_ observo, observes, observa, observem, observeu, observen _imp_ observava, observaves, observava, observàvem, observàveu, observaven _prt_ observí, observares, observà, observàrem, observàreu, observaren _fut_ observaré, observaràs, observarà, observarem, observareu, observaran _con_ observaria, observaries, observaria, observaríem, observaríeu, observarien • **sub** _pre_ observi, observis, observi, observem, observeu, observin _imp_ observés, observessis, observés, observéssim, observéssiu, observessin • **imp** -, observa, observi, observem, observeu, observin • **inf** observar • **ger** observant • **pp** _sing_ observat / observada _plur_ observats / observades

obtenir /get/ • **ind** _pre_ obtinc, obtens, obté, obtenim, obteniu, obtenen _imp_ obtenia, obtenies, obtenia, obteníem, obteníeu, obtenien _prt_ obtinguí, obtingueres, obtingué, obtinguérem, obtinguéreu, obtingueren _fut_ obtindré, obtindràs, obtindrà, obtindrem, obtindreu, obtindran _con_ obtindria, obtindries, obtindria, obtindríem, obtindríeu, obtindrien • **sub** _pre_ obtingui, obtinguis, obtingui, obtinguem, obtingueu, obtinguin _imp_ obtingués, obtinguessis, obtingués, obtinguéssim, obtinguéssiu, obtinguessin • **imp** -, obtén, obtingui, obtinguem, obteniu, obtinguin • **inf** obtenir • **ger** obtenint • **pp** _sing_ obtingut / obtinguda _plur_ obtinguts / obtingudes

obtindre /get, obtain/ • **ind** _pre_ obtinc, obtens, obté, obtenim, obteniu, obtenen _imp_ obtenia, obtenies, obtenia, obteníem, obteníeu, obtenien _prt_ obtinguí, obtingueres, obtingué, obtinguérem, obtinguéreu, obtingueren _fut_ obtindré, obtindràs, obtindrà, obtindrem, obtindreu, obtindran _con_ obtindria, obtindries, obtindria, obtindríem, obtindríeu, obtindrien • **sub** _pre_ obtingui, obtinguis, obtingui, obtinguem, obtingueu, obtinguin _imp_ obtingués, obtinguessis, obtingués, obtinguéssim, obtinguéssiu, obtinguessin • **imp** -, obtén, obtingui, obtinguem, obteniu, obtinguin • **inf** obtindre • **ger** obtenint • **pp** _sing_ obtingut / obtinguda _plur_ obtinguts / obtingudes

ocultar /hide/ • **ind** _pre_ oculto, ocultes, oculta, ocultem, oculteu, oculten _imp_ ocultava, ocultaves, ocultava, ocultàvem, ocultàveu, ocultaven _prt_ ocultí, ocultares, ocultà, ocultàrem, ocultàreu, ocultaren _fut_ ocultaré, ocultaràs, ocultarà, ocultarem, ocultareu, ocultaran _con_ ocultaria, ocultaries, ocultaria, ocultaríem, ocultaríeu, ocultarien • **sub** _pre_ oculti, ocultis, oculti, ocultem, oculteu, ocultin _imp_ ocultés, ocultessis, ocultés, ocultéssim, ocultéssiu, ocultessin • **imp** -, oculta, oculti, ocultem, oculteu, ocultin • **inf** ocultar • **ger** ocultant • **pp** _sing_ ocultat / ocultada _plur_ ocultats / ocultades

ocupar /occupy/ • **ind** _pre_ ocupo, ocupes, ocupa, ocupem, ocupeu, ocupen _imp_ ocupava, ocupaves, ocupava, ocupàvem, ocupàveu, ocupaven _prt_ ocupí, ocupares, ocupà, ocupàrem, ocupàreu, ocuparen _fut_ ocuparé, ocuparàs, ocuparà, ocuparem, ocupareu, ocuparan _con_ ocuparia, ocuparies, ocuparia, ocuparíem, ocuparíeu, ocuparien • **sub** _pre_ ocupi, ocupis, ocupi, ocupem, ocupeu, ocupin _imp_ ocupés, ocupessis, ocupés, ocupéssim, ocupéssiu, ocupessin • **imp** -, ocupa, ocupi, ocupem, ocupeu, ocupin • **inf** ocupar • **ger** ocupant • **pp** _sing_ ocupat / ocupada _plur_ ocupats / ocupades

odiar /hate/ • **ind** _pre_ odio, odies, odia, odiem, odieu, odien _imp_ odiava, odiaves, odiava, odiàvem, odiàveu, odiaven _prt_ odií, odiares, odià, odiàrem, odiàreu, odiaren _fut_ odiaré, odiaràs, odiarà, odiarem, odiareu, odiaran _con_ odiaria, odiaries, odiaria, odiaríem, odiaríeu, odiarien • **sub** _pre_ odiï, odiïs, odiï, odiem, odieu, odiïn _imp_ odiés, odiessis, odiés, odiéssim, odiéssiu, odiessin • **imp** -, odia, odïi, odiem, odieu, odïïn • **inf** odiar • **ger** odiant • **pp** _sing_ odiat / odiada _plur_ odiats / odiades

ofegar /drown/ • **ind** _pre_ ofego, ofegues, ofega, ofeguem, ofegueu, ofeguen _imp_ ofegava, ofegaves, ofegava, ofegàvem, ofegàveu, ofegaven _prt_ ofeguí, ofegares, ofegà, ofegàrem, ofegàreu, ofegaren _fut_ ofegaré, ofega- ràs, ofegarà, ofegarem, ofegareu, ofegaran _con_ ofegaria, ofegaries, ofe- garia, ofegaríem, ofegaríeu, ofegarien • **sub** _pre_ ofegui, ofeguis, ofegui, ofeguem, ofegueu, ofeguin _imp_ ofegués, ofeguessis, ofegués, ofeguéssim, ofeguéssiu, ofeguessin • **imp** -, ofega, ofegui, ofeguem, ofegueu, ofeguin • **inf** ofegar • **ger** ofegant • **pp** _sing_ ofegat / ofegada _plur_ ofegats / ofegades

ofendre /offend/ • **ind** _pre_ ofenc, ofens, ofèn, ofenem, ofeneu, ofe- nen _imp_ ofenia, ofenies, ofenia, ofeníem, ofeníeu, ofenien _prt_ ofenguí, ofengueres, ofengué, ofenguérem, ofenguéreu, ofengueren _fut_ ofendré, ofendràs, ofendrà, ofendrem, ofendreu, ofendran _con_ ofendria, ofendri- es, ofendria, ofendríem, ofendríeu, ofendrien • **sub** _pre_ ofengui, ofen- guis, ofengui, ofenguem, ofengueu, ofenguin _imp_ ofengués, ofenguessis, ofengués, ofenguéssim, ofenguéssiu, ofenguessin • **imp** -, ofèn, ofengui, ofenguem, ofeneu, ofenguin • **inf** ofendre • **ger** ofenent • **pp** _sing_ ofès / ofesa _plur_ ofesos / ofeses

oferir /offer/ • **ind** _pre_ ofereixo, ofereixes, ofereix, oferim, oferiu, ofereixen _imp_ oferia, oferies, oferia, oferíem, oferíeu, oferien _prt_ oferí, oferires, oferí, oferírem, oferíreu, oferiren _fut_ oferiré, oferiràs, oferirà, oferirem, oferireu, oferiran _con_ oferiria, oferiries, oferiria, oferiríem, oferiríeu, oferirien • **sub** _pre_ ofereixi, ofereixis, ofereixi, oferim, oferiu, ofereixin _imp_ oferís, oferissis, oferís, oferíssim, oferíssiu, oferissin • **imp** -, ofereix, ofereixi, oferim, oferiu, ofereixin • **inf** oferir • **ger** oferint • **pp** _sing_ ofert / oferta _plur_ oferts / ofertes

olorar /smell/ • **ind** _pre_ oloro, olores, olora, olorem, oloreu, oloren _imp_ olorava, oloraves, olorava, oloràvem, oloràveu, oloraven _prt_ olo- rí, olorares, olorà, oloràrem, oloràreu, oloraren _fut_ oloraré, oloraràs, olorarà, olorarem, olorareu, oloraran _con_ oloraria, oloraries, oloraria, oloraríem, oloraríeu, olorarien • **sub** _pre_ olori, oloris, olori, olorem, oloreu, olorin _imp_ olorés, oloressis, olorés, oloréssim, oloréssiu, olo- ressin • **imp** -, olora, olori, olorem, oloreu, olorin • **inf** olorar • **ger** olorant • **pp** _sing_ olorat / olorada _plur_ olorats / olorades

omplir /fill up/ • **ind** _pre_ omplo, omples, omple, omplim, ompliu, omplen _imp_ omplia, omplies, omplia, omplíem, omplíeu, omplien _prt_

omplí, omplires, omplí, omplírem, omplíreu, ompliren _fut_ ompliré, om-
pliràs, omplirà, omplirem, omplireu, ompliran _con_ ompliria, ompliries,
ompliria, omplíríem, omplíríeu, omplirien • **sub** _pre_ ompli, omplis, om-
pli, omplim, ompliu, omplin _imp_ omplís, omplissis, omplís, omplíssim,
omplíssiu, omplissin • **imp** -, omple, ompli, omplim, ompliu, omplin •
inf omplir • **ger** omplint • **pp** _sing_ omplert / omplerta _plur_ omplerts
/ omplertes

ordenar /order/ • **ind** _pre_ ordeno, ordenes, ordena, ordenem, ordeneu, ordenen _imp_ ordenava, ordenaves, ordenava, ordenàvem, orde-
nàveu, ordenaven _prt_ ordení, ordenares, ordenà, ordenàrem, ordenàreu,
ordenaren _fut_ ordenaré, ordenaràs, ordenarà, ordenarem, ordenareu,
ordenaran _con_ ordenaria, ordenaries, ordenaria, ordenaríem, ordenarí-
eu, ordenarien • **sub** _pre_ ordeni, ordenis, ordeni, ordenem, ordeneu,
ordenin _imp_ ordenés, ordenessis, ordenés, ordenéssim, ordenéssiu, or-
denessin • **imp** -, ordena, ordeni, ordenem, ordeneu, ordenin • **inf**
ordenar • **ger** ordenant • **pp** _sing_ ordenat / ordenada _plur_ ordenats /
ordenades

organitzar /organize/ • **ind** _pre_ organitzo, organitzes, organitza,
organitzem, organitzeu, organitzen _imp_ organitzava, organitzaves, organitzava, organitzàvem, organitzàveu, organitzaven _prt_ organitzí, organit-
zares, organitzà, organitzàrem, organitzàreu, organitzaren _fut_ organit-
zaré, organitzaràs, organitzarà, organitzarem, organitzareu, organitzaran
con organitzaria, organitzaries, organitzaria, organitzaríem, organitzarí-
eu, organitzarien • **sub** _pre_ organitzi, organitzis, organitzi, organitzem,
organitzeu, organitzin _imp_ organitzés, organitzessis, organitzés, organit-
zéssim, organitzéssiu, organitzessin • **imp** -, organitza, organitzi, organitzem, organitzeu, organitzin • **inf** organitzar • **ger** organitzant • **pp**
sing organitzat / organitzada _plur_ organitzats / organitzades

P

pagar /pay/ • **ind** _pre_ pago, pagues, paga, paguem, pagueu, paguen _imp_
pagava, pagaves, pagava, pagàvem, pagàveu, pagaven _prt_ paguí, pagares,
pagà, pagàrem, pagàreu, pagaren _fut_ pagaré, pagaràs, pagarà, pagarem,
pagareu, pagaran _con_ pagaria, pagaries, pagaria, pagaríem, pagaríeu, paga-
rien • **sub** _pre_ pagui, paguis, pagui, paguem, pagueu, paguin _imp_ pagués,
paguessis, pagués, paguéssim, paguéssiu, paguessin • **imp** -, paga, pagui,

paguem, pagueu, paguin • **inf** pagar • **ger** pagant • **pp** _sing_ pagat / pagada _plur_ pagats / pagades

parar /stop/ • **ind** _pre_ paro, pares, para, parem, pareu, paren _imp_ parava, paraves, parava, paràvem, paràveu, paraven _prt_ parí, parares, parà, paràrem, paràreu, pararen _fut_ pararé, pararàs, pararà, pararem, parareu, pararan _con_ pararia, pararies, pararia, pararíem, pararíeu, pararien • **sub** _pre_ pari, paris, pari, parem, pareu, parin _imp_ parés, paressis, parés, paréssim, paréssiu, paressin • **imp** -, para, pari, parem, pareu, parin • **inf** parar • **ger** parant • **pp** _sing_ parat / parada _plur_ parats / parades

parir /give birth/ • **ind** _pre_ pareixo, pareixes, pareix, parim, pariu, pareixen _imp_ paria, paries, paria, paríem, paríeu, parien _prt_ parí, parires, parí, parírem, paríreu, pariren _fut_ pariré, pariràs, parirà, parirem, parireu, pariran _con_ pariria, pariries, pariria, pariríem, pariríeu, paririen • **sub** _pre_ pareixi, pareixis, pareixi, parim, pariu, pareixin _imp_ parís, parissis, parís, paríssim, paríssiu, parissin • **imp** -, pareix, pareixi, parim, pariu, pareixin • **inf** parir • **ger** parint • **pp** _sing_ parit / parida _plur_ parits / parides

parlar /talk/ • **ind** _pre_ parlo, parles, parla, parlem, parleu, parlen _imp_ parlava, parlaves, parlava, parlàvem, parlàveu, parlaven _prt_ parlí, parlares, parlà, parlàrem, parlàreu, parlaren _fut_ parlaré, parlaràs, parlarà, parlarem, parlareu, parlaran _con_ parlaria, parlaries, parlaria, parlaríem, parlaríeu, parlarien • **sub** _pre_ parli, parlis, parli, parlem, parleu, parlin _imp_ parlés, parlessis, parlés, parléssim, parléssiu, parlessin • **imp** -, parla, parli, parlem, parleu, parlin • **inf** parlar • **ger** parlant • **pp** _sing_ parlat / parlada _plur_ parlats / parlades

participar /join in/ • **ind** _pre_ participo, participes, participa, participem, participeu, participen _imp_ participava, participaves, participava, participàvem, participàveu, participaven _prt_ participí, participares, participà, participàrem, participàreu, participaren _fut_ participaré, participaràs, participarà, participarem, participareu, participaran _con_ participaria, participaries, participaria, participaríem, participaríeu, participarien • **sub** _pre_ participi, participis, participi, participem, participeu, participin _imp_ participés, participessis, participés, participéssim, participéssiu, participessin • **imp** -, participa, participi, participem, participeu, participin • **inf** participar • **ger** participant • **pp** _sing_ participat / participada _plur_ participats / participades

partir /start off/ • **ind** _pre_ parteixo, parteixes, parteix, partim, partiu, parteixen _imp_ partia, parties, partia, partíem, partíeu, partien _prt_ partí, partires, partí, partírem, partíreu, partiren _fut_ partiré, partiràs, partirà, partirem, partireu, partiran _con_ partiria, partiries, partiria, partiríem, partiríeu, partirien • **sub** _pre_ parteixi, parteixis, parteixi, partim, partiu, parteixin _imp_ partís, partissis, partís, partíssim, partíssiu, partissin • **imp** -, parteix, parteixi, partim, partiu, parteixin • **inf** partir • **ger** partint • **pp** _sing_ partit / partida _plur_ partits / partides

passar /pass/ • **ind** _pre_ passo, passes, passa, passem, passeu, passen _imp_ passava, passaves, passava, passàvem, passàveu, passaven _prt_ pas- sí, passares, passà, passàrem, passàreu, passaren _fut_ passaré, passaràs, passarà, passarem, passareu, passaran _con_ passaria, passaries, passaria, passaríem, passaríeu, passarien • **sub** _pre_ passi, passis, passi, passem, passeu, passin _imp_ passés, passessis, passés, passéssim, passéssiu, pas- sessin • **imp** -, passa, passi, passem, passeu, passin • **inf** passar • **ger** passant • **pp** _sing_ passat / passada _plur_ passats / passades

passejar /take a walk/ • **ind** _pre_ passejo, passeges, passeja, passe- gem, passegeu, passegen _imp_ passejava, passejaves, passejava, passejà- vem, passejàveu, passejaven _prt_ passegí, passejares, passejà, passejàrem, passejàreu, passejaren _fut_ passejaré, passejaràs, passejarà, passejarem, passejareu, passejaran _con_ passejaria, passejaries, passejaria, passejaríem, passejaríeu, passejarien • **sub** _pre_ passegi, passegis, passegi, passegem, passegeu, passegin _imp_ passegés, passegessis, passegés, passegéssim, pas- segéssiu, passegessin • **imp** -, passeja, passegi, passegem, passegeu, pas- segin • **inf** passejar • **ger** passejant • **pp** _sing_ passejat / passejada _plur_ passejats / passejades

patir /suffer/ • **ind** _pre_ pateixo, pateixes, pateix, patim, patiu, patei- xen _imp_ patia, paties, patia, patíem, patíeu, patien _prt_ patí, patires, patí, patírem, patíreu, patiren _fut_ patiré, patiràs, patirà, patirem, patireu, pa- tiran _con_ patiria, patiries, patiria, patiríem, patiríeu, patirien • **sub** _pre_ pateixi, pateixis, pateixi, patim, patiu, pateixin _imp_ patís, patissis, patís, patíssim, patíssiu, patissin • **imp** -, pateix, pateixi, patim, patiu, pateixin • **inf** patir • **ger** patint • **pp** _sing_ patit / patida _plur_ patits / patides

pegar /paste/ • **ind** _pre_ pego, pegues, pega, peguem, pegueu, pe- guen _imp_ pegava, pegaves, pegava, pegàvem, pegàveu, pegaven _prt_ peguí, pegares, pegà, pegàrem, pegàreu, pegaren _fut_ pegaré, pegaràs, pegarà, pegarem, pegareu, pegaran _con_ pegaria, pegaries, pegaria, pegaríem, pe- garíeu, pegarien • **sub** _pre_ pegui, peguis, pegui, peguem, pegueu, peguin _imp_ pegués, peguessis, pegués, peguéssim, peguéssiu, peguessin • **imp** -, pega, pegui, peguem, pegueu, peguin • **inf** pegar • **ger** pegant • **pp**

sing pegat / pegada *plur* pegats / pegades

penjar /hang up/ • **ind** *pre* penjo, penges, penja, pengem, pengeu, pengen *imp* penjava, penjaves, penjava, penjàvem, penjàveu, penjaven *prt* pengí, penjares, penjà, penjàrem, penjàreu, penjaren *fut* penjaré, penjaràs, penjarà, penjarem, penjareu, penjaran *con* penjaria, penjaries, penjaria, penjaríem, penjaríeu, penjarien • **sub** *pre* pengi, pengis, pengi, pengem, pengeu, pengin *imp* pengés, pengessis, pengés, pengéssim, pengéssiu, pengessin • **imp** -, penja, pengi, pengem, pengeu, pengin • **inf** penjar • **ger** penjant • **pp** *sing* penjat / penjada *plur* penjats / penjades

pensar /think/ • **ind** *pre* penso, penses, pensa, pensem, penseu, pensen *imp* pensava, pensaves, pensava, pensàvem, pensàveu, pensaven *prt* pensí, pensares, pensà, pensàrem, pensàreu, pensaren *fut* pensaré, pensaràs, pensarà, pensarem, pensareu, pensaran *con* pensaria, pensaries, pensaria, pensaríem, pensaríeu, pensarien • **sub** *pre* pensi, pensis, pensi, pensem, penseu, pensin *imp* pensés, pensessis, pensés, penséssim, penséssiu, pensessin • **imp** -, pensa, pensi, pensem, penseu, pensin • **inf** pensar • **ger** pensant • **pp** *sing* pensat / pensada *plur* pensats / pensades

percebre /perceive/ • **ind** *pre* percebo, perceps, percep, percebem, percebeu, perceben *imp* percebia, percebies, percebia, percebíem, percebíeu, percebien *prt* percebí, perceberes, percebé, percebérem, percebéreu, perceberen *fut* percebré, percebràs, percebrà, percebrem, percebreu, percebran *con* percebria, percebries, percebria, percebríem, percebríeu, percebrien • **sub** *pre* percebi, percebis, percebi, percebem, percebeu, percebin *imp* percebés, percebessis, percebés, percebéssim, percebéssiu, percebessin • **imp** -, percep, percebi, percebem, percebeu, percebin • **inf** percebre • **ger** percebent • **pp** *sing* percebut / percebuda *plur* percebuts / percebudes

perdonar /forgive/ • **ind** *pre* perdono, perdones, perdona, perdonem, perdoneu, perdonen *imp* perdonava, perdonaves, perdonava, perdonàvem, perdonàveu, perdonaven *prt* perdoní, perdonares, perdonà, perdonàrem, perdonàreu, perdonaren *fut* perdonaré, perdonaràs, perdonarà, perdonarem, perdonareu, perdonaran *con* perdonaria, perdonaries, perdonaria, perdonaríem, perdonaríeu, perdonarien • **sub** *pre* perdoni, perdonis, perdoni, perdonem, perdoneu, perdonin *imp* perdonés, perdonessis, perdonés, perdonéssim, perdonéssiu, perdonessin • **imp** -, perdona, perdoni, perdonem, perdoneu, perdonin • **inf** perdonar • **ger** perdonant • **pp** *sing* perdonat / perdonada *plur* perdonats

/ perdonades

perdre /lose/ • **ind** _pre_ perdo, perds, perd, perdem, perdeu, perden _imp_ perdia, perdies, perdia, perdíem, perdíeu, perdien _prt_ perdí, perderes, perdé, perdérem, perdéreu, perderen _fut_ perdré, perdràs, perdrà, perdrem, perdreu, perdran _con_ perdria, perdries, perdria, perdríem, perdríeu, perdrien • **sub** _pre_ perdi, perdis, perdi, perdem, perdeu, perdin _imp_ perdés, perdessis, perdés, perdéssim, perdéssiu, perdessin • **imp** -, perd, perdi, perdem, perdeu, perdin • **inf** perdre • **ger** perdent • **pp** _sing_ perdut / perduda _plur_ perduts / perdudes

permetre /allow/ • **ind** _pre_ permeto, permets, permet, permetem, permeteu, permeten _imp_ permetia, permeties, permetia, permetíem, permetíeu, permetien _prt_ permetí, permeteres, permeté, permetérem, permetéreu, permeteren _fut_ permetré, permetràs, permetrà, permetrem, permetreu, permetran _con_ permetria, permetries, permetria, permetríem, permetríeu, permetrien • **sub** _pre_ permeti, permetis, permeti, permetem, permeteu, permetin _imp_ permetés, permetessis, permetés, permetéssim, permetéssiu, permetessin • **imp** -, permet, permeti, permetem, permeteu, permetin • **inf** permetre • **ger** permetent • **pp** _sing_ permès / permesa _plur_ permesos / permeses

perseguir /go after/ • **ind** _pre_ persegueixo, persegueixes, persegueix, perseguim, perseguiu, persegueixen _imp_ perseguia, perseguies, perseguia, perseguíem, perseguíeu, perseguien _prt_ perseguí, perseguires, perseguí, perseguírem, perseguíreu, perseguiren _fut_ perseguiré, perseguiràs, perseguirà, perseguirem, perseguireu, perseguiran _con_ perseguiria, perseguiries, perseguiria, perseguiríem, perseguiríeu, perseguirien • **sub** _pre_ persegueixi, persegueixis, persegueixi, perseguim, perseguiu, persegueixin _imp_ perseguís, perseguissis, perseguís, perseguíssim, perseguíssiu, perseguissin • **imp** -, persegueix, persegueixi, perseguim, perseguiu, persegueixin • **inf** perseguir • **ger** perseguint • **pp** _sing_ perseguit / perseguida _plur_ perseguits / perseguides

pesar /weigh/ • **ind** _pre_ peso, peses, pesa, pesem, peseu, pesen _imp_ pesava, pesaves, pesava, pesàvem, pesàveu, pesaven _prt_ pesí, pesares, pesà, pesàrem, pesàreu, pesaren _fut_ pesaré, pesaràs, pesarà, pesarem, pesareu, pesaran _con_ pesaria, pesaries, pesaria, pesaríem, pesaríeu, pesarien • **sub** _pre_ pesi, pesis, pesi, pesem, peseu, pesin _imp_ pesés, pesessis, pesés, peséssim, peséssiu, pesessin • **imp** -, pesa, pesi, pesem, peseu, pesin • **inf** pesar • **ger** pesant • **pp** _sing_ pesat / pesada _plur_ pesats / pesades

pescar /fish/ • **ind** _pre_   pesco, pesques, pesca, pesquem, pesqueu, pesquen _imp_ pescava, pescaves, pescava, pescàvem, pescàveu, pescaven _prt_ pesquí, pescares, pescà, pescàrem, pescàreu, pescaren _fut_ pescaré, pescaràs, pescarà, pescarem, pescareu, pescaran _con_ pescaria, pescaries, pescaria, pescaríem, pescaríeu, pescarien • **sub** _pre_ pesqui, pesquis, pesqui, pesquem, pesqueu, pesquin _imp_ pesqués, pesquessis, pesqués, pesquéssim, pesquéssiu, pesquessin • **imp** -, pesca, pesqui, pesquem, pesqueu, pesquin • **inf** pescar • **ger** pescant • **pp** _sing_ pescat / pescada _plur_ pescats / pescades

pintar /paint/ • **ind** _pre_   pinto, pintes, pinta, pintem, pinteu, pinten _imp_ pintava, pintaves, pintava, pintàvem, pintàveu, pintaven _prt_ pintí, pintares, pintà, pintàrem, pintàreu, pintaren _fut_ pintaré, pintaràs, pintarà, pintarem, pintareu, pintaran _con_ pintaria, pintaries, pintaria, pintaríem, pintaríeu, pintarien • **sub** _pre_ pinti, pintis, pinti, pintem, pinteu, pintin _imp_ pintés, pintessis, pintés, pintéssim, pintéssiu, pintessin • **imp** -, pinta, pinti, pintem, pinteu, pintin • **inf** pintar • **ger** pintant • **pp** _sing_ pintat / pintada _plur_ pintats / pintades

pixar /pee/ • **ind** _pre_   pixo, pixes, pixa, pixem, pixeu, pixen _imp_ pixava, pixaves, pixava, pixàvem, pixàveu, pixaven _prt_ pixí, pixares, pixà, pixàrem, pixàreu, pixaren _fut_ pixaré, pixaràs, pixarà, pixarem, pixareu, pixaran _con_ pixaria, pixaries, pixaria, pixaríem, pixaríeu, pixarien • **sub** _pre_ pixi, pixis, pixi, pixem, pixeu, pixin _imp_ pixés, pixessis, pixés, pixéssim, pixéssiu, pixessin • **imp** -, pixa, pixi, pixem, pixeu, pixin • **inf** pixar • **ger** pixant • **pp** _sing_ pixat / pixada _plur_ pixats / pixades

planejar /plan/ • **ind** _pre_   planejo, planeges, planeja, planegem, planegeu, planegen _imp_ planejava, planejaves, planejava, planejàvem, planejàveu, planejaven _prt_ planegí, planejares, planejà, planejàrem, planejàreu, planejaren _fut_ planejaré, planejaràs, planejarà, planejarem, planejareu, planejaran _con_ planejaria, planejaries, planejaria, planejaríem, planejaríeu, planejarien • **sub** _pre_ planegi, planegis, planegi, planegem, planegeu, planegin _imp_ planegés, planegessis, planegés, planegéssim, planegéssiu, planegessin • **imp** -, planeja, planegi, planegem, planegeu, planegin • **inf** planejar • **ger** planejant • **pp** _sing_ planejat / planejada _plur_ planejats / planejades

plantar /plant/ • **ind** _pre_   planto, plantes, planta, plantem, planteu, planten _imp_ plantava, plantaves, plantava, plantàvem, plantàveu, plantaven _prt_ plantí, plantares, plantà, plantàrem, plantàreu, plantaren _fut_ plantaré, plantaràs, plantarà, plantarem, plantareu, plantaran _con_ plantaria, plantaries, plantaria, plantaríem, plantaríeu, plantarien • **sub** _pre_ planti,

P

plantis, planti, plantem, planteu, plantin _imp_ plantés, plantessis, plantés, plantéssim, plantéssiu, plantessin • **imp** -, planta, planti, plantem, planteu, plantin • **inf** plantar • **ger** plantant • **pp** _sing_ plantat / plantada _plur_ plantats / plantades

plegar /fold up/ • **ind** _pre_ plego, plegues, plega, pleguem, plegueu, pleguen _imp_ plegava, plegaves, plegava, plegàvem, plegàveu, plegaven _prt_ pleguí, plegares, plegà, plegàrem, plegàreu, plegaren _fut_ plegaré, plegaràs, plegarà, plegarem, plegareu, plegaran _con_ plegaria, plegaries, plegaria, plegaríem, plegaríeu, plegarien • **sub** _pre_ plegui, pleguis, plegui, pleguem, plegueu, pleguin _imp_ plegués, pleguessis, plegués, pleguéssim, pleguéssiu, pleguessin • **imp** -, plega, plegui, pleguem, plegueu, pleguin • **inf** plegar • **ger** plegant • **pp** _sing_ plegat / plegada _plur_ plegats / plegades

plorar /cry/ • **ind** _pre_ ploro, plores, plora, plorem, ploreu, ploren _imp_ plorava, ploraves, plorava, ploràvem, ploràveu, ploraven _prt_ plorí, plorares, plorà, ploràrem, ploràreu, ploraren _fut_ ploraré, ploraràs, plorarà, plorarem, plorareu, ploraran _con_ ploraria, ploraries, ploraria, ploraríem, ploraríeu, plorarien • **sub** _pre_ plori, ploris, plori, plorem, ploreu, plorin _imp_ plorés, ploressis, plorés, ploréssim, ploréssiu, ploressin • **imp** -, plora, plori, plorem, ploreu, plorin • **inf** plorar • **ger** plorant • **pp** _sing_ plorat / plorada _plur_ plorats / plorades

poder /can/ • **ind** _pre_ puc, pots, pot, podem, podeu, poden _imp_ podia, podies, podia, podíem, podíeu, podien _prt_ poguí, pogueres, pogué, poguérem, poguéreu, pogueren _fut_ podré, podràs, podrà, podrem, podreu, podran _con_ podria, podries, podria, podríem, podríeu, podrien • **sub** _pre_ pugui, puguis, pugui, puguem, pugueu, puguin _imp_ pogués, poguessis, pogués, poguéssim, poguéssiu, poguessin • **imp** -, pugues, pugui, puguem, pugueu, puguin • **inf** poder • **ger** podent • **pp** _sing_ pogut / poguda _plur_ poguts / pogudes

portar /bring/ • **ind** _pre_ porto, portes, porta, portem, porteu, porten _imp_ portava, portaves, portava, portàvem, portàveu, portaven _prt_ portí, portares, portà, portàrem, portàreu, portaren _fut_ portaré, portaràs, portarà, portarem, portareu, portaran _con_ portaria, portaries, portaria, portaríem, portaríeu, portarien • **sub** _pre_ porti, portis, porti, portem, porteu, portin _imp_ portés, portessis, portés, portéssim, portéssiu, portessin • **imp** -, porta, porti, portem, porteu, portin • **inf** portar • **ger** portant • **pp** _sing_ portat / portada _plur_ portats / portades

posar /put/ • **ind** _pre_ poso, poses, posa, posem, poseu, posen _imp_ posava, posaves, posava, posàvem, posàveu, posaven _prt_ posí, posares, posà, posàrem, posàreu, posaren _fut_ posaré, posaràs, posarà, posarem, posareu, posaran _con_ posaria, posaries, posaria, posaríem, posaríeu, posarien • **sub** _pre_ posi, posis, posi, posem, poseu, posin _imp_ posés, posessis, posés, poséssim, poséssiu, posessin • **imp** -, posa, posi, posem, poseu, posin • **inf** posar • **ger** posant • **pp** _sing_ posat / posada _plur_ posats / posades

practicar /practice/ • **ind** _pre_ practico, practiques, practica, practiquem, practiqueu, practiquen _imp_ practicava, practicaves, practicava, practicàvem, practicàveu, practicaven _prt_ practiquí, practicares, practicà, practicàrem, practicàreu, practicaren _fut_ practicaré, practicaràs, practicarà, practicarem, practicareu, practicaran _con_ practicaria, practicaries, practicaria, practicaríem, practicaríeu, practicarien • **sub** _pre_ practiqui, practiquis, practiqui, practiquem, practiqueu, practiquin _imp_ practiqués, practiquessis, practiqués, practiquéssim, practiquéssiu, practiquessin • **imp** -, practica, practiqui, practiquem, practiqueu, practiquin • **inf** practicar • **ger** practicant • **pp** _sing_ practicat / practicada _plur_ practicats / practicades

pregar /pray/ • **ind** _pre_ prego, pregues, prega, preguem, pregueu, preguen _imp_ pregava, pregaves, pregava, pregàvem, pregàveu, pregaven _prt_ preguí, pregares, pregà, pregàrem, pregàreu, pregaren _fut_ pregaré, pregaràs, pregarà, pregarem, pregareu, pregaran _con_ pregaria, pregaries, pregaria, pregaríem, pregaríeu, pregarien • **sub** _pre_ pregui, preguis, pregui, preguem, pregueu, preguin _imp_ pregués, preguessis, pregués, preguéssim, preguéssiu, preguessin • **imp** -, prega, pregui, preguem, pregueu, preguin • **inf** pregar • **ger** pregant • **pp** _sing_ pregat / pregada _plur_ pregats / pregades

preguntar /ask/ • **ind** _pre_ pregunto, preguntes, pregunta, preguntem, pregunteu, pregunten _imp_ preguntava, preguntaves, preguntava, preguntàvem, preguntàveu, preguntaven _prt_ preguntí, preguntares, preguntà, preguntàrem, preguntàreu, preguntaren _fut_ preguntaré, preguntaràs, preguntarà, preguntarem, preguntareu, preguntaran _con_ preguntaria, preguntaries, preguntaria, preguntaríem, preguntaríeu, preguntarien • **sub** _pre_ pregunti, preguntis, pregunti, preguntem, pregunteu, preguntin _imp_ preguntés, preguntessis, preguntés, preguntéssim, preguntéssiu, preguntessin • **imp** -, pregunta, pregunti, preguntem, pregunteu, preguntin • **inf** preguntar • **ger** preguntant • **pp** _sing_ preguntat / preguntada _plur_ preguntats / preguntades

prendre /take/ • **ind** _pre_ prenc, prens, pren, prenem, preneu, prenen _imp_ prenia, prenies, prenia, preníem, preníeu, prenien _prt_ prenguí, prengueres, prengué, prenguérem, prenguéreu, prengueren *fut* prendré, prendràs, prendrà, prendrem, prendreu, prendran *con* prendria, prendries, prendria, prendríem, prendríeu, prendrien • **sub** *pre* prengui, prenguis, prengui, prenguem, prengueu, prenguin *imp* prengués, prenguessis, prengués, prenguéssim, prenguéssiu, prenguessin • **imp** -, pren, prengui, prenguem, preneu, prenguin • **inf** prendre • **ger** prenent • **pp** *sing* pres / presa *plur* presos / preses

preocupar /worry/ • **ind** *pre* preocupo, preocupes, preocupa, preocupem, preocupeu, preocupen *imp* preocupava, preocupaves, preocupava, preocupàvem, preocupàveu, preocupaven *prt* preocupí, preocupares, preocupà, preocupàrem, preocupàreu, preocuparen *fut* preocuparé, preocuparàs, preocuparà, preocuparem, preocupareu, preocuparan *con* preocuparia, preocuparies, preocuparia, preocuparíem, preocuparíeu, preocuparien • **sub** *pre* preocupi, preocupis, preocupi, preocupem, preocupeu, preocupin *imp* preocupés, preocupessis, preocupés, preocupéssim, preocupéssiu, preocupessin • **imp** -, preocupa, preocupi, preocupem, preocupeu, preocupin • **inf** preocupar • **ger** preocupant • **pp** *sing* preocupat / preocupada *plur* preocupats / preocupades

preparar /prepare/ • **ind** *pre* preparo, prepares, prepara, preparem, prepareu, preparen *imp* preparava, preparaves, preparava, preparàvem, preparàveu, preparaven *prt* preparí, preparares, preparà, preparàrem, preparàreu, prepararen *fut* prepararé, prepararàs, prepararà, prepararem, preparareu, prepararan *con* prepararia, prepararies, prepararia, prepararíem, prepararíeu, prepararien • **sub** *pre* prepari, preparis, prepari, preparem, prepareu, preparin *imp* preparés, preparessis, preparés, preparéssim, preparéssiu, preparessin • **imp** -, prepara, prepari, preparem, prepareu, preparin • **inf** preparar • **ger** preparant • **pp** *sing* preparat / preparada *plur* preparats / preparades

presentar /present/ • **ind** *pre* presento, presentes, presenta, presentem, presenteu, presenten *imp* presentava, presentaves, presentava, presentàvem, presentàveu, presentaven *prt* presentí, presentares, presentà, presentàrem, presentàreu, presentaren *fut* presentaré, presentaràs, presentarà, presentarem, presentareu, presentaran *con* presentaria, presentaries, presentaria, presentaríem, presentaríeu, presentarien • **sub** *pre* presenti, presentis, presenti, presentem, presenteu, presentin *imp* presentés, presentessis, presentés, presentéssim, presentéssiu, presentessin • **imp** -, presenta, presenti, presentem, presenteu, presentin • **inf** presentar • **ger** presentant • **pp** *sing* presentat / presentada *plur* presentats / presentades

prestar /lend/ • **ind** _pre_ presto, prestes, presta, prestem, presteu, presten _imp_ prestava, prestaves, prestava, prestàvem, prestàveu, prestaven _prt_ prestí, prestares, prestà, prestàrem, prestàreu, prestaren _fut_ prestaré, prestaràs, prestarà, prestarem, prestareu, prestaran _con_ prestaria, prestaries, prestaria, prestaríem, prestaríeu, prestarien • **sub** _pre_ presti, prestis, presti, prestem, presteu, prestin _imp_ prestés, prestessis, prestés, prestéssim, prestéssiu, prestessin • **imp** -, presta, presti, prestem, presteu, prestin • **inf** prestar • **ger** prestant • **pp** _sing_ prestat / prestada _plur_ prestats / prestades

produir /produce/ • **ind** _pre_ produeixo, produeixes, produeix, produïm, produïu, produeixen _imp_ produïa, produïes, produïa, produíem, produíeu, produïen _prt_ produí, produïres, produí, produírem, produíreu, produïren _fut_ produiré, produiràs, produirà, produirem, produireu, produiran _con_ produiria, produiries, produiria, produiríem, produiríeu, produirien • **sub** _pre_ produeixi, produeixis, produeixi, produïm, produïu, produeixin _imp_ produís, produïssis, produís, produíssim, produíssiu, produïssin • **imp** -, produeix, produeixi, produïm, produïu, produeixin • **inf** produir • **ger** produint • **pp** _sing_ produït / produïda _plur_ produïts / produïdes

prohibir /ban, prohibit/ • **ind** _pre_ prohibeixo, prohibeixes, prohibeix, prohibim, prohibiu, prohibeixen _imp_ prohibia, prohibies, prohibia, prohibíem, prohibíeu, prohibien _prt_ prohibí, prohibires, prohibí, prohibírem, prohibíreu, prohibiren _fut_ prohibiré, prohibiràs, prohibirà, prohibirem, prohibireu, prohibiran _con_ prohibiria, prohibiries, prohibiria, prohibiríem, prohibiríeu, prohibirien • **sub** _pre_ prohibeixi, prohibeixis, prohibeixi, prohibim, prohibiu, prohibeixin _imp_ prohibís, prohibissis, prohibís, prohibíssim, prohibíssiu, prohibissin • **imp** -, prohibeix, prohibeixi, prohibim, prohibiu, prohibeixin • **inf** prohibir • **ger** prohibint • **pp** _sing_ prohibit / prohibida _plur_ prohibits / prohibides

prometre /promise/ • **ind** _pre_ prometo, promets, promet, prometem, prometeu, prometen _imp_ prometia, prometies, prometia, prometíem, prometíeu, prometien _prt_ prometí, prometeres, prometé, prometérem, prometéreu, prometeren _fut_ prometré, prometràs, prometrà, prometrem, prometreu, prometran _con_ prometria, prometries, prometria, prometríem, prometríeu, prometrien • **sub** _pre_ prometi, prometis, prometi, prometem, prometeu, prometin _imp_ prometés, prometessis, prometés, prometéssim, prometéssiu, prometessin • **imp** -, promet, prometi, prometem, prometeu, prometin • **inf** prometre • **ger** prometent • **pp** _sing_ promès / promesa _plur_ promesos / promeses

proporcionar /provide/ • **ind** _pre_ proporciono, proporciones, proporciona, proporcionem, proporcioneu, proporcionen _imp_ proporcionava, proporcionaves, proporcionava, proporcionàvem, proporcionàveu, proporcionaven _prt_ proporcioní, proporcionares, proporcionà, proporcionàrem, proporcionàreu, proporcionaren _fut_ proporcionaré, proporcionaràs, proporcionarà, proporcionarem, proporcionareu, proporcionaran _con_ proporcionaria, proporcionaries, proporcionaria, proporcionaríem, proporcionaríeu, proporcionarien • **sub** _pre_ proporcioni, proporcionis, proporcioni, proporcionem, proporcioneu, proporcionin _imp_ proporcionés, proporcionessis, proporcionés, proporcionéssim, proporcionéssiu, proporcionessin • **imp** -, proporciona, proporcioni, proporcionem, proporcioneu, proporcionin • **inf** proporcionar • **ger** proporcionant • **pp** _sing_ proporcionat / proporcionada _plur_ proporcionats / proporcionades

proposar /proposed/ • **ind** _pre_ proposo, proposes, proposa, proposem, proposeu, proposen _imp_ proposava, proposaves, proposava, proposàvem, proposàveu, proposaven _prt_ proposí, proposares, proposà, proposàrem, proposàreu, proposaren _fut_ proposaré, proposaràs, proposarà, proposarem, proposareu, proposaran _con_ proposaria, proposaries, proposaria, proposaríem, proposaríeu, proposarien • **sub** _pre_ proposi, proposis, proposi, proposem, proposeu, proposin _imp_ proposés, proposessis, proposés, proposéssim, proposéssiu, proposessin • **imp** -, proposa, proposi, proposem, proposeu, proposin • **inf** proposar • **ger** proposant • **pp** _sing_ proposat / proposada _plur_ proposats / proposades

protegir /protect/ • **ind** _pre_ protegeixo, protegeixes, protegeix, protegim, protegiu, protegeixen _imp_ protegia, protegies, protegia, protegíem, protegíeu, protegien _prt_ protegí, protegires, protegí, protegírem, protegíreu, protegiren _fut_ protegiré, protegiràs, protegirà, protegirem, protegireu, protegiran _con_ protegiria, protegiries, protegiria, protegiríem, protegiríeu, protegirien • **sub** _pre_ protegeixi, protegeixis, protegeixi, protegim, protegiu, protegeixin _imp_ protegís, protegissis, protegís, protegíssim, protegíssiu, protegissin • **imp** -, protegeix, protegeixi, protegim, protegiu, protegeixin • **inf** protegir • **ger** protegint • **pp** _sing_ protegit / protegida _plur_ protegits / protegides

provar /prove/ • **ind** _pre_ provo, proves, prova, provem, proveu, proven _imp_ provava, provaves, provava, provàvem, provàveu, provaven _prt_ proví, provares, provà, provàrem, provàreu, provaren _fut_ provaré, provaràs, provarà, provarem, provareu, provaran _con_ provaria, provaries, provaria, provaríem, provaríeu, provarien • **sub** _pre_ provi, provis, provi, provem, proveu, provin *imp* provés, provessis, provés, provéssim, provéssiu, provessin • **imp** -, prova, provi, provem, proveu, provin • **inf** provar • **ger** provant • **pp** *sing* provat / provada *plur* provats / provades

provocar /provoke/ • **ind** *pre* provoco, provoques, provoca, provoquem, provoqueu, provoquen *imp* provocava, provocaves, provocava, provocàvem, provocàveu, provocaven *prt* provoquí, provocares, provocà, provocàrem, provocàreu, provocaren *fut* provocaré, provocaràs, provocarà, provocarem, provocareu, provocaran *con* provocaria, provocaries, provocaria, provocaríem, provocaríeu, provocarien • **sub** *pre* provoqui, provoquis, provoqui, provoquem, provoqueu, provoquin *imp* provoqués, provoquessis, provoqués, provoquéssim, provoquéssiu, provoquessin • **imp** -, provoca, provoqui, provoquem, provoqueu, provoquin • **inf** provocar • **ger** provocant • **pp** *sing* provocat / provocada *plur* provocats / provocades

publicar /publish/ • **ind** *pre* publico, publiques, publica, publiquem, publiqueu, publiquen *imp* publicava, publicaves, publicava, publicàvem, publicàveu, publicaven *prt* publiquí, publicares, publicà, publicàrem, publicàreu, publicaren *fut* publicaré, publicaràs, publicarà, publicarem, publicareu, publicaran *con* publicaria, publicaries, publicaria, publicaríem, publicaríeu, publicarien • **sub** *pre* publiqui, publiquis, publiqui, publiquem, publiqueu, publiquin *imp* publiqués, publiquessis, publiqués, publiquéssim, publiquéssiu, publiquessin • **imp** -, publica, publiqui, publiquem, publiqueu, publiquin • **inf** publicar • **ger** publicant • **pp** *sing* publicat / publicada *plur* publicats / publicades

pujar /go up, upload/ • **ind** *pre* pujo, puges, puja, pugem, pugeu, pugen *imp* pujava, pujaves, pujava, pujàvem, pujàveu, pujaven *prt* pugí, pujares, pujà, pujàrem, pujàreu, pujaren *fut* pujaré, pujaràs, pujarà, pujarem, pujareu, pujaran *con* pujaria, pujaries, pujaria, pujaríem, pujaríeu, pujarien • **sub** *pre* pugi, pugis, pugi, pugem, pugeu, pugin *imp* pugés, pugessis, pugés, pugéssim, pugéssiu, pugessin • **imp** -, puja, pugi, pugem, pugeu, pugin • **inf** pujar • **ger** pujant • **pp** *sing* pujat / pujada *plur* pujats / pujades

Q

quedar /remain, meet up/ • **ind** _pre_ quedo, quedes, queda, quedem, quedeu, queden _imp_ quedava, quedaves, quedava, quedàvem, quedàveu, quedaven _prt_ quedí, quedares, quedà, quedàrem, quedàreu, quedaren _fut_ quedaré, quedaràs, quedarà, quedarem, quedareu, quedaran _con_ quedaria, quedaries, quedaria, quedaríem, quedaríeu, quedarien • **sub** _pre_ quedi, quedis, quedi, quedem, quedeu, quedin _imp_ quedés, quedessis, quedés, quedéssim, quedéssiu, quedessin • **imp** -, queda, quedi, quedem, quedeu, quedin • **inf** quedar • **ger** quedant • **pp** _sing_ quedat / quedada _plur_ quedats / quedades

R

reaccionar /react/ • **ind** _pre_ reacciono, reacciones, reacciona, reaccionem, reaccioneu, reaccionen _imp_ reaccionava, reaccionaves, reaccionava, reaccionàvem, reaccionàveu, reaccionaven _prt_ reaccioní, reaccionares, reaccionà, reaccionàrem, reaccionàreu, reaccionaren _fut_ reaccionaré, reaccionaràs, reaccionarà, reaccionarem, reaccionareu, reaccionaran _con_ reaccionaria, reaccionaries, reaccionaria, reaccionaríem, reaccionaríeu, reaccionarien • **sub** _pre_ reaccioni, reaccionis, reaccioni, reaccionem, reaccioneu, reaccionin _imp_ reaccionés, reaccionessis, reaccionés, reaccionéssim, reaccionéssiu, reaccionessin • **imp** -, reacciona, reaccioni, reaccionem, reaccioneu, reaccionin • **inf** reaccionar • **ger** reaccionant • **pp** _sing_ reaccionat / reaccionada _plur_ reaccionats / reaccionades

realitzar /realize/ • **ind** _pre_ realitzo, realitzes, realitza, realitzem, realitzeu, realitzen _imp_ realitzava, realitzaves, realitzava, realitzàvem, realitzàveu, realitzaven _prt_ realitzí, realitzares, realitzà, realitzàrem, realitzàreu, realitzaren _fut_ realitzaré, realitzaràs, realitzarà, realitzarem, realitzareu, realitzaran _con_ realitzaria, realitzaries, realitzaria, realitzaríem, realitzaríeu, realitzarien • **sub** _pre_ realitzi, realitzis, realitzi, realitzem, realitzeu, realitzin _imp_ realitzés, realitzessis, realitzés, realitzéssim, realitzéssiu, realitzessin • **imp** -, realitza, realitzi, realitzem, realitzeu, realitzin • **inf** realitzar • **ger** realitzant • **pp** _sing_ realitzat / realitzada _plur_ realitzats / realitzades

rebre /receive/ • **ind** _pre_ rebo, reps, rep, rebem, rebeu, reben _imp_ rebia, rebies, rebia, rebíem, rebíeu, rebien _prt_ rebí, reberes, rebé, rebérem, rebéreu, reberen _fut_ rebré, rebràs, rebrà, rebrem, rebreu, rebran _con_ rebria, rebries, rebria, rebríem, rebríeu, rebrien • **sub** _pre_ rebi, rebis, rebi, rebem, rebeu, rebin *imp* rebés, rebessis, rebés, rebéssim, rebéssiu, rebessin • **imp** -, rep, rebi, rebem, rebeu, rebin • **inf** rebre • **ger** rebent • **pp** *sing* rebut / rebuda *plur* rebuts / rebudes

rebutjar /refuse/ • **ind** *pre* rebutjo, rebutges, rebutja, rebutgem, rebutgeu, rebutgen *imp* rebutjava, rebutjaves, rebutjava, rebutjàvem, rebutjàveu, rebutjaven *prt* rebutgí, rebutjares, rebutjà, rebutjàrem, rebutjàreu, rebutjaren *fut* rebutjaré, rebutjaràs, rebutjarà, rebutjarem, rebutjareu, rebutjaran *con* rebutjaria, rebutjaries, rebutjaria, rebutjaríem, rebutjaríeu, rebutjarien • **sub** *pre* rebutgi, rebutgis, rebutgi, rebutgem, rebutgeu, rebutgin *imp* rebutgés, rebutgessis, rebutgés, rebutgéssim, rebutgéssiu, rebutgessin • **imp** -, rebutja, rebutgi, rebutgem, rebutgeu, rebutgin • **inf** rebutjar • **ger** rebutjant • **pp** *sing* rebutjat / rebutjada *plur* rebutjats / rebutjades

reclamar /claim/ • **ind** *pre* reclamo, reclames, reclama, reclamem, reclameu, reclamen *imp* reclamava, reclamaves, reclamava, reclamàvem, reclamàveu, reclamaven *prt* reclamí, reclamares, reclamà, reclamàrem, reclamàreu, reclamaren *fut* reclamaré, reclamaràs, reclamarà, reclamarem, reclamareu, reclamaran *con* reclamaria, reclamaries, reclamaria, reclamaríem, reclamaríeu, reclamarien • **sub** *pre* reclami, reclamis, reclami, reclamem, reclameu, reclamin *imp* reclamés, reclamessis, reclamés, reclaméssim, reclaméssiu, reclamessin • **imp** -, reclama, reclami, reclamem, reclameu, reclamin • **inf** reclamar • **ger** reclamant • **pp** *sing* reclamat / reclamada *plur* reclamats / reclamades

recollir /pick up/ • **ind** *pre* recullo, reculls, recull, recollim, recolliu, recullen *imp* recollia, recollies, recollia, recollíem, recollíeu, recollien *prt* recollí, recollires, recollí, recollírem, recollíreu, recolliren *fut* recolliré, recolliràs, recollirà, recollirem, recollireu, recolliran *con* recolliria, recolliries, recolliria, recolliríem, recolliríeu, recollirien • **sub** *pre* reculli, recullis, reculli, recollim, recolliu, recullin *imp* recollís, recollissis, recollís, recollíssim, recollíssiu, recollissin • **imp** -, recull, reculli, recollim, recolliu, recullin • **inf** recollir • **ger** recollint • **pp** *sing* recollit / recollida *plur* recollits / recollides

recolzar /support/ • **ind** *pre* recolzo, recolzes, recolza, recolzem, recolzeu, recolzen *imp* recolzava, recolzaves, recolzava, recolzàvem, recolzàveu, recolzaven *prt* recolzí, recolzares, recolzà, recolzàrem, recolzàreu, recolzaren *fut* recolzaré, recolzaràs, recolzarà, recolzarem, recolzareu, recolzaran *con* recolzaria, recolzaries, recolzaria, recolzaríem, recolzaríeu, recolzarien • **sub** *pre* recolzi, recolzis, recolzi, recolzem, recolzeu, recolzin *imp* recolzés, recolzessis, recolzés, recolzéssim, re-

R

colzéssiu, recolzessin • **imp** -, recolza, recolzi, recolzem, recolzeu, recolzin • **inf** recolzar • **ger** recolzant • **pp** _sing_ recolzat / recolzada
plur recolzats / recolzades

reconstruir /rebuild/ • **ind** _pre_ reconstrueixo, reconstrueixes, reconstrueix, reconstruïm, reconstruïu, reconstrueixen _imp_ reconstruïa, reconstruïes, reconstruïa, reconstruíem, reconstruíeu, reconstruïen
prt reconstruí, reconstruïres, reconstruí, reconstruírem, reconstruíreu,
reconstruïren _fut_ reconstruiré, reconstruiràs, reconstruirà, reconstrui-
rem, reconstruireu, reconstruiran _con_ reconstruiria, reconstruiries, reconstruiria, reconstruiríem, reconstruiríeu, reconstruirien • **sub** _pre_ reconstrueixi, reconstrueixis, reconstrueixi, reconstruïm, reconstruïu, reconstrueixin _imp_ reconstruís, reconstruïssis, reconstruís, reconstruís-
sim, reconstruíssiu, reconstruïssin • **imp** -, reconstrueix, reconstrueixi, reconstruïm, reconstruïu, reconstrueixin • **inf** reconstruir • **ger**
reconstruint • **pp** _sing_ reconstruït / reconstruïda _plur_ reconstruïts /
reconstruïdes

recordar /remember/ • **ind** _pre_ recordo, recordes, recorda, recordem, recordeu, recorden _imp_ recordava, recordaves, recordava, re-
cordàvem, recordàveu, recordaven _prt_ recordí, recordares, recordà,
recordàrem, recordàreu, recordaren _fut_ recordaré, recordaràs, recor-
darà, recordarem, recordareu, recordaran _con_ recordaria, recordaries,
recordaria, recordaríem, recordaríeu, recordarien • **sub** _pre_ recordi,
recordis, recordi, recordem, recordeu, recordin _imp_ recordés, recor-
dessis, recordés, recordéssim, recordéssiu, recordessin • **imp** -, recorda, recordi, recordem, recordeu, recordin • **inf** recordar • **ger**
recordant • **pp** _sing_ recordat / recordada _plur_ recordats / recordades

recuperar /recover/ • **ind** _pre_ recupero, recuperes, recupera, recuperem, recupereu, recuperen _imp_ recuperava, recuperaves, recuperava, recuperàvem, recuperàveu, recuperaven _prt_ recuperí, recuperares,
recuperà, recuperàrem, recuperàreu, recuperaren _fut_ recuperaré, recu-
peraràs, recuperarà, recuperarem, recuperareu, recuperaran _con_ recuperaria, recuperaries, recuperaria, recuperaríem, recuperaríeu, recupe-
rarien • **sub** _pre_ recuperi, recuperis, recuperi, recuperem, recupereu,
recuperin _imp_ recuperés, recuperessis, recuperés, recuperéssim, recu-
peréssiu, recuperessin • **imp** -, recupera, recuperi, recuperem, recupereu, recuperin • **inf** recuperar • **ger** recuperant • **pp** _sing_ recuperat
/ recuperada _plur_ recuperats / recuperades

reduir /cut down/ • **ind** _pre_ redueixo, redueixes, redueix, reduïm,
reduïu, redueixen _imp_ reduïa, reduïes, reduïa, reduíem, reduíeu, reduï-

en _prt_ reduí, reduïres, reduí, reduírem, reduíreu, reduïren _fut_ reduiré, reduiràs, reduirà, reduirem, reduireu, reduiran _con_ reduiria, reduiries, reduiria, reduiríem, reduiríeu, reduirien • **sub** _pre_ redueixi, redueixis, redueixi, reduïm, reduïu, redueixin _imp_ reduís, reduïssis, reduís, reduíssim, reduíssiu, reduïssin • **imp** -, redueix, redueixi, reduïm, reduïu, redueixin • **inf** reduir • **ger** reduint • **pp** _sing_ reduït / reduïda _plur_ reduïts / reduïdes

regalar /give away/ • **ind** _pre_ regalo, regales, regala, regalem, regaleu, regalen _imp_ regalava, regalaves, regalava, regalàvem, regalàveu, regalaven _prt_ regalí, regalares, regalà, regalàrem, regalàreu, regalaren _fut_ regalaré, regalaràs, regalarà, regalarem, regalareu, regalaran _con_ regalaria, regalaries, regalaria, regalaríem, regalaríeu, regalarien • **sub** _pre_ regali, regalis, regali, regalem, regaleu, regalin _imp_ regalés, regalessis, regalés, regaléssim, regaléssiu, regalessin • **imp** -, regala, regali, regalem, regaleu, regalin • **inf** regalar • **ger** regalant • **pp** _sing_ regalat / regalada _plur_ regalats / regalades

registrar /register/ • **ind** _pre_ registro, registres, registra, registrem, registreu, registren _imp_ registrava, registraves, registrava, registràvem, registràveu, registraven _prt_ registrí, registrares, registrà, registràrem, registràreu, registraren _fut_ registraré, registraràs, registrarà, registrarem, registrareu, registraran _con_ registraria, registraries, registraria, registraríem, registraríeu, registrarien • **sub** _pre_ registri, registris, registri, registrem, registreu, registrin _imp_ registrés, registressis, registrés, registréssim, registréssiu, registressin • **imp** -, registra, registri, registrem, registreu, registrin • **inf** registrar • **ger** registrant • **pp** _sing_ registrat / registrada _plur_ registrats / registrades

regular /regulate/ • **ind** _pre_ regulo, regules, regula, regulem, reguleu, regulen _imp_ regulava, regulaves, regulava, regulàvem, regulàveu, regulaven _prt_ regulí, regulares, regulà, regulàrem, regulàreu, regularen _fut_ regularé, regularàs, regularà, regularem, regulareu, regularan _con_ regularia, regularies, regularia, regularíem, regularíeu, regularien • **sub** _pre_ reguli, regulis, reguli, regulem, reguleu, regulin _imp_ regulés, regulessis, regulés, reguléssim, reguléssiu, regulessin • **imp** -, regula, reguli, regulem, reguleu, regulin • **inf** regular • **ger** regulant • **pp** _sing_ regulat / regulada _plur_ regulats / regulades

rendir /give up/ • **ind** _pre_ rendeixo, rendeixes, rendeix, rendim, rendiu, rendeixen _imp_ rendia, rendies, rendia, rendíem, rendíeu, rendien _prt_ rendí, rendires, rendí, rendírem, rendíreu, rendiren _fut_ rendiré, rendiràs, rendirà, rendirem, rendireu, rendiran _con_ rendiria, rendiries, rendiria,

R

rendiríem, rendiríeu, rendirien • **sub** _pre_ rendeixi, rendeixis, rendeixi, rendim, rendiu, rendeixin _imp_ rendís, rendissis, rendís, rendíssim, rendíssiu, rendissin • **imp** -, rendeix, rendeixi, rendim, rendiu, rendeixin • **inf** rendir • **ger** rendint • **pp** _sing_ rendit / rendida _plur_ rendits / rendides

rentar /wash/ • **ind** _pre_ rento, rentes, renta, rentem, renteu, renten _imp_ rentava, rentaves, rentava, rentàvem, rentàveu, rentaven _prt_ rentí, rentares, rentà, rentàrem, rentàreu, rentaren _fut_ rentaré, rentaràs, rentarà, rentarem, rentareu, rentaran _con_ rentaria, rentaries, rentaria, rentaríem, rentaríeu, rentarien • **sub** _pre_ renti, rentis, renti, rentem, renteu, rentin _imp_ rentés, rentessis, rentés, rentéssim, rentéssiu, rentessin • **imp** -, renta, renti, rentem, renteu, rentin • **inf** rentar • **ger** rentant • **pp** _sing_ rentat / rentada _plur_ rentats / rentades

renunciar /give up/ • **ind** _pre_ renuncio, renuncies, renuncia, renunciem, renuncieu, renuncien _imp_ renunciava, renunciaves, renunciava, renunciàvem, renunciàveu, renunciaven _prt_ renunciï, renunciares, renuncià, renunciàrem, renunciàreu, renunciaren _fut_ renunciaré, renunciaràs, renunciarà, renunciarem, renunciareu, renunciaran _con_ renunciaria, renunciaries, renunciaria, renunciaríem, renunciaríeu, renunciarien • **sub** _pre_ renunciï, renunciïs, renunciï, renunciem, renuncieu, renunciïn _imp_ renunciés, renunciessis, renunciés, renunciéssim, renunciéssiu, renunciessin • **imp** -, renuncia, renunciï, renunciem, renuncieu, renunciï • **inf** renunciar • **ger** renunciant • **pp** _sing_ renunciat / renunciada _plur_ renunciats / renunciades

reparar /repair/ • **ind** _pre_ reparo, repares, repara, reparem, repareu, reparen _imp_ reparava, reparaves, reparava, reparàvem, reparàveu, reparaven _prt_ reparí, reparares, reparà, reparàrem, reparàreu, repararen _fut_ repararé, repararàs, repararà, repararem, reparareu, repararan _con_ repararia, repararies, repararia, repararíem, repararíeu, repararien • **sub** _pre_ repari, reparis, repari, reparem, repareu, reparin _imp_ reparés, reparessis, reparés, reparéssim, reparéssiu, reparessin • **imp** -, repara, repari, reparem, repareu, reparin • **inf** reparar • **ger** reparant • **pp** _sing_ reparat / reparada _plur_ reparats / reparades

repartir /distribute/ • **ind** _pre_ reparteixo, reparteixes, reparteix, repartim, repartiu, reparteixen _imp_ repartia, reparties, repartia, repartíem, repartíeu, repartien _prt_ repartí, repartires, repartí, repartírem, repartíreu, repartiren _fut_ repartiré, repartiràs, repartirà, repartirem, repartireu, repartiran _con_ repartiria, repartiries, repartiria, repartiríem, repartiríeu, repartirien • **sub** _pre_ reparteixi, reparteixis, reparteixi, repartim, repartiu, reparteixin _imp_ repartís, repartissis, repartís, repartíssim, repartíssiu, repartissin • **imp** -, reparteix, reparteixi, repartim, repartiu, reparteixin • **inf** repartir • **ger** repartint • **pp** _sing_ repartit / repartida _plur_ repartits / repartides

repetir /repeat/ • **ind** _pre_ repeteixo, repeteixes, repeteix, repetim, repetiu, repeteixen _imp_ repetia, repeties, repetia, repetíem, repetíeu, repetien _prt_ repetí, repetires, repetí, repetírem, repetíreu, repetiren _fut_ repetiré, repetiràs, repetirà, repetirem, repetireu, repetiran _con_ repetiria, repetiries, repetiria, repetiríem, repetiríeu, repetirien • **sub** _pre_ repeteixi, repeteixis, repeteixi, repetim, repetiu, repeteixin _imp_ repetís, repetissis, repetís, repetíssim, repetíssiu, repetissin • **imp** -, repeteix, repeteixi, repetim, repetiu, repeteixin • **inf** repetir • **ger** repetint • **pp** _sing_ repetit / repetida _plur_ repetits / repetides

representar /represent/ • **ind** _pre_ represento, representes, representa, representem, representeu, representen _imp_ representava, representaves, representava, representàvem, representàveu, representaven _prt_ representí, representares, representà, representàrem, representàreu, representaren _fut_ representaré, representaràs, representarà, representarem, representareu, representaran _con_ representaria, representaries, representaria, representaríem, representaríeu, representarien • **sub** _pre_ representi, representis, representi, representem, representeu, representin _imp_ representés, representessis, representés, representéssim, representéssiu, representessin • **imp** -, representa, representi, representem, representeu, representin • **inf** representar • **ger** representant • **pp** _sing_ representat / representada _plur_ representats / representades

resar /pray/ • **ind** _pre_ reso, reses, resa, resem, reseu, resen _imp_ resava, resaves, resava, resàvem, resàveu, resaven _prt_ resí, resares, resà, resàrem, resàreu, resaren _fut_ resaré, resaràs, resarà, resarem, resareu, resaran _con_ resaria, resaries, resaria, resaríem, resaríeu, resarien • **sub** _pre_ resi, resis, resi, resem, reseu, resin _imp_ resés, resessis, resés, reséssim, reséssiu, resessin • **imp** -, resa, resi, resem, reseu, resin • **inf** resar • **ger** resant • **pp** _sing_ resat / resada _plur_ resats / resades

rescatar /rescue/ • **ind** _pre_ rescato, rescates, rescata, rescatem, rescateu, rescaten _imp_ rescatava, rescataves, rescatava, rescatàvem, rescatàveu, rescataven _prt_ rescatí, rescatares, rescatà, rescatàrem, rescatàreu, rescataren _fut_ rescataré, rescataràs, rescatarà, rescatarem, rescatareu, rescataran _con_ rescataria, rescataries, rescataria, rescataríem, rescataríeu, rescatarien • **sub** _pre_ rescati, rescatis, rescati, rescatem, rescateu, rescatin *imp* rescatés, rescatessis, rescatés, rescatéssim, rescatéssiu, rescatessin • **imp** -, rescata, rescati, rescatem, rescateu, rescatin • **inf** rescatar • **ger** rescatant • **pp** *sing* rescatat / rescatada *plur* rescatats / rescatades

resistir /resist/ • **ind** *pre* resisteixo, resisteixes, resisteix, resistim, resistiu, resisteixen *imp* resistia, resisties, resistia, resistíem, resistíeu, resistien *prt* resistí, resistires, resistí, resistírem, resistíreu, resistiren *fut* resistiré, resistiràs, resistirà, resistirem, resistireu, resistiran *con* resistiria, resistiries, resistiria, resistiríem, resistiríeu, resistirien • **sub** *pre* resisteixi, resisteixis, resisteixi, resistim, resistiu, resisteixin *imp* resistís, resistissis, resistís, resistíssim, resistíssiu, resistissin • **imp** -, resisteix, resisteixi, resistim, resistiu, resisteixin • **inf** resistir • **ger** resistint • **pp** *sing* resistit / resistida *plur* resistits / resistides

resoldre /solve/ • **ind** *pre* resolc, resols, resol, resolem, resoleu, resolen *imp* resolia, resolies, resolia, resolíem, resolíeu, resolien *prt* resolguí, resolgueres, resolgué, resolguérem, resolguéreu, resolgueren *fut* resoldré, resoldràs, resoldrà, resoldrem, resoldreu, resoldran *con* resoldria, resoldries, resoldria, resoldríem, resoldríeu, resoldrien • **sub** *pre* resolgui, resolguis, resolgui, resolguem, resolgueu, resolguin *imp* resolgués, resolguessis, resolgués, resolguéssim, resolguéssiu, resolguessin • **imp** -, resol, resolgui, resolguem, resoleu, resolguin • **inf** resoldre • **ger** resolent • **pp** *sing* resolt / resolta *plur* resolts / resoltes

respectar /respect/ • **ind** *pre* respecto, respectes, respecta, respectem, respecteu, respecten *imp* respectava, respectaves, respectava, respectàvem, respectàveu, respectaven *prt* respectí, respectares, respectà, respectàrem, respectàreu, respectaren *fut* respectaré, respectaràs, respectarà, respectarem, respectareu, respectaran *con* respectaria, respectaries, respectaria, respectaríem, respectaríeu, respectarien • **sub** *pre* respecti, respectis, respecti, respectem, respecteu, respectin *imp* respectés, respectessis, respectés, respectéssim, respectéssiu, respectessin • **imp** -, respecta, respecti, respectem, respecteu, respectin • **inf** respectar • **ger** respectant • **pp** *sing* respectat / respectada *plur* respectats / respectades

respirar /breathe/ • **ind** *pre* respiro, respires, respira, respirem, respireu, respiren *imp* respirava, respiraves, respirava, respiràvem, respiràveu, respiraven *prt* respirí, respirares, respirà, respiràrem, respiràreu, respiraren *fut* respiraré, respiraràs, respirarà, respirarem, respirareu, respiraran *con* respiraria, respiraries, respiraria, respiraríem, respiraríeu, respirarien • **sub** *pre* respiri, respiris, respiri, respirem, respireu,

respirin *imp* respirés, respiressis, respirés, respiréssim, respiréssiu, res-
piressin • **imp** -, respira, respiri, respirem, respireu, respirin • **inf** respirar • **ger** respirant • **pp** *sing* respirat / respirada *plur* respirats /
respirades

respondre /answer/ • **ind** *pre* responc, respons, respon, respo-
nem, responeu, responen *imp* responia, responies, responia, responí-
em, responíeu, responien *prt* respunguí, respongueres, respongué, res-
ponguérem, responguéreu, respongueren *fut* respondré, respondràs,
respondrà, respondrem, respondreu, respondran *con* respondria, res-
pondries, respondria, respondríem, respondríeu, respondrien • **sub** *pre*
respongui, responguis, respongui, responguem, respongueu, responguin
imp respongués, responguessis, respongués, responguéssim, respon-
guéssiu, responguessin • **imp** -, respon, respongui, responguem, responeu, responguin • **inf** respondre • **ger** responent • **pp** *sing* respost /
resposta *plur* respostos / respostes

restar /subtract/ • **ind** *pre* resto, restes, resta, restem, resteu, resten
imp restava, restaves, restava, restàvem, restàveu, restaven *prt* restí,
restares, restà, restàrem, restàreu, restaren *fut* restaré, restaràs, restarà,
restarem, restareu, restaran *con* restaria, restaries, restaria, restaríem,
restaríeu, restarien • **sub** *pre* resti, restis, resti, restem, resteu, restin
imp restés, restessis, restés, restéssim, restéssiu, restessin • **imp** -,
resta, resti, restem, resteu, restin • **inf** restar • **ger** restant • **pp** *sing*
restat / restada *plur* restats / restades

resultar /turn out/ • **ind** *pre* resulto, resultes, resulta, resultem,
resulteu, resulten *imp* resultava, resultaves, resultava, resultàvem, resul-
tàveu, resultaven *prt* resultí, resultares, resultà, resultàrem, resultàreu,
resultaren *fut* resultaré, resultaràs, resultarà, resultarem, resultareu, re-
sultaran *con* resultaria, resultaries, resultaria, resultaríem, resultaríeu,
resultarien • **sub** *pre* resulti, resultis, resulti, resultem, resulteu, resultin *imp* resultés, resultessis, resultés, resultéssim, resultéssiu, resultessin
• **imp** -, resulta, resulti, resultem, resulteu, resultin • **inf** resultar • **ger**
resultant • **pp** *sing* resultat / resultada *plur* resultats / resultades

retenir /hold back/ • **ind** *pre* retinc, retens, reté, retenim, reteniu,
retenen *imp* retenia, retenies, retenia, reteníem, reteníeu, retenien *prt*
retinguí, retingueres, retingué, retinguérem, retinguéreu, retingueren *fut*
retindré, retindràs, retindrà, retindrem, retindreu, retindran *con* retindria, retindries, retindria, retindríem, retindríeu, retindrien • **sub** *pre*
retingui, retinguis, retingui, retinguem, retingueu, retinguin *imp* retingués, retinguessis, retingués, retinguéssim, retinguéssiu, retinguessin •

R

imp -, retén, retingui, retinguem, reteniu, retinguin • **inf** retenir • **ger** retenint • **pp** _sing_ retingut / retinguda _plur_ retinguts / retingudes

retirar /withdraw/ • **ind** _pre_ retiro, retires, retira, retirem, retireu, retiren _imp_ retirava, retiraves, retirava, retiràvem, retiràveu, retiraven _prt_ retirí, retirares, retirà, retiràrem, retiràreu, retiraren _fut_ retiraré, retiraràs, retirarà, retirarem, retirareu, retiraran _con_ retiraria, retiraries, retiraria, retiraríem, retiraríeu, retirarien • **sub** _pre_ retiri, retiris, retiri, retirem, retireu, retirin _imp_ retirés, retiressis, retirés, retiréssim, retiréssiu, retiressin • **imp** -, retira, retiri, retirem, retireu, retirin • **inf** retirar • **ger** retirant • **pp** _sing_ retirat / retirada _plur_ retirats / retirades

retornar /return/ • **ind** _pre_ retorno, retornes, retorna, retornem, retorneu, retornen _imp_ retornava, retornaves, retornava, retornàvem, retornàveu, retornaven _prt_ retorní, retornares, retornà, retornàrem, retornàreu, retornaren _fut_ retornaré, retornaràs, retornarà, retornarem, retornareu, retornaran _con_ retornaria, retornaries, retornaria, retornaríem, retornaríeu, retornarien • **sub** _pre_ retorni, retornis, retorni, retornem, retorneu, retornin _imp_ retornés, retornessis, retornés, retornéssim, retornéssiu, retornessin • **imp** -, retorna, retorni, retornem, retorneu, retornin • **inf** retornar • **ger** retornant • **pp** _sing_ retornat / retornada _plur_ retornats / retornades

reunir /bring together/ • **ind** _pre_ reuneixo, reuneixes, reuneix, reunim, reuniu, reuneixen _imp_ reunia, reunies, reunia, reuníem, reuníeu, reunien _prt_ reuní, reunires, reuní, reunírem, reuníreu, reuniren _fut_ reuniré, reuniràs, reunirà, reunirem, reunireu, reuniran _con_ reuniria, reuniries, reuniria, reuniríem, reuniríeu, reunirien • **sub** _pre_ reuneixi, reuneixis, reuneixi, reunim, reuniu, reuneixin _imp_ reunís, reunissis, reunís, reuníssim, reuníssiu, reunissin • **imp** -, reuneix, reuneixi, reunim, reuniu, reuneixin • **inf** reunir • **ger** reunint • **pp** _sing_ reunit / reunida _plur_ reunits / reunides

revelar /reveal/ • **ind** _pre_ revelo, reveles, revela, revelem, reveleu, revelen _imp_ revelava, revelaves, revelava, revelàvem, revelàveu, revelaven _prt_ revelí, revelares, revelà, revelàrem, revelàreu, revelaren _fut_ revelaré, revelaràs, revelarà, revelarem, revelareu, revelaran _con_ revelaria, revelaries, revelaria, revelaríem, revelaríeu, revelarien • **sub** _pre_ reveli, revelis, reveli, revelem, reveleu, revelin _imp_ revelés, revelessis, revelés, reveléssim, reveléssiu, revelessin • **imp** -, revela, reveli, revelem, reveleu, revelin • **inf** revelar • **ger** revelant • **pp** _sing_ revelat / revelada _plur_ revelats / revelades

revisar /review/ • **ind** _pre_ reviso, revises, revisa, revisem, reviseu, revisen _imp_ revisava, revisaves, revisava, revisàvem, revisàveu, revisaven _prt_ revisí, revisares, revisà, revisàrem, revisàreu, revisaren _fut_ revisaré, revisaràs, revisarà, revisarem, revisareu, revisaran _con_ revisaria, revisaries, revisaria, revisaríem, revisaríeu, revisarien • **sub** _pre_ revisi, revisis, revisi, revisem, reviseu, revisin _imp_ revisés, revisessis, revisés, reviséssim, reviséssiu, revisessin • **imp** -, revisa, revisi, revisem, reviseu, revisin • **inf** revisar • **ger** revisant • **pp** _sing_ revisat / revisada _plur_ revisats / revisades

riure /laugh/ • **ind** _pre_ ric, rius, riu, riem, rieu, riuen _imp_ reia, reies, reia, rèiem, rèieu, reien _prt_ riguí, rigueres, rigué, riguérem, riguéreu, rigueren _fut_ riuré, riuràs, riurà, riurem, riureu, riuran _con_ riuria, riuries, riuria, riuríem, riuríeu, riurien • **sub** _pre_ rigui, riguis, rigui, riguem, rigueu, riguin _imp_ rigués, riguessis, rigués, riguéssim, riguéssiu, riguessin • **imp** -, riu, rigui, riguem, rieu, riguin • **inf** riure • **ger** rient • **pp** _sing_ rigut / riguda _plur_ riguts / rigudes

robar /steal/ • **ind** _pre_ robo, robes, roba, robem, robeu, roben _imp_ robava, robaves, robava, robàvem, robàveu, robaven _prt_ robí, robares, robà, robàrem, robàreu, robaren _fut_ robaré, robaràs, robarà, robarem, robareu, robaran _con_ robaria, robaries, robaria, robaríem, robaríeu, robarien • **sub** _pre_ robi, robis, robi, robem, robeu, robin _imp_ robés, robessis, robés, robéssim, robéssiu, robessin • **imp** -, roba, robi, robem, robeu, robin • **inf** robar • **ger** robant • **pp** _sing_ robat / robada _plur_ robats / robades

rodar /roll/ • **ind** _pre_ rodo, rodes, roda, rodem, rodeu, roden _imp_ rodava, rodaves, rodava, rodàvem, rodàveu, rodaven _prt_ rodí, rodares, rodà, rodàrem, rodàreu, rodaren _fut_ rodaré, rodaràs, rodarà, rodarem, rodareu, rodaran _con_ rodaria, rodaries, rodaria, rodaríem, rodaríeu, rodarien • **sub** _pre_ rodi, rodis, rodi, rodem, rodeu, rodin _imp_ rodés, rodessis, rodés, rodéssim, rodéssiu, rodessin • **imp** -, roda, rodi, rodem, rodeu, rodin • **inf** rodar • **ger** rodant • **pp** _sing_ rodat / rodada _plur_ rodats / rodades

romandre /stay/ • **ind** _pre_ romanc, romans, roman, romanem, romaneu, romanen _imp_ romania, romanies, romania, romaníem, romaníeu, romanien _prt_ romanguí, romangueres, romangué, romanguérem, romanguéreu, romangueren _fut_ romandré, romandràs, romandrà, romandrem, romandreu, romandran _con_ romandria, romandries, romandria, romandríem, romandríeu, romandrien • **sub** _pre_ romangui, romanguis, romangui, romanguem, romangueu, romanguin _imp_ romangués, romanguessis,

R

romangués, romanguéssim, romanguéssiu, romanguessin • **imp** -, roman, romangui, romanguem, romaneu, romanguin • **inf** romandre • **ger** romanent • **pp** _sing_ romàs / romasa _plur_ romasos / romases

S

saber /know/ • **ind** _pre_ sé, saps, sap, sabem, sabeu, saben _imp_ sabia, sabies, sabia, sabíem, sabíeu, sabien _prt_ sabí, saberes, sabé, sabérem, sabéreu, saberen _fut_ sabré, sabràs, sabrà, sabrem, sabreu, sabran _con_ sabria, sabries, sabria, sabríem, sabríeu, sabrien • **sub** _pre_ sàpiga, sàpigues, sàpiga, sapiguem, sapigueu, sàpiguen _imp_ sabés, sabessis, sabés, sabéssim, sabéssiu, sabessin • **imp** -, sàpigues, sàpiga, sapiguem, sapigueu, sàpiguen • **inf** saber • **ger** sabent • **pp** _sing_ sabut / sabuda _plur_ sabuts / sabudes

sacrificar /sacrifice/ • **ind** _pre_ sacrifico, sacrifiques, sacrifica, sacrifiquem, sacrifiqueu, sacrifiquen _imp_ sacrificava, sacrificaves, sacrificava, sacrificàvem, sacrificàveu, sacrificaven _prt_ sacrifiquí, sacrificares, sacrificà, sacrificàrem, sacrificàreu, sacrificaren _fut_ sacrificaré, sacrificaràs, sacrificarà, sacrificarem, sacrificareu, sacrificaran _con_ sacrificaria, sacrificaries, sacrificaria, sacrificaríem, sacrificaríeu, sacrificarien • **sub** _pre_ sacrifiqui, sacrifiquis, sacrifiqui, sacrifiquem, sacrifiqueu, sacrifiquin _imp_ sacrifiqués, sacrifiquessis, sacrifiqués, sacrifiquéssim, sacrifiquéssiu, sacrifiquessin • **imp** -, sacrifica, sacrifiqui, sacrifiquem, sacrifiqueu, sacrifiquin • **inf** sacrificar • **ger** sacrificant • **pp** _sing_ sacrificat / sacrificada _plur_ sacrificats / sacrificades

sagnar /bleed/ • **ind** _pre_ sagno, sagnes, sagna, sagnem, sagneu, sagnen _imp_ sagnava, sagnaves, sagnava, sagnàvem, sagnàveu, sagnaven _prt_ sagní, sagnares, sagnà, sagnàrem, sagnàreu, sagnaren _fut_ sagnaré, sagnaràs, sagnarà, sagnarem, sagnareu, sagnaran _con_ sagnaria, sagnaries, sagnaria, sagnaríem, sagnaríeu, sagnarien • **sub** _pre_ sagni, sagnis, sagni, sagnem, sagneu, sagnin _imp_ sagnés, sagnessis, sagnés, sagnéssim, sagnéssiu, sagnessin • **imp** -, sagna, sagni, sagnem, sagneu, sagnin • **inf** sagnar • **ger** sagnant • **pp** _sing_ sagnat / sagnada _plur_ sagnats / sagnades

saltar /jump/ • **ind** _pre_ salto, saltes, salta, saltem, salteu, salten _imp_ saltava, saltaves, saltava, saltàvem, saltàveu, saltaven _prt_ saltí, saltares, saltà, saltàrem, saltàreu, saltaren _fut_ saltaré, saltaràs, saltarà, saltarem, saltareu, saltaran _con_ saltaria, saltaries, saltaria, saltaríem, saltaríeu, salta-rien • **sub** _pre_ salti, saltis, salti, saltem, salteu, saltin _imp_ saltés, saltessis, saltés, saltéssim, saltéssiu, saltessin • **imp** -, salta, salti, saltem, salteu, saltin • **inf** saltar • **ger** saltant • **pp** _sing_ saltat / saltada _plur_ saltats / saltades

saludar /greet/ • **ind** _pre_ saludo, saludes, saluda, saludem, saludeu, saluden _imp_ saludava, saludaves, saludava, saludàvem, saludàveu, salu-daven _prt_ saludí, saludares, saludà, saludàrem, saludàreu, saludaren _fut_ saludaré, saludaràs, saludarà, saludarem, saludareu, saludaran _con_ salu-daria, saludaries, saludaria, saludaríem, saludaríeu, saludarien • **sub** _pre_ saludi, saludis, saludi, saludem, saludeu, saludin _imp_ saludés, saludessis, saludés, saludéssim, saludéssiu, saludessin • **imp** -, saluda, saludi, salu-dem, saludeu, saludin • **inf** saludar • **ger** saludant • **pp** _sing_ saludat / saludada _plur_ saludats / saludades

salvar /save/ • **ind** _pre_ salvo, salves, salva, salvem, salveu, salven _imp_ salvava, salvaves, salvava, salvàvem, salvàveu, salvaven _prt_ salví, salvares, salvà, salvàrem, salvàreu, salvaren _fut_ salvaré, salvaràs, salvarà, salvarem, salvareu, salvaran _con_ salvaria, salvaries, salvaria, salvaríem, salvaríeu, salvarien • **sub** _pre_ salvi, salvis, salvi, salvem, salveu, salvin _imp_ salvés, salvessis, salvés, salvéssim, salvéssiu, salvessin • **imp** -, salva, salvi, sal-vem, salveu, salvin • **inf** salvar • **ger** salvant • **pp** _sing_ salvat / salvada _plur_ salvats / salvades

saquejar /sack/ • **ind** _pre_ saquejo, saqueges, saqueja, saquegem, saquegeu, saquegen _imp_ saquejava, saquejaves, saquejava, saquejàvem, saquejàveu, saquejaven _prt_ saquejí, saquejares, saquejà, saquejàrem, sa-quejàreu, saquejaren _fut_ saquejaré, saquejaràs, saquejarà, saquejarem, sa-quejareu, saquejaran _con_ saquejaria, saquejaries, saquejaria, saquejaríem, saquejaríeu, saquejarien • **sub** _pre_ saquegi, saquegis, saquegi, saquegem, saquegeu, saquegin _imp_ saquegés, saquegessis, saquegés, saquegéssim, saquegéssiu, saquegessin • **imp** -, saqueja, saquegi, saquegem, saquegeu, saquegin • **inf** saquejar • **ger** saquejant • **pp** _sing_ saquejat / saquejada _plur_ saquejats / saquejades

satisfer /meet/ • **ind** _pre_ satisfaig, satisfàs, satisfà, satisfem, satisfeu, satisfan _imp_ satisfeia, satisfeies, satisfeia, satisfèiem, satisfèieu, satisfeien _prt_ satisfiu, satisferes, satiséfu, satisférem, satiséreu, satisferen _fut_ satis-faré, satisfaràs, satisfarà, satisfarem, satisfareu, satisfaran _con_ satisfaria, satisfaries, satisfaria, satisfariem, satisfarieu, satisfarien • **sub** _pre_ satisfa-ci, satisfacis, satisfaci, satisfem, satisfeu, satisfacin _imp_ satisfés, satisfessis, satisfés, satisféssim, satisféssiu, satisfessin • **imp** -, satisfés, satisfaci, satisfem, satisfeu, satisfacin • **inf** satisfer • **ger** satisfent • **pp** _sing_ satisfet / satisfeta _plur_ satisfets / satisfetes

segrestar /kidnap/ • **ind** _pre_ segresto, segrestes, segresta, segrestem, segresteu, segresten _imp_ segrestava, segrestaves, segrestava, segrestàvem, segrestàveu, segrestaven _prt_ segrestí, segrestares, segrestà, segrestàrem, segrestàreu, segrestaren _fut_ segrestaré, segrestaràs, segrestarà, segrestarem, segrestareu, segrestaran _con_ segrestaria, segrestaries, segrestaria, segrestaríem, segrestaríeu, segrestarien • **sub** _pre_ segresti, segrestis, segresti, segrestem, segresteu, segrestin _imp_ segrestés, segrestessis, segrestés, segrestéssim, segrestéssiu, segrestessin • **imp** -, segresta, segresti, segrestem, segresteu, segrestin • **inf** segrestar • **ger** segrestant • **pp** _sing_ segrestat / segrestada _plur_ segrestats / segrestades

seguir /follow/ • **ind** _pre_ segueixo, segueixes, segueix, seguim, seguiu, segueixen _imp_ seguia, seguies, seguia, seguíem, seguíeu, seguien _prt_ seguí, seguires, seguí, seguírem, seguíreu, seguiren _fut_ seguiré, seguiràs, seguirà, seguirem, seguireu, seguiran _con_ seguiria, seguiries, seguiria, seguiríem, seguiríeu, seguirien • **sub** _pre_ segueixi, segueixis, segueixi, seguim, seguiu, segueixin _imp_ seguís, seguissis, seguís, seguíssim, seguíssiu, seguissin • **imp** -, segueix, segueixi, seguim, seguiu, segueixin • **inf** seguir • **ger** seguint • **pp** _sing_ seguit / seguida _plur_ seguits / seguides

semblar /look like/ • **ind** _pre_ semblo, sembles, sembla, semblem, sembleu, semblen _imp_ semblava, semblaves, semblava, semblàvem, semblàveu, semblaven _prt_ semblí, semblares, semblà, semblàrem, semblàreu, semblaren _fut_ semblaré, semblaràs, semblarà, semblarem, semblareu, semblaran _con_ semblaria, semblaries, semblaria, semblaríem, semblaríeu, semblarien • **sub** _pre_ sembli, semblis, sembli, semblem, sembleu, semblin _imp_ semblés, semblessis, semblés, sembléssim, sembléssiu, semblessin • **imp** -, sembla, sembli, semblem, sembleu, semblin • **inf** semblar • **ger** semblant • **pp** _sing_ semblat / semblada _plur_ semblats / semblades

sentir /feel/ • **ind** _pre_ sento, sents, sent, sentim, sentiu, senten _imp_ sentia, senties, sentia, sentíem, sentíeu, sentien _prt_ sentí, sentires, sentí, sentírem, sentíreu, sentiren _fut_ sentiré, sentiràs, sentirà, sentirem, sentireu, sentiran _con_ sentiria, sentiries, sentiria, sentiríem, sentiríeu, sentirien • **sub** _pre_ senti, sentis, senti, sentim, sentiu, sentin _imp_ sentís, sentissis, sentís, sentíssim, sentíssiu, sentissin • **imp** -, sent, senti, sentim, sentiu, sentin • **inf** sentir • **ger** sentint • **pp** _sing_ sentit / sentida _plur_ sentits / sentides

separar /split up/ • **ind** _pre_ separo, separes, separa, separem, separeu, separen _imp_ separava, separaves, separava, separàvem, separàveu, separaven _prt_ separí, separares, separà, separàrem, separàreu, separaren _fut_ separaré, separaràs, separarà, separarem, separareu, separaran _con_ separaria, separaries, separaria, separaríem, separaríeu, separarien • **sub** _pre_ separi, separis, separi, separem, separeu, separin _imp_ separés, separessis, separés, separéssim, separéssiu, separessin • **imp** -, separa, separi, separem, separeu, separin • **inf** separar • **ger** separant • **pp** _sing_ separat / separada _plur_ separats / separades

ser /be/ • **ind** _pre_ sóc só, ets, és, som, sou, són _imp_ era, eres, era, érem, éreu, eren _prt_ fui, fores, fou, fórem, fóreu, foren _fut_ seré, seràs, serà, serem, sereu, seran _con_ seria fóra, series fores, seria fóra, seríem fórem, seríeu fóreu, serien foren • **sub** _pre_ sigui siga, siguis, sigui siga, siguem, sigueu, siguin _imp_ fos sigués, fossis siguessis, fos sigués, fóssim siguéssim, fóssiu siguéssiu, fossin siguessin • **imp** -, sigues, sigui siga, siguem, sou, siguin • **inf** ser • **ger** sent essent • **pp** _sing_ estat sigut / estada siguda _plur_ estats siguts / estades sigudes

servir /serve/ • **ind** _pre_ serveixo, serveixes, serveix, servim, serviu, serveixen _imp_ servia, servies, servia, servíem, servíeu, servien _prt_ serví, servires, serví, servírem, servíreu, serviren _fut_ serviré, serviràs, servirà, servirem, servireu, serviran _con_ serviria, serviries, serviria, serviríem, serviríeu, servirien • **sub** _pre_ serveixi, serveixis, serveixi, servim, serviu, serveixin _imp_ servís, servissis, servís, servíssim, servíssiu, servissin • **imp** -, serveix, serveixi, servim, serviu, serveixin • **inf** servir • **ger** servint • **pp** _sing_ servit / servida _plur_ servits / servides

seure /sit/ • **ind** _pre_ sec, seus, seu, seiem, seieu, seuen _imp_ seia, seies, seia, sèiem, sèieu, seien _prt_ seguí, segueres, segué, seguérem, seguéreu, segueren _fut_ seuré, seuràs, seurà, seurem, seureu, seuran _con_ seuria, seuries, seuria, seuríem, seuríeu, seurien • **sub** _pre_ segui, seguis, segui, seguem, segueu, seguin _imp_ segués, seguessis, segués, seguéssim, seguéssiu, seguessin • **imp** -, seu, segui, seguem, seieu, seguin • **inf** seure • **ger** seient • **pp** _sing_ segut / seguda _plur_ seguts / segudes

signar /sign/ • **ind** _pre_ signo, signes, signa, signem, signeu, signen _imp_ signava, signaves, signava, signàvem, signàveu, signaven _prt_ signí, signares, signà, signàrem, signàreu, signaren _fut_ signaré, signaràs, signarà, signarem, signareu, signaran _con_ signaria, signaries, signaria, signaríem, signaríeu, signarien • **sub** _pre_ signi, signis, signi, signem, signeu, signin _imp_ signés, signessis, signés, signéssim, signéssiu, signessin • **imp** -, signa, signi, signem, signeu, signin • **inf** signar • **ger** signant • **pp** _sing_ signat

/ signada *plur* signats / signades

significar /mean/ • **ind** *pre* significo, signifiques, significa, signifiquem, signifiqueu, signifiquen *imp* significava, significaves, significava, significàvem, significàveu, significaven *prt* signifiquí, significares, significà, significàrem, significàreu, significaren *fut* significaré, significaràs, significarà, significarem, significareu, significaran *con* significaria, significaries, significaria, significaríem, significaríeu, significarien • **sub** *pre* signifiqui, signifiquis, signifiqui, signifiquem, signifiqueu, signifiquin *imp* signifiqués, signifiquessis, signifiqués, signifiquéssim, signifiquéssiu, signifiquessin • **imp** -, significa, signifiqui, signifiquem, signifiqueu, signifiquin • **inf** significar • **ger** significant • **pp** *sing* significat / significada *plur* significats / significades

sobreviure /survive/ • **ind** *pre* sobrevisc, sobrevius, sobreviu, sobrevivim, sobreviviu, sobreviuen *imp* sobrevivia, sobrevivies, sobrevivia, sobrevivíem, sobrevivíeu, sobrevivien *prt* sobrevisquí, sobrevisqueres, sobrevisqué, sobrevisquérem, sobrevisquéreu, sobrevisqueren *fut* sobreviuré, sobreviuràs, sobreviurà, sobreviurem, sobreviureu, sobreviuran *con* sobreviuria, sobreviuries, sobreviuria, sobreviuríem, sobreviuríeu, sobreviurien • **sub** *pre* sobrevisqui, sobrevisquis, sobrevisqui, sobrevisquem, sobrevisqueu, sobrevisquin *imp* sobrevisqués, sobrevisquessis, sobrevisqués, sobrevisquéssim, sobrevisquéssiu, sobrevisquessin • **imp** -, sobreviu, sobrevisqui, sobrevisquem, sobreviviu, sobrevisquin • **inf** sobreviure • **ger** sobrevivint • **pp** *sing* sobreviscut / sobreviscuda *plur* sobreviscuts / sobreviscudes

solucionar /solve/ • **ind** *pre* soluciono, soluciones, soluciona, solucionem, solucioneu, solucionen *imp* solucionava, solucionaves, solucionava, solucionàvem, solucionàveu, solucionaven *prt* solucioní, solucionares, solucionà, solucionàrem, solucionàreu, solucionaren *fut* solucionaré, solucionaràs, solucionarà, solucionarem, solucionareu, solucionaran *con* solucionaria, solucionaries, solucionaria, solucionaríem, solucionaríeu, solucionarien • **sub** *pre* solucioni, solucionis, solucioni, solucionem, solucioneu, solucionin *imp* solucionés, solucionessis, solucionés, solucionéssim, solucionéssiu, solucionessin • **imp** -, soluciona, solucioni, solucionem, solucioneu, solucionin • **inf** solucionar • **ger** solucionant • **pp** *sing* solucionat / solucionada *plur* solucionats / solucionades

somiar /dream/ • **ind** *pre* somio, somies, somia, somiem, somieu, somien *imp* somiava, somiaves, somiava, somiàvem, somiàveu, somiaven *prt* somií, somiares, somià, somiàrem, somiàreu, somiaren *fut* somiaré, somiaràs, somiarà, somiarem, somiareu, somiaran *con* somiaria, somiaries, somiaria, somiaríem, somiaríeu, somiarien • **sub** _pre_ somïi, somïis, somïi, somiem, somieu, somïin _imp_ somiés, somiessis, somiés, somiéssim, somiéssiu, somiessin • **imp** -, somia, somïi, somiem, somieu, somïin • **inf** somiar • **ger** somiant • **pp** _sing_ somiat / somiada _plur_ somiats / somiades

somriure /smile/ • **ind** _pre_ somric, somrius, somriu, somriem, somrieu, somriuen _imp_ somreia, somreies, somreia, somrèiem, somrèieu, somreien _prt_ somriguí, somrigueres, somrigué, somriguérem, somriguéreu, somrigueren _fut_ somriuré, somriuràs, somriurà, somriurem, somriureu, somriuran _con_ somriuria, somriuries, somriuria, somriuríem, somriuríeu, somriurien • **sub** _pre_ somrigui, somriguis, somrigui, somriguem, somrigueu, somriguin _imp_ somrigués, somriguessis, somrigués, somriguéssim, somriguéssiu, somriguessin • **imp** -, somriu, somrigui, somriguem, somrieu, somriguin • **inf** somriure • **ger** somrient • **pp** _sing_ somrigut / somriguda _plur_ somriguts / somrigudes

sonar /sound/ • **ind** _pre_ sono, sones, sona, sonem, soneu, sonen _imp_ sonava, sonaves, sonava, sonàvem, sonàveu, sonaven _prt_ soní, sonares, sonà, sonàrem, sonàreu, sonaren _fut_ sonaré, sonaràs, sonarà, sonarem, sonareu, sonaran _con_ sonaria, sonaries, sonaria, sonaríem, sonaríeu, sonarien • **sub** _pre_ soni, sonis, soni, sonem, soneu, sonin _imp_ sonés, sonessis, sonés, sonéssim, sonéssiu, sonessin • **imp** -, sona, soni, sonem, soneu, sonin • **inf** sonar • **ger** sonant • **pp** _sing_ sonat / sonada _plur_ sonats / sonades

sopar /dine/ • **ind** _pre_ sopo, sopes, sopa, sopem, sopeu, sopen _imp_ sopava, sopaves, sopava, sopàvem, sopàveu, sopaven _prt_ sopí, sopares, sopà, sopàrem, sopàreu, soparen _fut_ soparé, soparàs, soparà, soparem, sopareu, soparan _con_ soparia, soparies, soparia, soparíem, soparíeu, soparien • **sub** _pre_ sopi, sopis, sopi, sopem, sopeu, sopin _imp_ sopés, sopessis, sopés, sopéssim, sopéssiu, sopessin • **imp** -, sopa, sopi, sopem, sopeu, sopin • **inf** sopar • **ger** sopant • **pp** _sing_ sopat / sopada _plur_ sopats / sopades

sorprendre /surprise/ • **ind** _pre_ sorprenc, sorprens, sorprèn, sorprenem, sorpreneu, sorprenen _imp_ sorprenia, sorprenies, sorprenia, sorpreníem, sorpreníeu, sorprenien _prt_ sorprenguí, sorprengueres, sorprengué, sorprenguérem, sorprenguéreu, sorprengueren _fut_ sorprendré, sorprendràs, sorprendrà, sorprendrem, sorprendreu, sorprendran _con_ sorprendria, sorprendries, sorprendria, sorprendríem, sorprendríeu, sorprendrien • **sub** _pre_ sorprengui, sorprenguis, sorprengui, sorprenguem, sorprengueu, sorprenguin _imp_ sorprengués, sorprenguessis, sorprengués, sorprenguéssim, sorprenguéssiu, sorprenguessin • **imp** -, sorprèn, sorprengui, sorprenguem, sorpreneu, sorprenguin • **inf** sorprendre • **ger** sorprenent • **pp** _sing_ sorprès / sorpresa _plur_ sorpresos / sorpreses

sortir /go out/ • **ind** _pre_ surto, surts, surt, sortim, sortiu, surten _imp_ sortia, sorties, sortia, sortíem, sortíeu, sortien _prt_ sortí, sortires, sortí, sortírem, sortíreu, sortiren _fut_ sortiré, sortiràs, sortirà, sortirem, sortireu, sortiran _con_ sortiria, sortiries, sortiria, sortiríem, sortiríeu, sortirien • **sub** _pre_ surti, surtis, surti, sortim, sortiu, surtin _imp_ sortís, sortissis, sortís, sortíssim, sortíssiu, sortissin • **imp** -, surt, surti, sortim, sortiu, surtin • **inf** sortir • **ger** sortint • **pp** _sing_ sortit / sortida _plur_ sortits / sortides

substituir /replace/ • **ind** _pre_ substitueixo, substitueixes, substitueix, substituïm, substituïu, substitueixen _imp_ substituïa, substituïes, substituïa, substituíem, substituíeu, substituïen _prt_ substituí, substituïres, substituí, substituírem, substituíreu, substituïren _fut_ substituiré, substituiràs, substituirà, substituirem, substituireu, substituiran _con_ substituiria, substituiries, substituiria, substituiríem, substituiríeu, substituirien • **sub** _pre_ substitueixi, substitueixis, substitueixi, substituïm, substituïu, substitueixin _imp_ substituís, substituïssis, substituís, substituíssim, substituíssiu, substituïssin • **imp** -, substitueix, substitueixi, substituïm, substituïu, substitueixin • **inf** substituir • **ger** substituint • **pp** _sing_ substituït / substituïda _plur_ substituïts / substituïdes

succeir /happen/ • **ind** _pre_ succeeixo, succeeixes, succeeix, succeïm, succeïu, succeeixen _imp_ succeïa, succeïes, succeïa, succeíem, succeíeu, succeïen _prt_ succeí, succeïres, succeí, succeírem, succeíreu, succeïren _fut_ succeiré, succeiràs, succeirà, succeirem, succeireu, succeiran _con_ succeiria, succeiries, succeiria, succeiríem, succeiríeu, succeirien • **sub** _pre_ succeeixi, succeeixis, succeeixi, succeïm, succeïu, succeeixin _imp_ succeís, succeïssis, succeís, succeíssim, succeíssiu, succeïssin • **imp** -, succeeix, succeeixi, succeïm, succeïu, succeeixin • **inf** succeir • **ger** succeint • **pp** _sing_ succeït / succeïda _plur_ succeïts / succeïdes

suggerir /suggest/ • **ind** _pre_ suggereixo, suggereixes, suggereix, suggerim, suggeriu, suggereixen _imp_ suggeria, suggeries, suggeria, suggeríem, suggeríeu, suggerien _prt_ suggerí, suggerires, suggerí, suggerírem, suggeríreu, suggeriren _fut_ suggeriré, suggeriràs, suggerirà, suggerirem, suggerireu, suggeriran _con_ suggeriria, suggeriries, suggeriria, suggeriríem, suggeriríeu, suggeririen • **sub** _pre_ suggereixi, suggereixis, suggereixi, suggerim, suggeriu, suggereixin _imp_ suggerís, suggerissis, suggerís, suggeríssim, suggeríssiu, suggerissin • **imp** -, suggereix, suggereixi, suggerim, suggeriu, suggereixin • **inf** suggerir • **ger** suggerint • **pp** *sing* suggerit / suggerida *plur* suggerits / suggerides

superar /get over/ • **ind** *pre* supero, superes, supera, superem, supereu, superen *imp* superava, superaves, superava, superàvem, superàveu, superaven *prt* superí, superares, superà, superàrem, superàreu, superaren *fut* superaré, superaràs, superarà, superarem, superareu, superaran *con* superaria, superaries, superaria, superaríem, superaríeu, superarien • **sub** *pre* superi, superis, superi, superem, supereu, superin *imp* superés, superessis, superés, superéssim, superéssiu, superessin • **imp** -, supera, superi, superem, supereu, superin • **inf** superar • **ger** superant • **pp** *sing* superat / superada *plur* superats / superades

suplicar /beg/ • **ind** *pre* suplico, supliques, suplica, supliquem, supliqueu, supliquen *imp* suplicava, suplicaves, suplicava, suplicàvem, suplicàveu, suplicaven *prt* supliquí, suplicares, suplicà, suplicàrem, suplicàreu, suplicaren *fut* suplicaré, suplicaràs, suplicarà, suplicarem, suplicareu, suplicaran *con* suplicaria, suplicaries, suplicaria, suplicaríem, suplicaríeu, suplicarien • **sub** *pre* supliqui, supliquis, supliqui, supliquem, supliqueu, supliquin *imp* supliqués, supliquessis, supliqués, supliquéssim, supliquéssiu, supliquessin • **imp** -, suplica, supliqui, supliquem, supliqueu, supliquin • **inf** suplicar • **ger** suplicant • **pp** *sing* suplicat / suplicada *plur* suplicats / suplicades

suportar /bear/ • **ind** *pre* suporto, suportes, suporta, suportem, suporteu, suporten *imp* suportava, suportaves, suportava, suportàvem, suportàveu, suportaven *prt* suportí, suportares, suportà, suportàrem, suportàreu, suportaren *fut* suportaré, suportaràs, suportarà, suportarem, suportareu, suportaran *con* suportaria, suportaries, suportaria, suportaríem, suportaríeu, suportarien • **sub** *pre* suporti, suportis, suporti, suportem, suporteu, suportin *imp* suportés, suportessis, suportés, suportéssim, suportéssiu, suportessin • **imp** -, suporta, suporti, suportem, suporteu, suportin • **inf** suportar • **ger** suportant • **pp** *sing* suportat / suportada *plur* suportats / suportades

suposar /suppose/ • **ind** *pre* suposo, suposes, suposa, suposem, suposeu, suposen *imp* suposava, suposaves, suposava, suposàvem, suposàveu, suposaven *prt* suposí, suposares, suposà, suposàrem, suposàreu, suposaren *fut* suposaré, suposaràs, suposarà, suposarem, suposareu, suposaran *con* suposaria, suposaries, suposaria, suposaríem, suposaríeu, suposarien • **sub** *pre* suposi, suposis, suposi, suposem, suposeu, suposin *imp* suposés, suposessis, suposés, suposéssim, suposéssiu, suposes-

sin • **imp** -, suposa, suposi, suposem, suposeu, suposin • **inf** suposar •
ger suposant • **pp** _sing_ suposat / suposada _plur_ suposats / suposades

T

tallar /cut down/ • **ind** _pre_ tallo, talles, talla, tallem, talleu, tallen _imp_
tallava, tallaves, tallava, tallàvem, tallàveu, tallaven _prt_ tallí, tallares, tallà,
tallàrem, tallàreu, tallaren _fut_ tallaré, tallaràs, tallarà, tallarem, tallareu,
tallaran _con_ tallaria, tallaries, tallaria, tallaríem, tallaríeu, tallarien • **sub**
pre talli, tallis, talli, tallem, talleu, tallin _imp_ tallés, tallessis, tallés, tallés-
sim, talléssiu, tallessin • **imp** -, talla, talli, tallem, talleu, tallin • **inf** tallar
• **ger** tallant • **pp** _sing_ tallat / tallada _plur_ tallats / tallades

tancar /close/ • **ind** _pre_ tanco, tanques, tanca, tanquem, tanqueu,
tanquen _imp_ tancava, tancaves, tancava, tancàvem, tancàveu, tancaven
prt tanquí, tancares, tancà, tancàrem, tancàreu, tancaren _fut_ tancaré,
tancaràs, tancarà, tancarem, tancareu, tancaran _con_ tancaria, tancaries,
tancaria, tancaríem, tancaríeu, tancarien • **sub** _pre_ tanqui, tanquis, tanqui, tanquem, tanqueu, tanquin _imp_ tanqués, tanquessis, tanqués, tan-
quéssim, tanquéssiu, tanquessin • **imp** -, tanca, tanqui, tanquem, tanqueu, tanquin • **inf** tancar • **ger** tancant • **pp** _sing_ tancat / tancada
plur tancats / tancades

tastar /taste/ • **ind** _pre_ tasto, tastes, tasta, tastem, tasteu, tasten _imp_
tastava, tastaves, tastava, tastàvem, tastàveu, tastaven _prt_ tastí, tastares,
tastà, tastàrem, tastàreu, tastaren _fut_ tastaré, tastaràs, tastarà, tastarem,
tastareu, tastaran _con_ tastaria, tastaries, tastaria, tastaríem, tastaríeu,
tastarien • **sub** _pre_ tasti, tastis, tasti, tastem, tasteu, tastin _imp_ tastés,
tastessis, tastés, tastéssim, tastéssiu, tastessin • **imp** -, tasta, tasti, tastem, tasteu, tastin • **inf** tastar • **ger** tastant • **pp** _sing_ tastat / tastada
plur tastats / tastades

telefonar /telephone/ • **ind** _pre_ telefono, telefones, telefona, telefonem, telefoneu, telefonen _imp_ telefonava, telefonaves, telefonava,
telefonàvem, telefonàveu, telefonaven _prt_ telefoní, telefonares, telefonà,
telefonàrem, telefonàreu, telefonaren _fut_ telefonaré, telefonaràs, telefo-
narà, telefonarem, telefonareu, telefonaran _con_ telefonaria, telefonaries,
telefonaria, telefonaríem, telefonaríeu, telefonarien • **sub** _pre_ telefoni,
telefonis, telefoni, telefonem, telefoneu, telefonin _imp_ telefonés, tele-
fonessis, telefonés, telefonéssim, telefonéssiu, telefonessin • **imp** -, te-

lefona, telefoni, telefonem, telefoneu, telefonin • **inf** telefonar • **ger** telefonant • **pp** _sing_ telefonat / telefonada _plur_ telefonats / telefonades

tenir /have/ • **ind** _pre_ tinc, tens, té, tenim, teniu, tenen _imp_ tenia, tenies, tenia, teníem, teníeu, tenien _prt_ tinguí, tingueres, tingué, tinguérem, tinguéreu, tingueren _fut_ tindré, tindràs, tindrà, tindrem, tindreu, tindran _con_ tindria, tindries, tindria, tindríem, tindríeu, tindrien • **sub** _pre_ tingui, tinguis, tingui, tinguem, tingueu, tinguin _imp_ tingués, tinguessis, tingués, tinguéssim, tinguéssiu, tinguessin • **imp** -, té, tingui, tinguem, teniu, tinguin • **inf** tenir • **ger** tenint • **pp** _sing_ tingut / tinguda _plur_ tinguts / tingudes

terminar /end/ • **ind** _pre_ termino, termines, termina, terminem, termineu, terminen _imp_ terminava, terminaves, terminava, terminàvem, terminàveu, terminaven _prt_ terminí, terminares, terminà, terminàrem, terminàreu, terminaren _fut_ terminaré, terminaràs, terminarà, terminarem, terminareu, terminaran _con_ terminaria, terminaries, terminaria, terminaríem, terminaríeu, terminarien • **sub** _pre_ termini, terminis, termini, terminem, termineu, terminin _imp_ terminés, terminessis, terminés, terminéssim, terminéssiu, terminessin • **imp** -, termina, termini, terminem, termineu, terminin • **inf** terminar • **ger** terminant • **pp** _sing_ terminat / terminada _plur_ terminats / terminades

tirar /throw/ • **ind** _pre_ tiro, tires, tira, tirem, tireu, tiren _imp_ tirava, tiraves, tirava, tiràvem, tiràveu, tiraven _prt_ tirí, tirares, tirà, tiràrem, tiràreu, tiraren _fut_ tiraré, tiraràs, tirarà, tirarem, tirareu, tiraran _con_ tiraria, tiraries, tiraria, tiraríem, tiraríeu, tirarien • **sub** _pre_ tiri, tiris, tiri, tirem, tireu, tirin _imp_ tirés, tiressis, tirés, tiréssim, tiréssiu, tiressin • **imp** -, tira, tiri, tirem, tireu, tirin • **inf** tirar • **ger** tirant • **pp** _sing_ tirat / tirada _plur_ tirats / tirades

tocar /touch/ • **ind** _pre_ toco, toques, toca, toquem, toqueu, toquen _imp_ tocava, tocaves, tocava, tocàvem, tocàveu, tocaven _prt_ toquí, tocares, tocà, tocàrem, tocàreu, tocaren _fut_ tocaré, tocaràs, tocarà, tocarem, tocareu, tocaran _con_ tocaria, tocaries, tocaria, tocaríem, tocaríeu, tocarien • **sub** _pre_ toqui, toquis, toqui, toquem, toqueu, toquin _imp_ toqués, toquessis, toqués, toquéssim, toquéssiu, toquessin • **imp** -, toca, toqui, toquem, toqueu, toquin • **inf** tocar • **ger** tocant • **pp** _sing_ tocat / tocada _plur_ tocats / tocades

tornar /come back/ • **ind** _pre_ torno, tornes, torna, tornem, torneu, tornen _imp_ tornava, tornaves, tornava, tornàvem, tornàveu, tornaven _prt_ torní, tornares, tornà, tornàrem, tornàreu, tornaren _fut_ tornaré, tornaràs, tornarà, tornarem, tornareu, tornaran _con_ tornaria, tornaries, tornaria, tornaríem, tornaríeu, tornarien • **sub** _pre_ torni, tornis, torni, tornem, torneu, tornin _imp_ tornés, tornessis, tornés, tornéssim, tornéssiu, tornessin • **imp** -, torna, torni, tornem, torneu, tornin • **inf** tornar • **ger** tornant • **pp** _sing_ tornat / tornada _plur_ tornats / tornades

torturar /torture/ • **ind** _pre_ torturo, tortures, tortura, torturem, tortureu, torturen _imp_ torturava, torturaves, torturava, torturàvem, torturàveu, torturaven _prt_ torturí, torturares, torturà, torturàrem, torturàreu, torturaren _fut_ torturaré, torturaràs, torturarà, torturarem, torturareu, torturaran _con_ torturaria, torturaries, torturaria, torturaríem, torturaríeu, torturarien • **sub** _pre_ torturi, torturis, torturi, torturem, tortureu, torturin _imp_ torturés, torturessis, torturés, torturéssim, torturéssiu, torturessin • **imp** -, tortura, torturi, torturem, tortureu, torturin • **inf** torturar • **ger** torturant • **pp** _sing_ torturat / torturada _plur_ torturats / torturades

tractar /treat/ • **ind** _pre_ tracto, tractes, tracta, tractem, tracteu, tracten _imp_ tractava, tractaves, tractava, tractàvem, tractàveu, tractaven _prt_ tractí, tractares, tractà, tractàrem, tractàreu, tractaren _fut_ tractaré, tractaràs, tractarà, tractarem, tractareu, tractaran _con_ tractaria, tractaries, tractaria, tractaríem, tractaríeu, tractarien • **sub** _pre_ tracti, tractis, tracti, tractem, tracteu, tractin _imp_ tractés, tractessis, tractés, tractéssim, tractéssiu, tractessin • **imp** -, tracta, tracti, tractem, tracteu, tractin • **inf** tractar • **ger** tractant • **pp** _sing_ tractat / tractada _plur_ tractats / tractades

trair /betray/ • **ind** _pre_ traeixo, traeixes, traeix, traïm, traïu, traeixen _imp_ traïa, traïes, traïa, traíem, traíeu, traïen _prt_ traí, traïres, traí, traírem, traíreu, traïren _fut_ trairé, trairàs, trairà, trairem, traireu, trairan _con_ trairia, trairies, trairia, trairíem, trairíeu, trairien • **sub** _pre_ traeixi, traeixis, traeixi, traïm, traïu, traeixin _imp_ traís, traïssis, traís, traíssim, traíssiu, traïssin • **imp** -, traeix, traeixi, traïm, traïu, traeixin • **inf** trair • **ger** traint • **pp** _sing_ traït / traïda _plur_ traïts / traïdes

traslladar /move/ • **ind** _pre_ trasllado, trasllades, trasllada, traslladem, traslladeu, traslladen _imp_ traslladava, traslladaves, traslladava, traslladàvem, traslladàveu, traslladaven _prt_ traslladí, traslladares, traslladà, traslladàrem, traslladàreu, traslladaren _fut_ traslladaré, traslladaràs, traslladarà, traslladarem, traslladareu, traslladaran _con_ traslladaria, traslladaries, traslladaria, traslladaríem, traslladaríeu, traslladarien • **sub** _pre_ traslladi, traslladis, traslladi, traslladem, traslladeu, traslladin _imp_ traslladés, traslladessis, traslladés, traslladéssim, traslladéssiu, traslladessin •

imp -, trasllada, traslladi, traslladem, traslladeu, traslladin • **inf** traslladar • **ger** traslladant • **pp** _sing_ traslladat / traslladada _plur_ traslladats / trasllades

traure /draw/ • **ind** _pre_ trac, traus, trau, traiem, traieu, trauen _imp_ treia, treies, treia, trèiem, trèieu, treien _prt_ traguí, tragueres, tragué, traguérem, traguéreu, tragueren _fut_ trauré, trauràs, traurà, traurem, traureu, trauran _con_ trauria, trauries, trauria, trauríem, trauríeu, traurien • **sub** _pre_ tragui, traguis, tragui, traguem, tragueu, traguin _imp_ tragués, traguessis, tragués, traguéssim, traguéssiu, traguessin • **imp** -, trau, tragui, traguem, traieu, traguin • **inf** traure • **ger** traient • **pp** _sing_ tret / treta _plur_ trets / tretes

travessar /cross/ • **ind** _pre_ travesso, travesses, travessa, travessem, travesseu, travessen _imp_ travessava, travessaves, travessava, travessàvem, travessàveu, travessaven _prt_ travessí, travessares, travessà, travessàrem, travessàreu, travessaren _fut_ travessaré, travessaràs, travessarà, travessarem, travessareu, travessaran _con_ travessaria, travessaries, travessaria, travessaríem, travessaríeu, travessarien • **sub** _pre_ travessi, travessis, travessi, travessem, travesseu, travessin _imp_ travessés, travessessis, travessés, travesséssim, travesséssiu, travessessin • **imp** -, travessa, travessi, travessem, travesseu, travessin • **inf** travessar • **ger** travessant • **pp** _sing_ travessat / travessada _plur_ travessats / travessades

treballar /work/ • **ind** _pre_ treballo, treballes, treballa, treballem, treballeu, treballen _imp_ treballava, treballaves, treballava, treballàvem, treballàveu, treballaven _prt_ treballí, treballares, treballà, treballàrem, treballàreu, treballaren _fut_ treballaré, treballaràs, treballarà, treballarem, treballareu, treballaran _con_ treballaria, treballaries, treballaria, treballaríem, treballaríeu, treballarien • **sub** _pre_ treballi, treballis, treballi, treballem, treballeu, treballin _imp_ treballés, treballessis, treballés, treballéssim, treballéssiu, treballessin • **imp** -, treballa, treballi, treballem, treballeu, treballin • **inf** treballar • **ger** treballant • **pp** _sing_ treballat / treballada _plur_ treballats / treballades

tremolar /tremble/ • **ind** _pre_ tremolo, tremoles, tremola, tremolem, tremoleu, tremolen _imp_ tremolava, tremolaves, tremolava, tremolàvem, tremolàveu, tremolaven _prt_ tremolí, tremolares, tremolà, tremolàrem, tremolàreu, tremolaren _fut_ tremolaré, tremolaràs, tremolarà, tremolarem, tremolareu, tremolaran _con_ tremolaria, tremolaries, tremolaria, tremolaríem, tremolaríeu, tremolarien • **sub** _pre_ tremoli, tremolis, tremoli, tremolem, tremoleu, tremolin _imp_ tremolés, tremolessis, tremolés, tremoléssim, tremoléssiu, tremolessin • **imp** -, tremola, tre-

T

moli, tremolem, tremoleu, tremolin • **inf** tremolar • **ger** tremolant •
pp _sing_ tremolat / tremolada _plur_ tremolats / tremolades

trencar /break/ • **ind** _pre_ trenco, trenques, trenca, trenquem, trenqueu, trenquen _imp_ trencava, trencaves, trencava, trencàvem, trencàveu,
trencaven _prt_ trenquí, trencares, trencà, trencàrem, trencàreu, trenca-
ren _fut_ trencaré, trencaràs, trencarà, trencarem, trencareu, trencaran
con trencaria, trencaries, trencaria, trencaríem, trencaríeu, trencarien
• **sub** _pre_ trenqui, trenquis, trenqui, trenquem, trenqueu, trenquin _imp_
trenqués, trenquessis, trenqués, trenquéssim, trenquéssiu, trenquessin •
imp -, trenca, trenqui, trenquem, trenqueu, trenquin • **inf** trencar •
ger trencant • **pp** _sing_ trencat / trencada _plur_ trencats / trencades

treure /remove/ • **ind** _pre_ trec, treus, treu, traiem, traieu, treuen
imp treia, treies, treia, trèiem, trèieu, treien _prt_ traguí, tragueres, tragué, traguérem, traguéreu, tragueren _fut_ trauré, trauràs, traurà, traurem, traureu, trauran _con_ trauria, trauries, trauria, trauríem, trauríeu,
traurien • **sub** _pre_ tregui, treguis, tregui, traguem, tragueu, treguin _imp_
tragués, traguessis, tragués, traguéssim, traguéssiu, traguessin • **imp** -,
treu, tregui, traguem, traieu, treguin • **inf** treure • **ger** traient • **pp**
sing tret / treta _plur_ trets / tretes

triar /pick, decide, choose/ • **ind** _pre_ trio, tries, tria, triem, trieu,
trien _imp_ triava, triaves, triava, triàvem, triàveu, triaven _prt_ trií, triares,
trià, triàrem, triàreu, triaren _fut_ triaré, triaràs, triarà, triarem, triareu,
triaran _con_ triaria, triaries, triaria, triaríem, triaríeu, triarien • **sub** _pre_
trïí, trïís, trïí, triem, trieu, trïïn _imp_ triés, triessis, triés, triéssim, triéssiu,
triessin • **imp** -, tria, trïí, triem, trieu, trïïn • **inf** triar • **ger** triant •
pp _sing_ triat / triada _plur_ triats / triades

trigar /take it/ • **ind** _pre_ trigo, trigues, triga, triguem, trigueu, tri-
guen _imp_ trigava, trigaves, trigava, trigàvem, trigàveu, trigaven _prt_ triguí,
trigares, trigà, trigàrem, trigàreu, trigaren _fut_ trigaré, trigaràs, trigarà,
trigarem, trigareu, trigaran _con_ trigaria, trigaries, trigaria, trigaríem, tri-
garíeu, trigarien • **sub** _pre_ trigui, triguis, trigui, triguem, trigueu, triguin
imp trigués, triguessis, trigués, triguéssim, triguéssiu, triguessin • **imp**
-, triga, trigui, triguem, trigueu, triguin • **inf** trigar • **ger** trigant • **pp**
sing trigat / trigada _plur_ trigats / trigades

trobar /find/ • **ind** _pre_ trobo, trobes, troba, trobem, trobeu, troben
imp trobava, trobaves, trobava, trobàvem, trobàveu, trobaven _prt_ tro-
bí, trobares, trobà, trobàrem, trobàreu, trobaren _fut_ trobaré, trobaràs,
trobarà, trobarem, trobareu, trobaran _con_ trobaria, trobaries, trobaria,

trobaríem, trobaríeu, trobarien • **sub** _pre_ trobi, trobis, trobi, trobem, trobeu, trobin _imp_ trobés, trobessis, trobés, trobéssim, trobéssiu, trobessin • **imp** -, troba, trobi, trobem, trobeu, trobin • **inf** trobar • **ger** trobant • **pp** _sing_ trobat / trobada _plur_ trobats / trobades

trucar /call/ • **ind** _pre_ truco, truques, truca, truquem, truqueu, truquen _imp_ trucava, trucaves, trucava, trucàvem, trucàveu, trucaven _prt_ truquí, trucares, trucà, trucàrem, trucàreu, trucaren _fut_ trucaré, trucaràs, trucarà, trucarem, trucareu, trucaran _con_ trucaria, trucaries, trucaria, trucaríem, trucaríeu, trucarien • **sub** _pre_ truqui, truquis, truqui, truquem, truqueu, truquin _imp_ truqués, truquessis, truqués, truquéssim, truquéssiu, truquessin • **imp** -, truca, truqui, truquem, truqueu, truquin • **inf** trucar • **ger** trucant • **pp** _sing_ trucat / trucada _plur_ trucats / trucades

U

unir /join/ • **ind** _pre_ uneixo, uneixes, uneix, unim, uniu, uneixen _imp_ unia, unies, unia, uníem, uníeu, unien _prt_ uní, unires, uní, unírem, uníreu, uniren _fut_ uniré, uniràs, unirà, unirem, unireu, uniran _con_ uniria, uniries, uniria, uniríem, uniríeu, unirien • **sub** _pre_ uneixi, uneixis, uneixi, unim, uniu, uneixin _imp_ unís, unissis, unís, uníssim, uníssiu, unissin • **imp** -, uneix, uneixi, unim, uniu, uneixin • **inf** unir • **ger** unint • **pp** _sing_ unit / unida _plur_ units / unides

usar /use/ • **ind** _pre_ uso, uses, usa, usem, useu, usen _imp_ usava, usaves, usava, usàvem, usàveu, usaven _prt_ usí, usares, usà, usàrem, usàreu, usaren _fut_ usaré, usaràs, usarà, usarem, usareu, usaran _con_ usaria, usaries, usaria, usaríem, usaríeu, usarien • **sub** _pre_ usi, usis, usi, usem, useu, usin _imp_ usés, usessis, usés, uséssim, uséssiu, usessin • **imp** -, usa, usi, usem, useu, usin • **inf** usar • **ger** usant • **pp** _sing_ usat / usada _plur_ usats / usades

utilitzar /use/ • **ind** _pre_ utilitzo, utilitzes, utilitza, utilitzem, utilitzeu, utilitzen _imp_ utilitzava, utilitzaves, utilitzava, utilitzàvem, utilitzàveu, utilitzaven _prt_ utilitzí, utilitzares, utilitzà, utilitzàrem, utilitzàreu, utilitzaren _fut_ utilitzaré, utilitzaràs, utilitzarà, utilitzarem, utilitzareu, utilitzaran _con_ utilitzaria, utilitzaries, utilitzaria, utilitzaríem, utilitzaríeu, utilitzarien • **sub** _pre_ utilitzi, utilitzis, utilitzi, utilitzem, utilitzeu, utilitzin _imp_ utilitzés, utilitzessis, utilitzés, utilitzéssim, utilitzéssiu, utilitzessin • **imp** -,

T
U

utilitza, utilitzi, utilitzem, utilitzeu, utilitzin • **inf** utilitzar • **ger** utilitzant
• **pp** _sing_ utilitzat / utilitzada _plur_ utilitzats / utilitzades

V

vendre /sell/ • **ind** _pre_ venc, vens, ven, venem, veneu, venen _imp_
venia, venies, venia, veníem, veníeu, venien _prt_ venguí, vengueres, vengué,
venguérem, venguéreu, vengueren _fut_ vendré, vendràs, vendrà, vendrem,
vendreu, vendran _con_ vendria, vendries, vendria, vendríem, vendríeu,
vendrien • **sub** _pre_ vengui, venguis, vengui, venguem, vengueu, venguin
imp vengués, venguessis, vengués, venguéssim, venguéssiu, venguessin •
imp -, ven, vengui, venguem, veneu, venguin • **inf** vendre • **ger** venent
• **pp** _sing_ venut / venuda _plur_ venuts / venudes

venir /come/ • **ind** _pre_ vinc, véns, ve, venim, veniu, vénen _imp_ venia,
venies, venia, veníem, veníeu, venien _prt_ vinguí, vingueres, vingué, vingué-
rem, vinguéreu, vingueren _fut_ vindré, vindràs, vindrà, vindrem, vindreu,
vindran _con_ vindria, vindries, vindria, vindríem, vindríeu, vindrien • **sub**
pre vingui, vinguis, vingui, vinguem, vingueu, vinguin _imp_ vingués, vin-
guessis, vingués, vinguéssim, vinguéssiu, vinguessin • **imp** -, vine, vingui,
vinguem, veniu, vinguin • **inf** venir • **ger** venint • **pp** _sing_ vingut /
vinguda _plur_ vinguts / vingudes

venjar /revenge/ • **ind** _pre_ venjo, venges, venja, vengem, vengeu,
vengen _imp_ venjava, venjaves, venjava, venjàvem, venjàveu, venjaven _prt_
vengí, venjares, venjà, venjàrem, venjàreu, venjaren _fut_ venjaré, venjaràs,
venjarà, venjarem, venjareu, venjaran _con_ venjaria, venjaries, venjaria,
venjaríem, venjaríeu, venjarien • **sub** _pre_ vengi, vengis, vengi, vengem,
vengeu, vengin _imp_ vengés, vengessis, vengés, vengéssim, vengéssiu, ven-
gessin • **imp** -, venja, vengi, vengem, vengeu, vengin • **inf** venjar • **ger**
venjant • **pp** _sing_ venjat / venjada _plur_ venjats / venjades

vessar /spill/ • **ind** _pre_ vesso, vesses, vessa, vessem, vesseu, vessen
imp vessava, vessaves, vessava, vessàvem, vessàveu, vessaven _prt_ ves-
sí, vessares, vessà, vessàrem, vessàreu, vessaren _fut_ vessaré, vessaràs,
vessarà, vessarem, vessareu, vessaran _con_ vessaria, vessaries, vessaria,
vessaríem, vessaríeu, vessarien • **sub** _pre_ vessi, vessis, vessi, vessem,
vesseu, vessin _imp_ vessés, vessessis, vessés, vesséssim, vesséssiu, ves-
sessin • **imp** -, vessa, vessi, vessem, vesseu, vessin • **inf** vessar • **ger**
vessant • **pp** _sing_ vessat / vessada _plur_ vessats / vessades

veure /see/ • **ind** _pre_ veig, veus, veu, veiem, veieu, veuen _imp_ veia, veies, veia, vèiem, vèieu, veien _prt_ viu, veieres, veié, veiérem, veiéreu, veieren _fut_ veuré, veuràs, veurà, veurem, veureu, veuran _con_ veuria, veuries, veuria, veuríem, veuríeu, veurien • **sub** _pre_ vegi, vegis, vegi, vegem, vegeu, vegin _imp_ veiés, veiessis, veiés, veiéssim, veiéssiu, veiessin • **imp** -, veges, vegi, vegem, veieu, vegin • **inf** veure • **ger** veient • **pp** _sing_ vist / vista _plur_ vistos / vistes

viatjar /travel/ • **ind** _pre_ viatjo, viatges, viatja, viatgem, viatgeu, viatgen _imp_ viatjava, viatjaves, viatjava, viatjàvem, viatjàveu, viatjaven _prt_ viatgí, viatjares, viatjà, viatjàrem, viatjàreu, viatjaren _fut_ viatjaré, viatjaràs, viatjarà, viatjarem, viatjareu, viatjaran _con_ viatjaria, viatjaries, viatjaria, viatjaríem, viatjaríeu, viatjarien • **sub** _pre_ viatgi, viatgis, viatgi, viatgem, viatgeu, viatgin _imp_ viatgés, viatgessis, viatgés, viatgéssim, viatgéssiu, viatgessin • **imp** -, viatja, viatgi, viatgem, viatgeu, viatgin • **inf** viatjar • **ger** viatjant • **pp** _sing_ viatjat / viatjada _plur_ viatjats / viatjades

vigilar /watch over/ • **ind** _pre_ vigilo, vigiles, vigila, vigilem, vigileu, vigilen _imp_ vigilava, vigilaves, vigilava, vigilàvem, vigilàveu, vigilaven _prt_ vigilí, vigilares, vigilà, vigilàrem, vigilàreu, vigilaren _fut_ vigilaré, vigilaràs, vigilarà, vigilarem, vigilareu, vigilaran _con_ vigilaria, vigilaries, vigilaria, vigilaríem, vigilaríeu, vigilarien • **sub** _pre_ vigili, vigilis, vigili, vigilem, vigileu, vigilin _imp_ vigilés, vigilessis, vigilés, vigiléssim, vigiléssiu, vigilessin • **imp** -, vigila, vigili, vigilem, vigileu, vigilin • **inf** vigilar • **ger** vigilant • **pp** _sing_ vigilat / vigilada _plur_ vigilats / vigilades

violar /rape, violate/ • **ind** _pre_ violo, violes, viola, violem, violeu, violen _imp_ violava, violaves, violava, violàvem, violàveu, violaven _prt_ violí, violares, violà, violàrem, violàreu, violaren _fut_ violaré, violaràs, violarà, violarem, violareu, violaran _con_ violaria, violaries, violaria, violaríem, violaríeu, violarien • **sub** _pre_ violi, violis, violi, violem, violeu, violin _imp_ violés, violessis, violés, violéssim, violéssiu, violessin • **imp** -, viola, violi, violem, violeu, violin • **inf** violar • **ger** violant • **pp** _sing_ violat / violada _plur_ violats / violades

visitar /visit/ • **ind** _pre_ visito, visites, visita, visitem, visiteu, visiten _imp_ visitava, visitaves, visitava, visitàvem, visitàveu, visitaven _prt_ visití, visitares, visità, visitàrem, visitàreu, visitaren _fut_ visitaré, visitaràs, visitarà, visitarem, visitareu, visitaran _con_ visitaria, visitaries, visitaria, visitaríem, visitaríeu, visitarien • **sub** _pre_ visiti, visitis, visiti, visitem, visiteu, visitin _imp_ visités, visitessis, visités, visitéssim, visitéssiu, visitessin • **imp** -, visita, visiti, visitem, visiteu, visitin • **inf** visitar • **ger** visitant • **pp** _sing_ visitat / visitada _plur_ visitats / visitades

V

viure /live/ • **ind** _pre_ visc, vius, viu, vivim, viviu, viuen _imp_ vivia, vivies, vivia, vivíem, vivíeu, vivien _prt_ visquí, visqueres, visqué, visquérem, visquéreu, visqueren _fut_ viuré, viuràs, viurà, viurem, viureu, viuran _con_ viuria, viuries, viuria, viuríem, viuríeu, viurien • **sub** _pre_ visqui, visquis, visqui, visquem, visqueu, visquin _imp_ visqués, visquessis, visqués, visquéssim, visquéssiu, visquessin • **imp** -, viu, visqui, visquem, viviu, visquin • **inf** viure • **ger** visquent • **pp** _sing_ viscut / viguda _plur_ viguts / vigudes

volar /fly/ • **ind** _pre_ volo, voles, vola, volem, voleu, volen _imp_ volava, volaves, volava, volàvem, volàveu, volaven _prt_ volí, volares, volà, volàrem, volàreu, volaren _fut_ volaré, volaràs, volarà, volarem, volareu, volaran _con_ volaria, volaries, volaria, volaríem, volaríeu, volarien • **sub** _pre_ voli, volis, voli, volem, voleu, volin _imp_ volés, volessis, volés, voléssim, voléssiu, volessin • **imp** -, vola, voli, volem, voleu, volin • **inf** volar • **ger** volant • **pp** _sing_ volat / volada _plur_ volats / volades

voler /want/ • **ind** _pre_ vull, vols, vol, volem, voleu, volen _imp_ volia, volies, volia, volíem, volíeu, volien _prt_ volguí, volgueres, volgué, volguérem, volguéreu, volgueren _fut_ voldré, voldràs, voldrà, voldrem, voldreu, voldran _con_ voldria, voldries, voldria, voldríem, voldríeu, voldrien • **sub** _pre_ vulgui, vulguis, vulgui, vulguem, vulgueu, vulguin _imp_ volgués, volguessis, volgués, volguéssim, volguéssiu, volguessin • **imp** -, vulgues, vulgui, vulguem, vulgueu, vulguin • **inf** voler • **ger** volent • **pp** _sing_ volgut / volgut _plur_ volguts / volgudes

vomitar /vomit/ • **ind** _pre_ vomito, vomites, vomita, vomitem, vomiteu, vomiten _imp_ vomitava, vomitaves, vomitava, vomitàvem, vomitàveu, vomitaven _prt_ vomití, vomitares, vomità, vomitàrem, vomitàreu, vomitaren _fut_ vomitaré, vomitaràs, vomitarà, vomitarem, vomitareu, vomitaran _con_ vomitaria, vomitaries, vomitaria, vomitaríem, vomitaríeu, vomitarien • **sub** _pre_ vomiti, vomitis, vomiti, vomitem, vomiteu, vomitin _imp_ vomités, vomitessis, vomités, vomitéssim, vomitéssiu, vomitessin • **imp** -, vomita, vomiti, vomitem, vomiteu, vomitin • **inf** vomitar • **ger** vomitant • **pp** _sing_ vomitat / vomitada _plur_ vomitats / vomitades

votar /vote/ • **ind** _pre_ voto, votes, vota, votem, voteu, voten _imp_ votava, votaves, votava, votàvem, votàveu, votaven _prt_ votí, votares, votà, votàrem, votàreu, votaren _fut_ votaré, votaràs, votarà, votarem, votareu, votaran _con_ votaria, votaries, votaria, votaríem, votaríeu, votarien • **sub** _pre_ voti, votis, voti, votem, voteu, votin _imp_ votés, votessis, votés, votéssim, votéssiu, votessin • **imp** -, vota, voti, votem, voteu, votin • **inf** votar • **ger** votant • **pp** _sing_ votat / votada _plur_ votats / votades

V

X

xerrar /chat/ • **ind** _pre_ xerro, xerres, xerra, xerrem, xerreu, xerren _imp_ xerrava, xerraves, xerrava, xerràvem, xerràveu, xerraven _prt_ xerrí, xerrares, xerrà, xerràrem, xerràreu, xerraren _fut_ xerraré, xerraràs, xerrarà, xerrarem, xerrareu, xerraran _con_ xerraria, xerraries, xerraria, xerraríem, xerraríeu, xerrarien • **sub** _pre_ xerri, xerris, xerri, xerrem, xerreu, xerrin _imp_ xerrés, xerressis, xerrés, xerréssim, xerréssiu, xerressin • **imp** -, xerra, xerri, xerrem, xerreu, xerrin • **inf** xerrar • **ger** xerrant • **pp** _sing_ xerrat / xerrada _plur_ xerrats / xerrades

xocar /crash/ • **ind** _pre_ xoco, xoques, xoca, xoquem, xoqueu, xoquen _imp_ xocava, xocaves, xocava, xocàvem, xocàveu, xocaven _prt_ xoquí, xocares, xocà, xocàrem, xocàreu, xocaren _fut_ xocaré, xocaràs, xocarà, xocarem, xocareu, xocaran _con_ xocaria, xocaries, xocaria, xocaríem, xocaríeu, xocarien • **sub** _pre_ xoqui, xoquis, xoqui, xoquem, xoqueu, xoquin _imp_ xoqués, xoquessis, xoqués, xoquéssim, xoquéssiu, xoquessin • **imp** -, xoca, xoqui, xoquem, xoqueu, xoquin • **inf** xocar • **ger** xocant • **pp** _sing_ xocat / xocada _plur_ xocats / xocades

Made in the USA
Las Vegas, NV
27 July 2023

75296287R00077